W9-AYK-552

GEORGE A. ROMERO
EMPIRE OF THE DEAD

ACT ONE

COLOR ARTIST:
MATT HOLLINGSWORTH

LETTERER:
VC'S CORY PETIT

PRODUCER:
PETER GRUNWALD

ASSISTANT EDITOR:
JAKE THOMAS

EDITOR:
BILL ROSEMANN

Special thanks to JORGE ZAFFINO,
whose art influenced my approach
on this book – Alex Maleev

COLLECTION EDITOR: **MARK D. BEAZLEY**
ASSISTANT EDITOR: **SARAH BRUNSTAD**
ASSOCIATE MANAGING EDITOR: **ALEX STARBUCK**
EDITOR, SPECIAL PROJECTS: **JENNIFER GRÜNWALD**
SENIOR EDITOR, SPECIAL PROJECTS: **JEFF YOUNGQUIST**
BOOK DESIGNER: **RODOLFO MURAGUCHI**
SVP PRINT, SALES & MARKETING: **DAVID GABRIEL**

EDITOR IN CHIEF: **AXEL ALONSO**
CHIEF CREATIVE OFFICER: **JOE QUESADA**
PUBLISHER: **DAN BUCKLEY**

GEORGE ROMERO'S EMPIRE OF THE DEAD: ACT ONE. Contains material originally published in magazine form as GEORGE ROMERO'S EMPIRE OF THE DEAD: ACT ONE #1-5. First printing 2014. ISBN# 978-0-7851-8517-8. Published by MARVEL WORLDWIDE, INC., a subsidiary of MARVEL ENTERTAINMENT, LLC. OFFICE OF PUBLICATION: 135 West 50th Street, New York, NY 10020. Copyright © **2014** Romero-Grunwald Productions. All rights reserved. All characters featured in this issue and the distinctive names and likenesses thereof, and all related indicia are trademarks of Romero-Grunwald Productions. No similarity between any of the names, characters, persons, and/or institutions in this magazine with those of any living or dead person or institution is intended, and any such similarity which may exist is purely coincidental. Marvel and its logos are TM & © Marvel Characters, Inc. **Printed in Canada.** ALAN FINE, EVP - Office of the President, Marvel Worldwide, Inc. and EVP & CMO Marvel Characters B.V.; DAN BUCKLEY, Publisher & President - Print, Animation & Digital Divisions; JOE QUESADA, Chief Creative Officer; TOM BREVOORT, SVP of Publishing; DAVID BOGART, SVP of Operations & Procurement, Publishing; C.B. CEBULSKI, SVP of Creator & Content Development; DAVID GABRIEL, SVP Print, Sales & Marketing; JIM O'KEEFE, VP of Operations & Logistics; DAN CARR, Executive Director of Publishing Technology; SUSAN CRESPI, Editorial Operations Manager; ALEX MORALES, Publishing Operations Manager; STAN LEE, Chairman Emeritus. For information regarding advertising in Marvel Comics or on Marvel.com, please contact Niza Disla, Director of Marvel Partnerships, at ndisla@marvel.com. For Marvel subscription inquiries, please call 800-217-9158. **Manufactured between 5/16/2014 and 6/23/2014 by SOLISCO PRINTERS, SCOTT, QC, CANADA.**

10 9 8 7 6 5 4 3 2 1

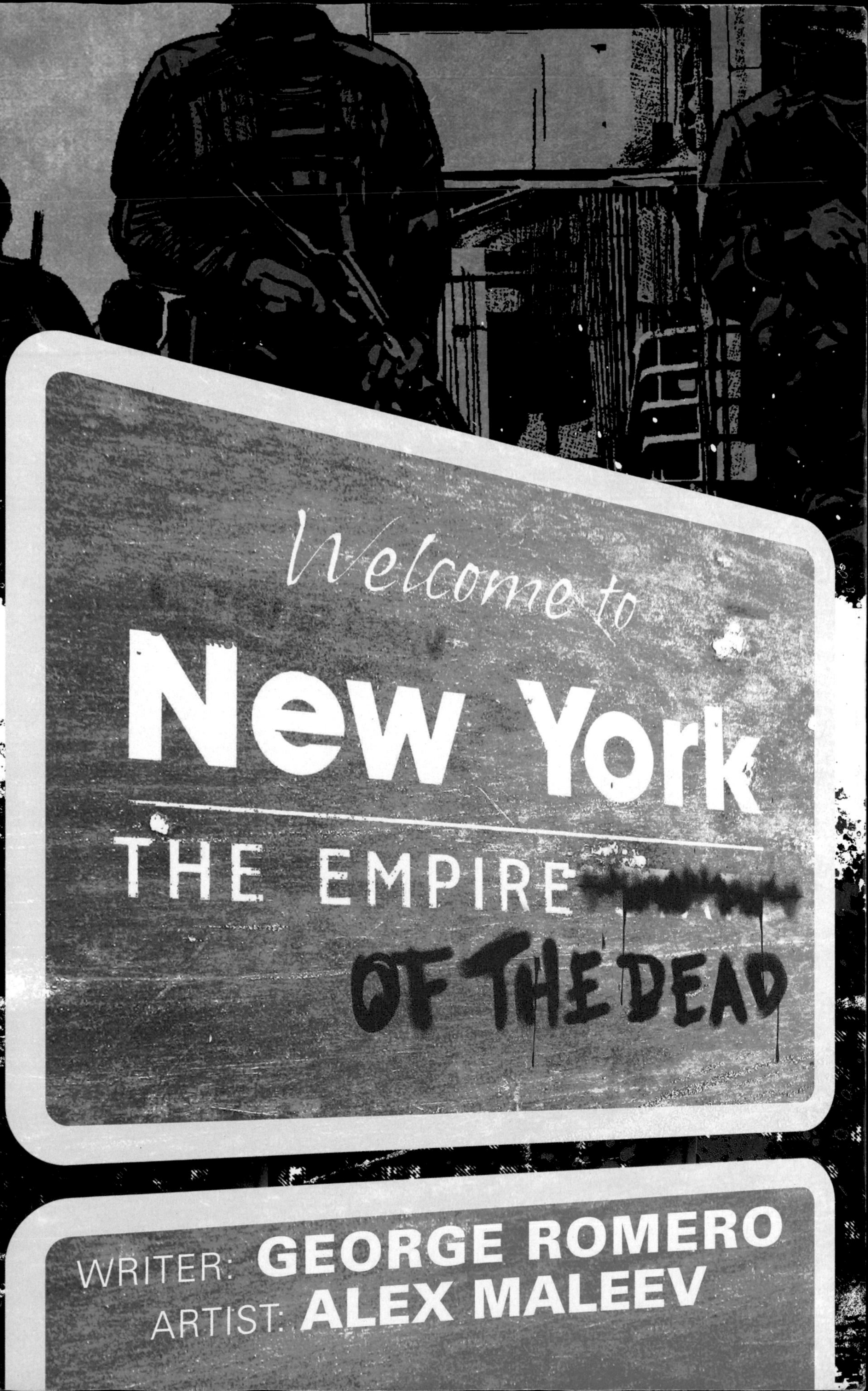
Welcome to
New York
THE EMPIRE
OF THE DEAD
WRITER: GEORGE ROMERO
ARTIST: ALEX MALEEV

INTRODUCTION
BY STAN LEE

One reason I like telling stories about super heroes is that between the pages of heroic action and great derring-do you can sneak in discussions of larger social themes and political issues without sounding like you're preaching.

In my time, I was able to talk about drugs in *Amazing Spider-Man*, civil rights in *Captain America*, and cold war politics in *Iron Man*. But regardless of the message, I always tried to keep human drama at the center of the story.

Well, at the same time the Marvel Age of Comics was hitting its stride, George Romero burst onto the scene with *Night of the Living Dead*. Right out of the gate he revolutionized monster movies with his take on zombies — moving away from voodoo and creating terrifying mobs of creatures who destroyed everything in their path and looked a little too much like everyone else.

While George was creating a ripping good yarn, he also had a deeper message to spread. His film explored the political climate of the '60s and took on civil rights directly by casting an African-American actor as the hero at a time when such things weren't done.

And he wasn't done yet! His movies since, both the zombie films like *Dawn of the Dead*, *Day of the Dead* and *Land of the Dead*, as well as movies like the vampire tale *Martin* and the government-created nightmare of *The Crazies*, have continued looking at social issues while telling entertaining stories.

With *Empire of the Dead*, George has teamed up with Marvel and artist extraordinaire Alex Maleev to delve deeper into his world of the Dead in a whole new medium. George's creations are sinking their teeth right into the Big Apple itself.

EXCELSIOR!

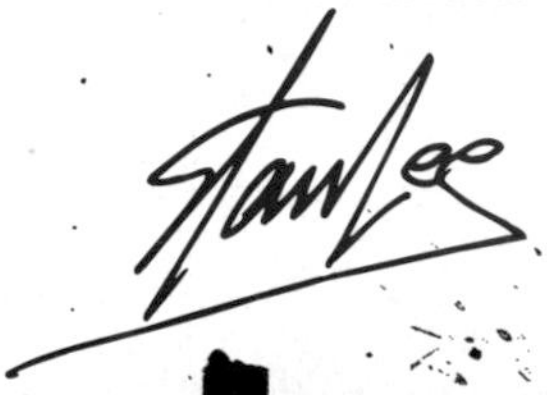

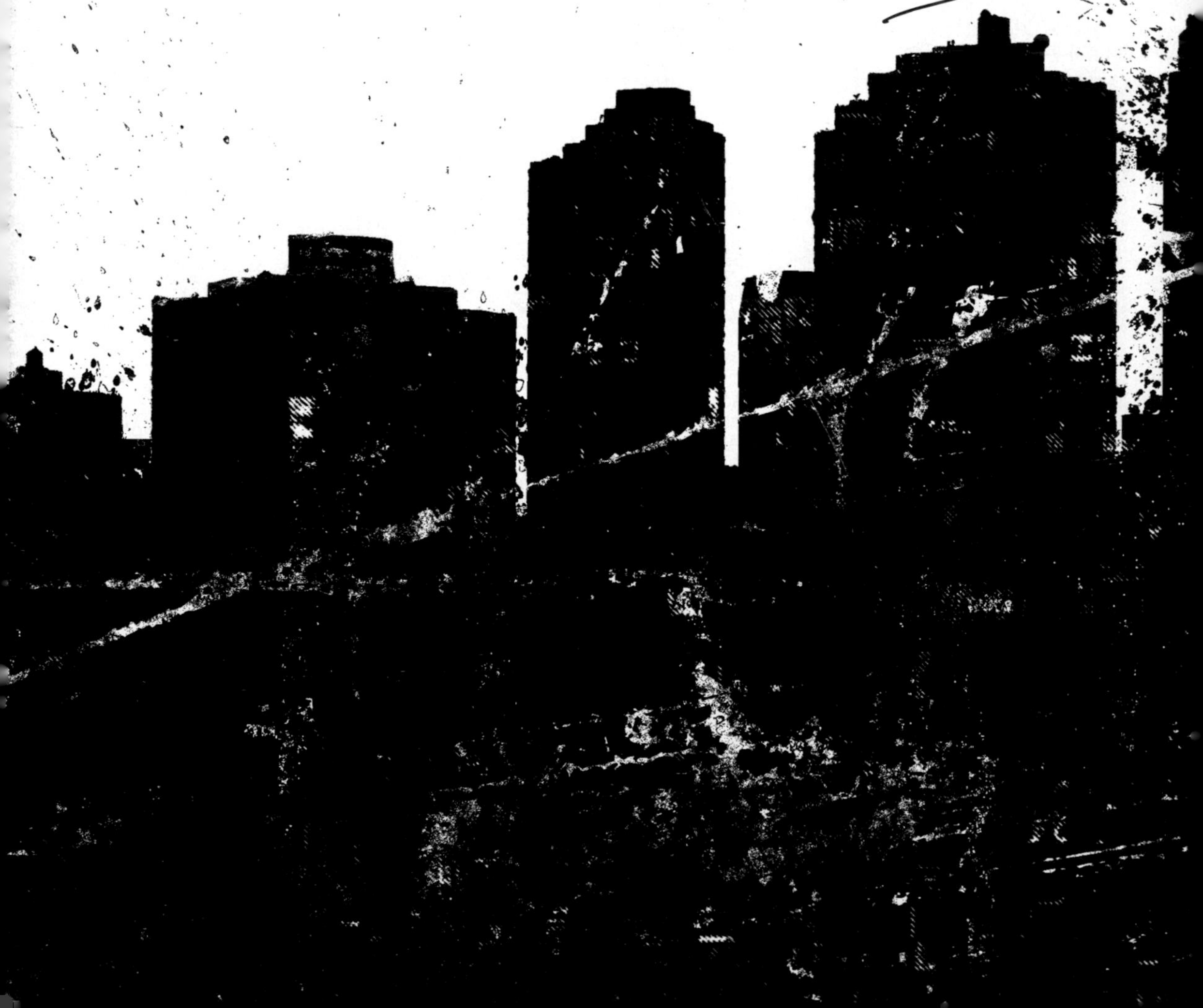

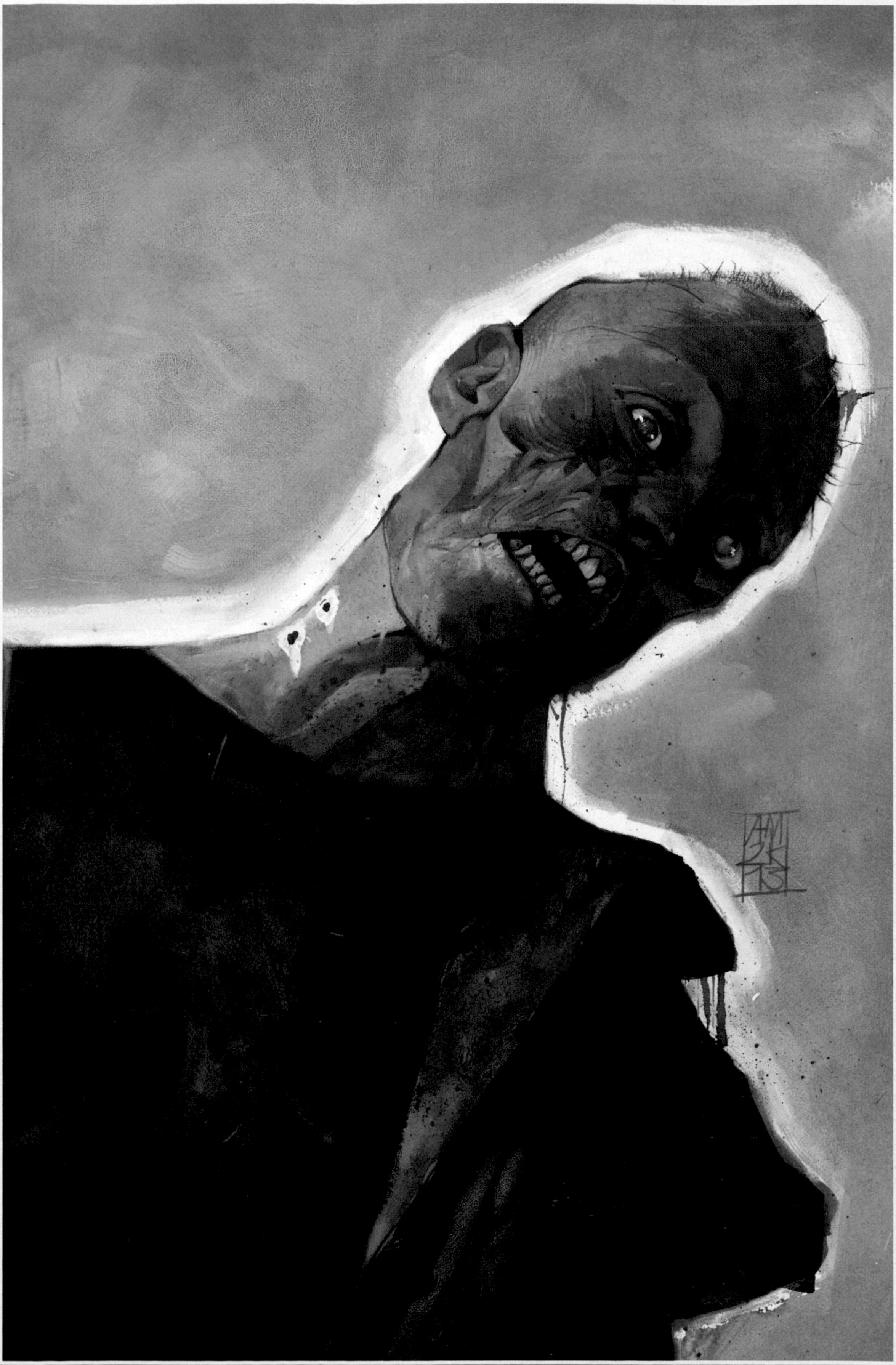

ONE

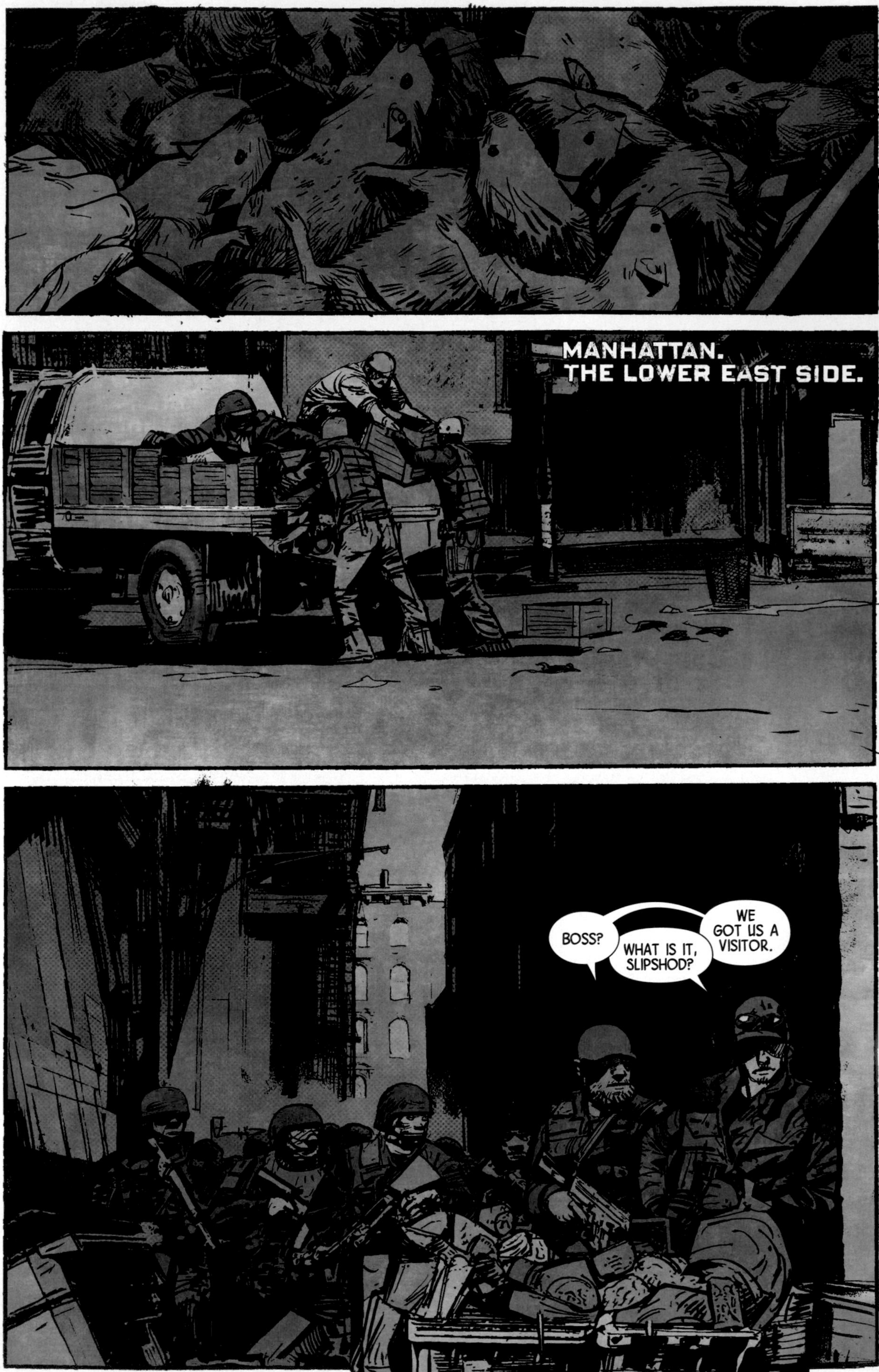
MANHATTAN.
THE LOWER EAST SIDE.
BOSS?
WHAT IS IT, SLIPSHOD?
WE GOT US A VISITOR.

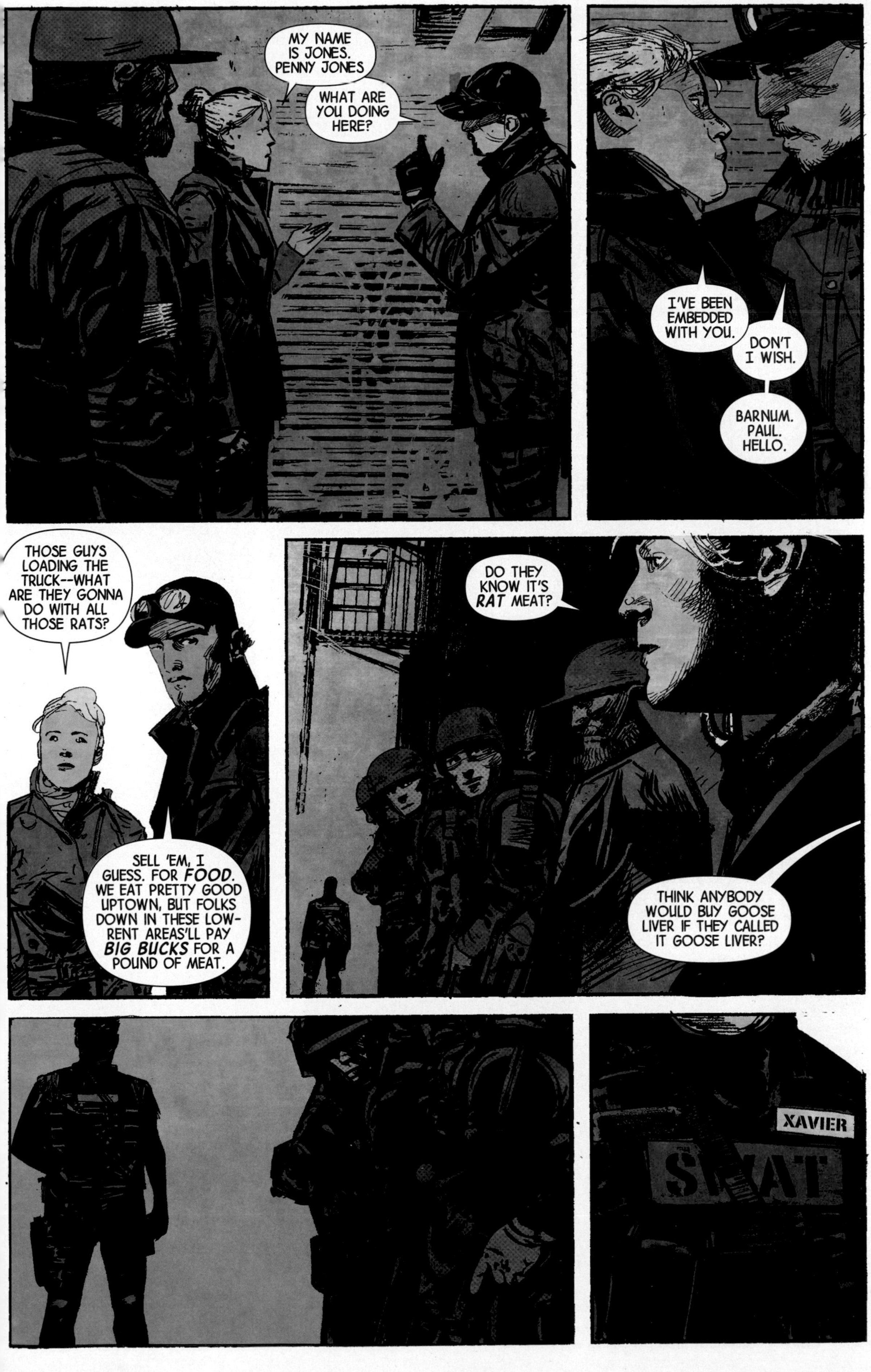
MY NAME IS JONES. PENNY JONES
WHAT ARE YOU DOING HERE?
I'VE BEEN EMBEDDED WITH YOU.
DON'T I WISH.
BARNUM. PAUL. HELLO.
THOSE GUYS LOADING THE TRUCK--WHAT ARE THEY GONNA DO WITH ALL THOSE RATS?
SELL 'EM, I GUESS. FOR FOOD. WE EAT PRETTY GOOD UPTOWN, BUT FOLKS DOWN IN THESE LOW-RENT AREAS'LL PAY BIG BUCKS FOR A POUND OF MEAT.
DO THEY KNOW IT'S RAT MEAT?
THINK ANYBODY WOULD BUY GOOSE LIVER IF THEY CALLED IT GOOSE LIVER?
XAVIER

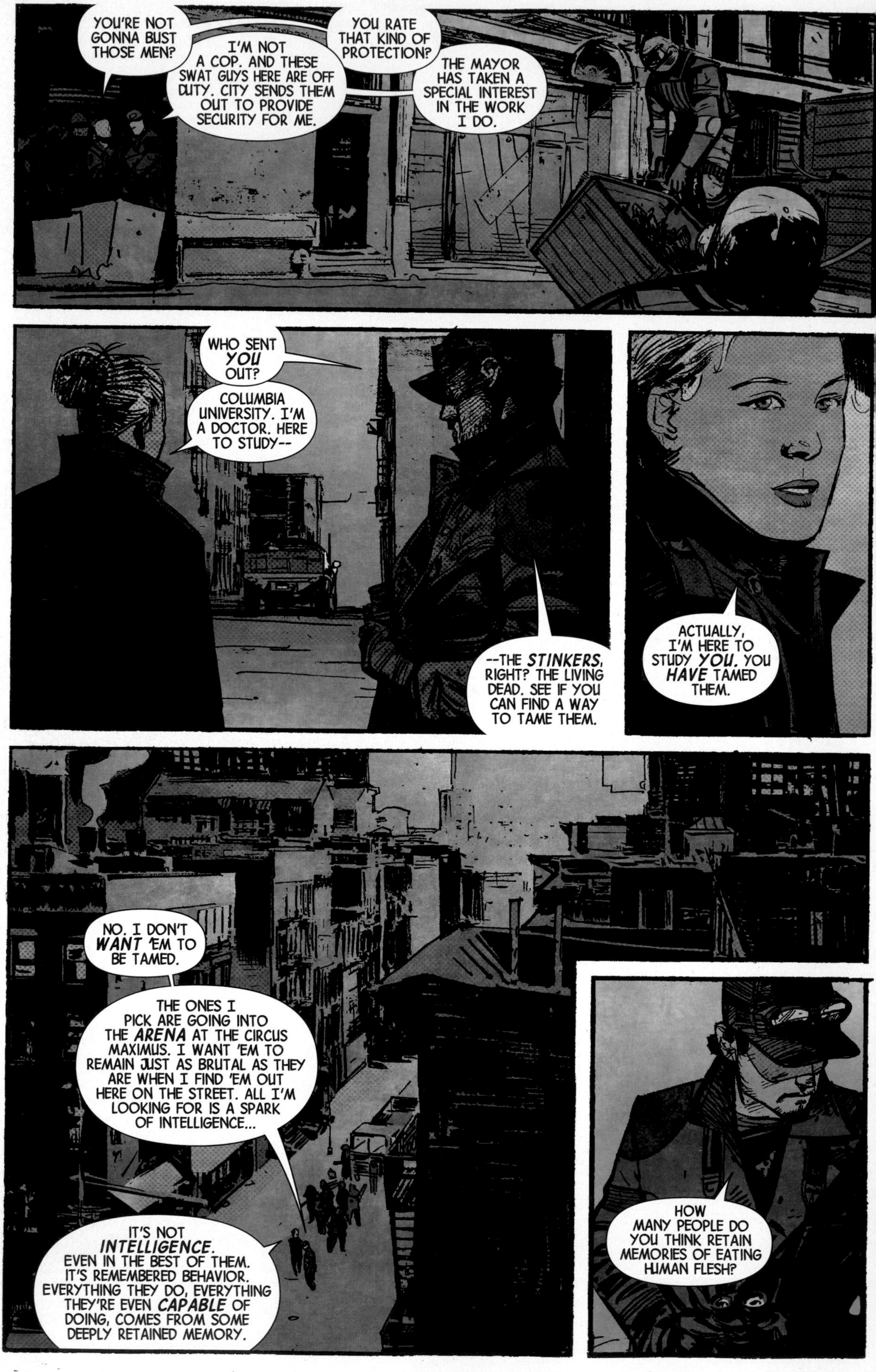
YOU'RE NOT GONNA BUST THOSE MEN?
I'M NOT A COP. AND THESE SWAT GUYS HERE ARE OFF DUTY. CITY SENDS THEM OUT TO PROVIDE SECURITY FOR ME.
YOU RATE THAT KIND OF PROTECTION?
THE MAYOR HAS TAKEN A SPECIAL INTEREST IN THE WORK I DO.
WHO SENT *YOU* OUT?
COLUMBIA UNIVERSITY. I'M A DOCTOR. HERE TO STUDY--
--THE *STINKERS*, RIGHT? THE LIVING DEAD. SEE IF YOU CAN FIND A WAY TO TAME THEM.
ACTUALLY, I'M HERE TO STUDY *YOU*. YOU *HAVE* TAMED THEM.
NO. I DON'T *WANT* 'EM TO BE TAMED.
THE ONES I PICK ARE GOING INTO THE *ARENA* AT THE CIRCUS MAXIMUS. I WANT 'EM TO REMAIN JUST AS BRUTAL AS THEY ARE WHEN I FIND 'EM OUT HERE ON THE STREET. ALL I'M LOOKING FOR IS A SPARK OF INTELLIGENCE...
IT'S NOT *INTELLIGENCE*. EVEN IN THE BEST OF THEM. IT'S REMEMBERED BEHAVIOR. EVERYTHING THEY DO, EVERYTHING THEY'RE EVEN *CAPABLE* OF DOING, COMES FROM SOME DEEPLY RETAINED MEMORY.
HOW MANY PEOPLE DO YOU THINK RETAIN MEMORIES OF EATING HUMAN FLESH?

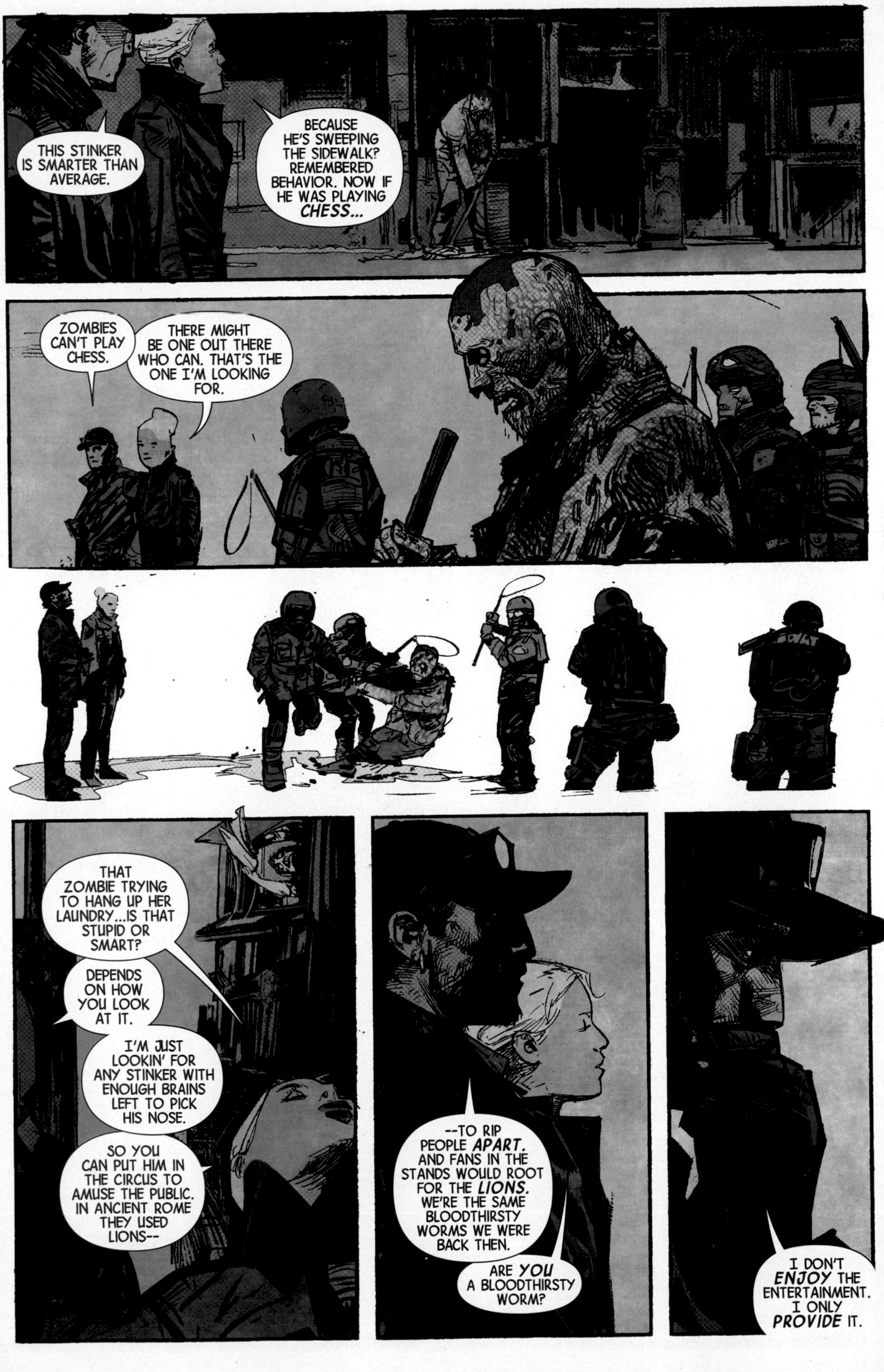
THIS STINKER IS SMARTER THAN AVERAGE.
BECAUSE HE'S SWEEPING THE SIDEWALK? REMEMBERED BEHAVIOR. NOW IF HE WAS PLAYING CHESS...
ZOMBIES CAN'T PLAY CHESS.
THERE MIGHT BE ONE OUT THERE WHO CAN. THAT'S THE ONE I'M LOOKING FOR.
THAT ZOMBIE TRYING TO HANG UP HER LAUNDRY...IS THAT STUPID OR SMART?
DEPENDS ON HOW YOU LOOK AT IT.
I'M JUST LOOKIN' FOR ANY STINKER WITH ENOUGH BRAINS LEFT TO PICK HIS NOSE.
SO YOU CAN PUT HIM IN THE CIRCUS TO AMUSE THE PUBLIC. IN ANCIENT ROME THEY USED LIONS--
--TO RIP PEOPLE APART. AND FANS IN THE STANDS WOULD ROOT FOR THE LIONS. WE'RE THE SAME BLOODTHIRSTY WORMS WE WERE BACK THEN.
ARE YOU A BLOODTHIRSTY WORM?
I DON'T ENJOY THE ENTERTAINMENT. I ONLY PROVIDE IT.

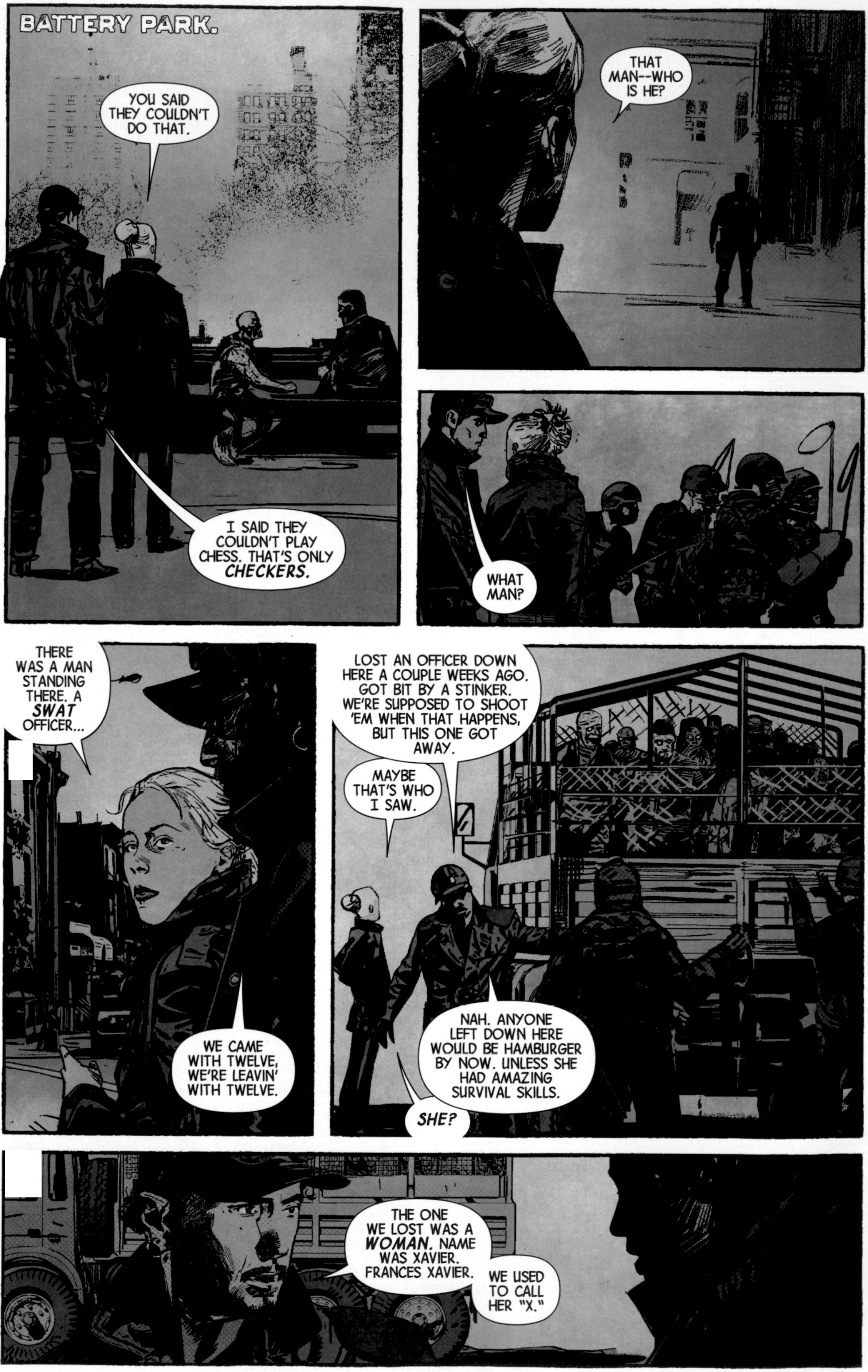
BATTERY PARK.
YOU SAID THEY COULDN'T DO THAT.
I SAID THEY COULDN'T PLAY CHESS. THAT'S ONLY CHECKERS.
THAT MAN--WHO IS HE?
WHAT MAN?
THERE WAS A MAN STANDING THERE. A SWAT OFFICER...
WE CAME WITH TWELVE, WE'RE LEAVIN' WITH TWELVE.
LOST AN OFFICER DOWN HERE A COUPLE WEEKS AGO. GOT BIT BY A STINKER. WE'RE SUPPOSED TO SHOOT 'EM WHEN THAT HAPPENS, BUT THIS ONE GOT AWAY.
MAYBE THAT'S WHO I SAW.
NAH. ANYONE LEFT DOWN HERE WOULD BE HAMBURGER BY NOW. UNLESS SHE HAD AMAZING SURVIVAL SKILLS.
SHE?
THE ONE WE LOST WAS A WOMAN. NAME WAS XAVIER. FRANCES XAVIER.
WE USED TO CALL HER "X."

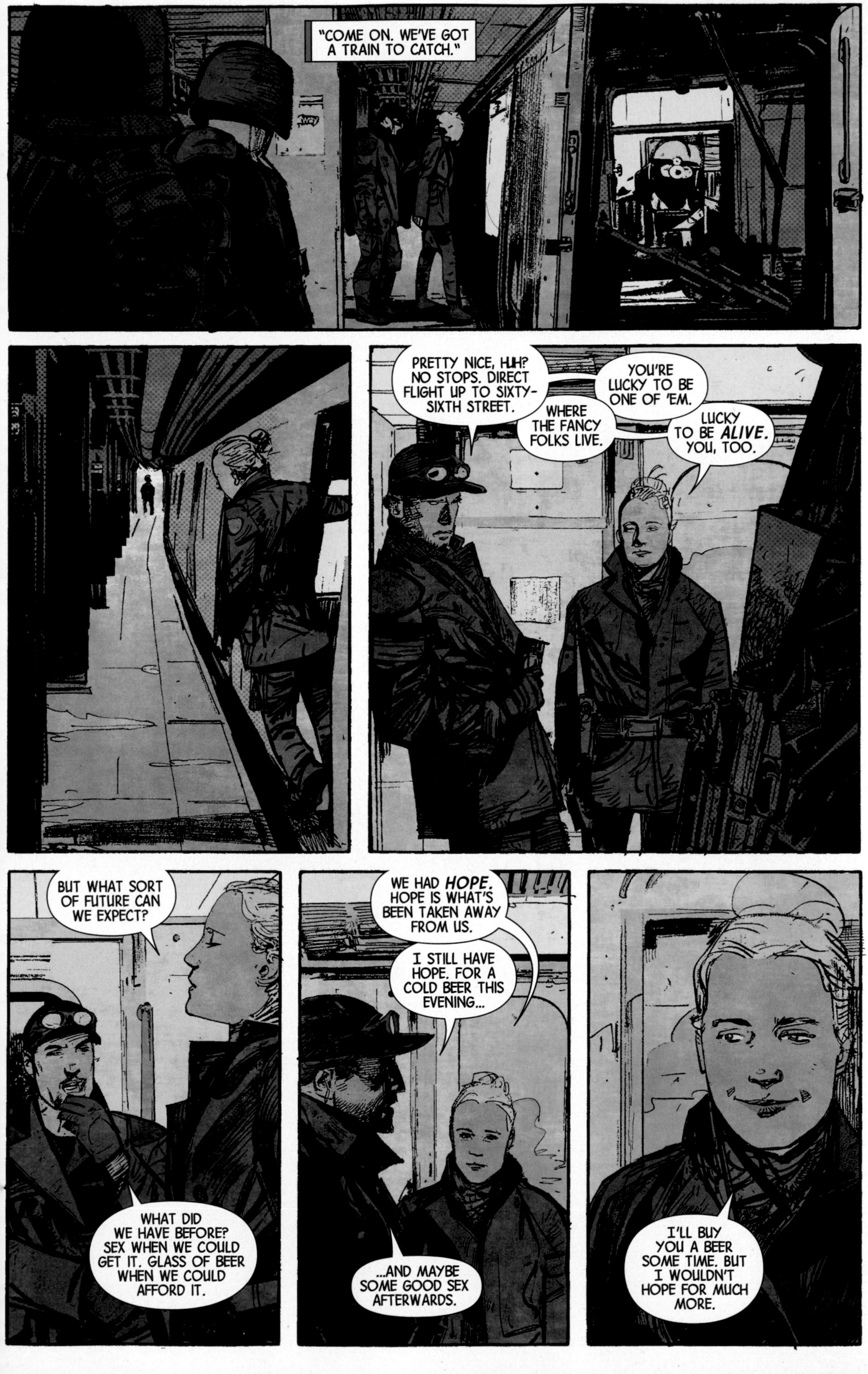
"COME ON. WE'VE GOT A TRAIN TO CATCH."
PRETTY NICE, HUH? NO STOPS. DIRECT FLIGHT UP TO SIXTY-SIXTH STREET.
WHERE THE FANCY FOLKS LIVE.
YOU'RE LUCKY TO BE ONE OF 'EM.
LUCKY TO BE ALIVE. YOU, TOO.
BUT WHAT SORT OF FUTURE CAN WE EXPECT?
WHAT DID WE HAVE BEFORE? SEX WHEN WE COULD GET IT. GLASS OF BEER WHEN WE COULD AFFORD IT.
WE HAD HOPE. HOPE IS WHAT'S BEEN TAKEN AWAY FROM US.
I STILL HAVE HOPE. FOR A COLD BEER THIS EVENING...
...AND MAYBE SOME GOOD SEX AFTERWARDS.
I'LL BUY YOU A BEER SOME TIME. BUT I WOULDN'T HOPE FOR MUCH MORE.

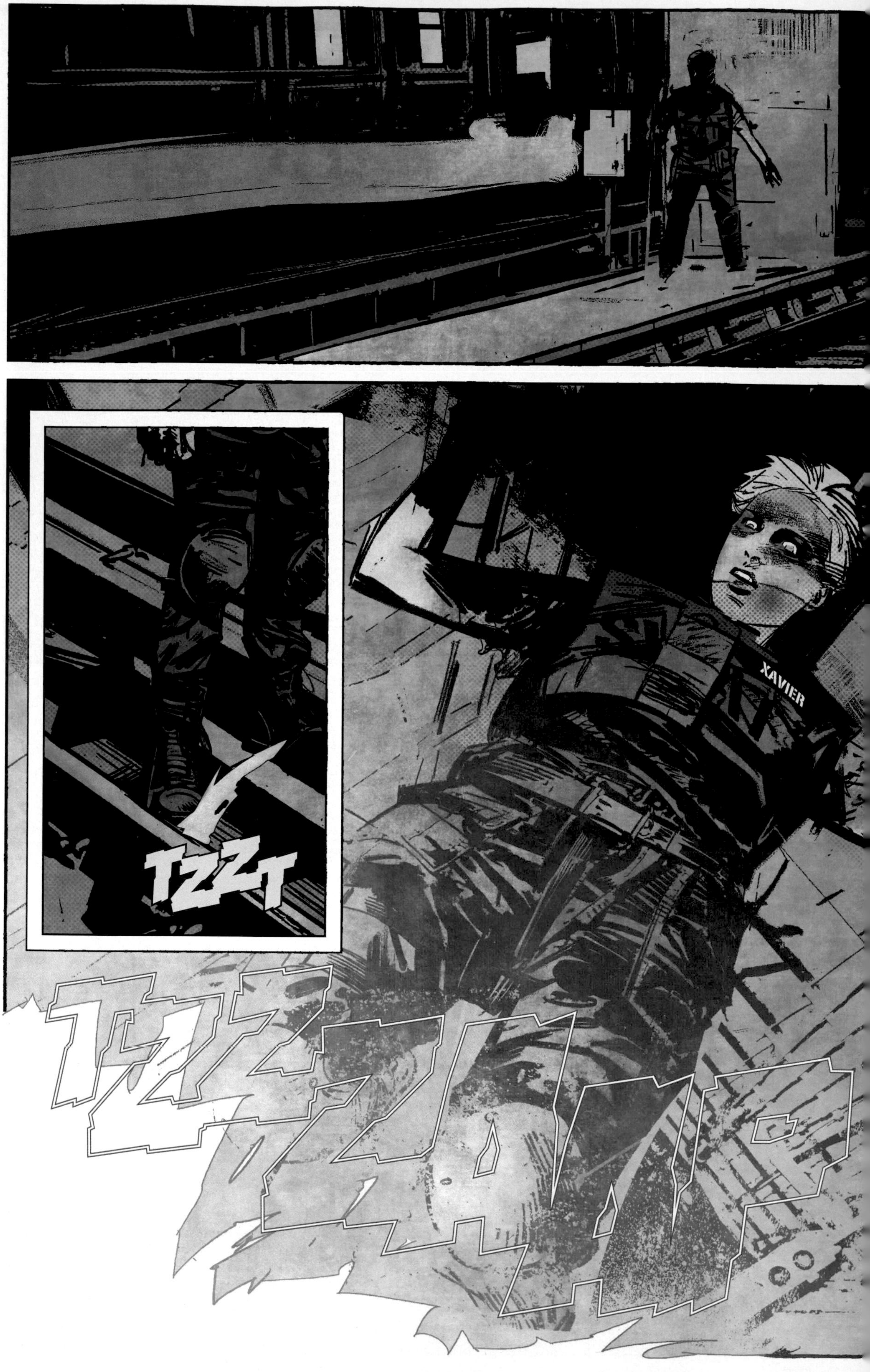
TZZT
XAVIER
TZZZAP

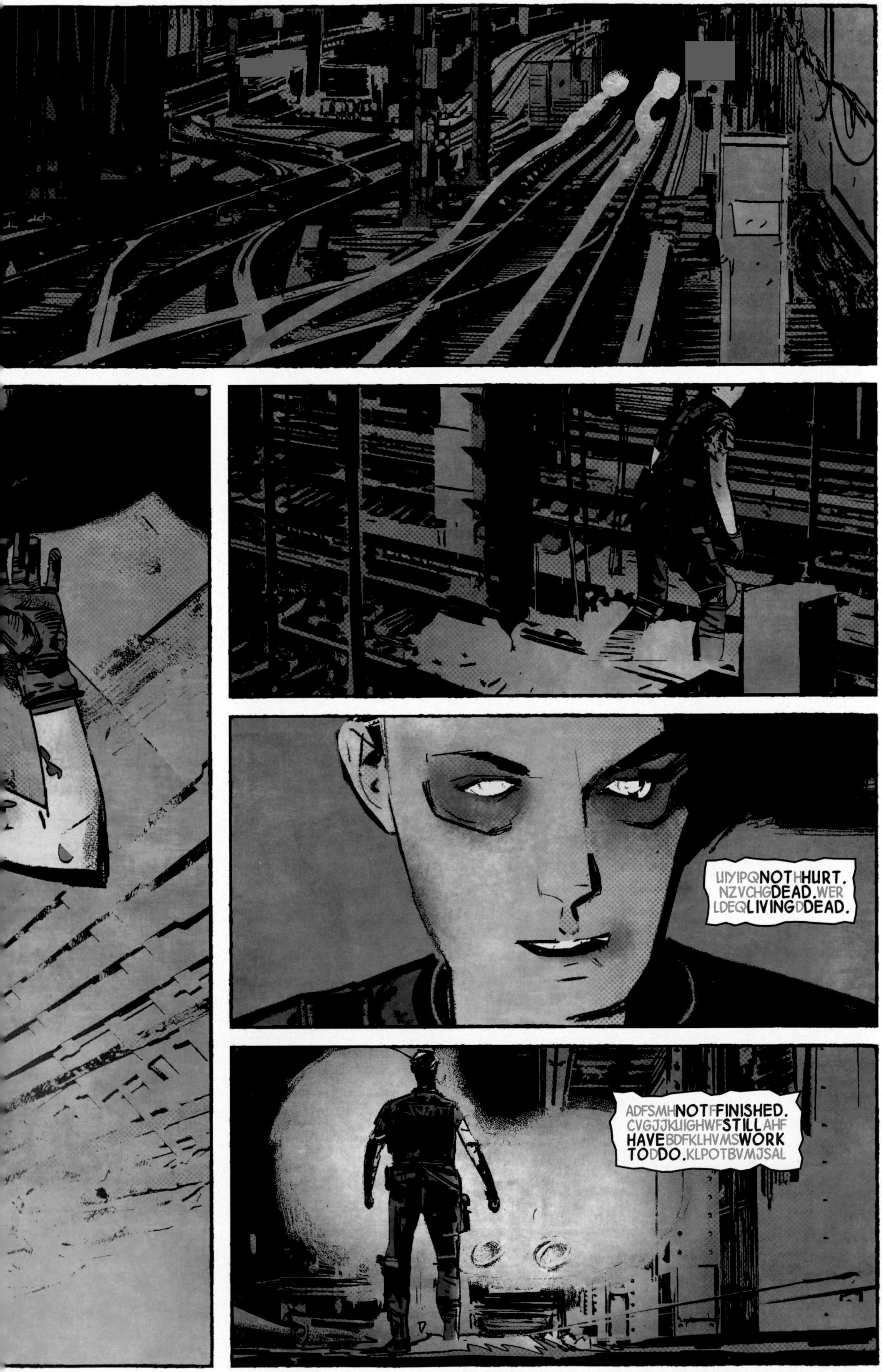
UIYIPQNOTHHURT. NZVCHGDEAD.WER LDEQLIVINGDDEAD.
ADFSMHNOTFFINISHED. CVGJJKUIGHWFSTILLAHF HAVEBDFKLHVMSWORK TODDO.KLPOTBVMJSAL

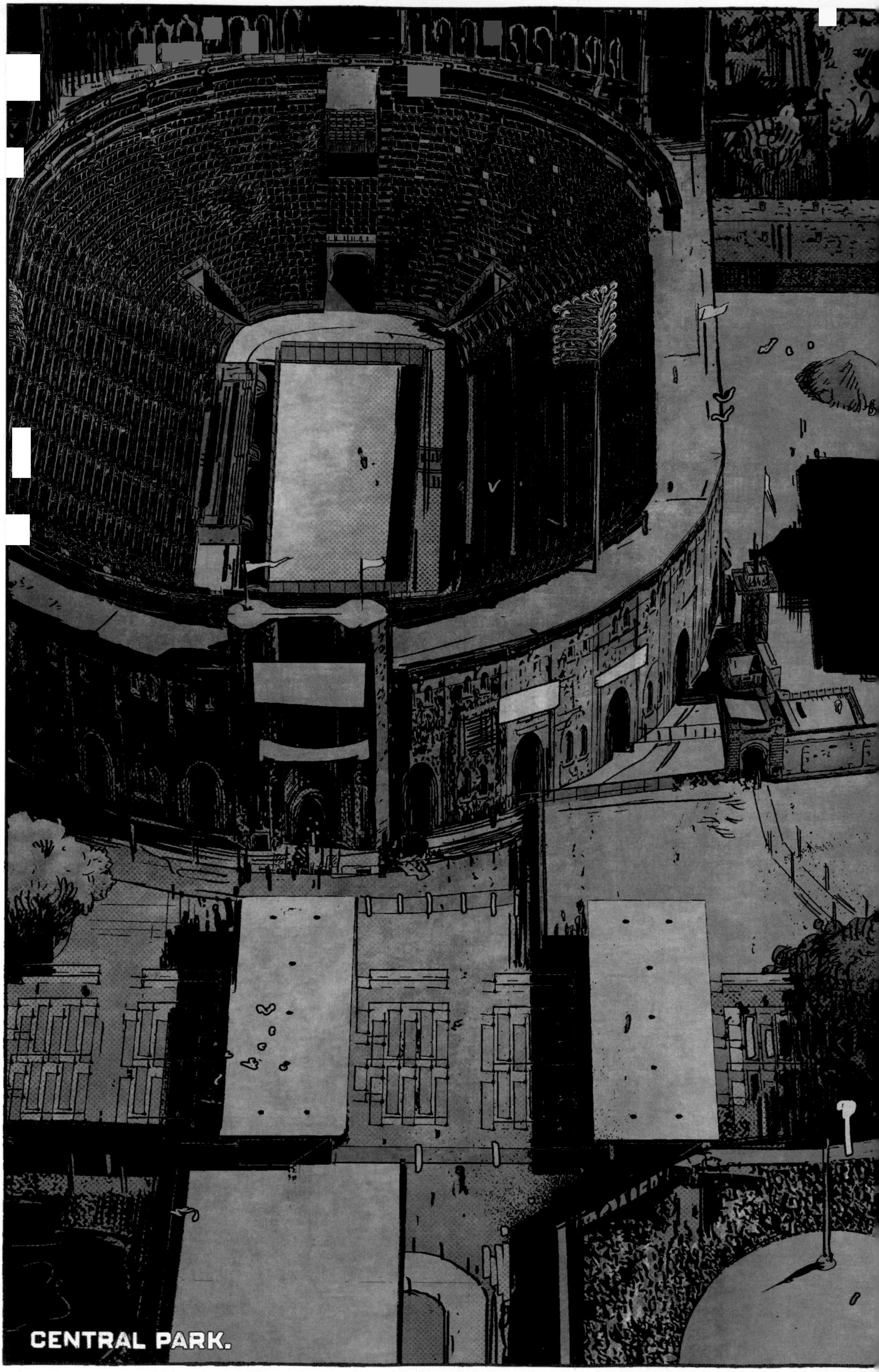
CENTRAL PARK.

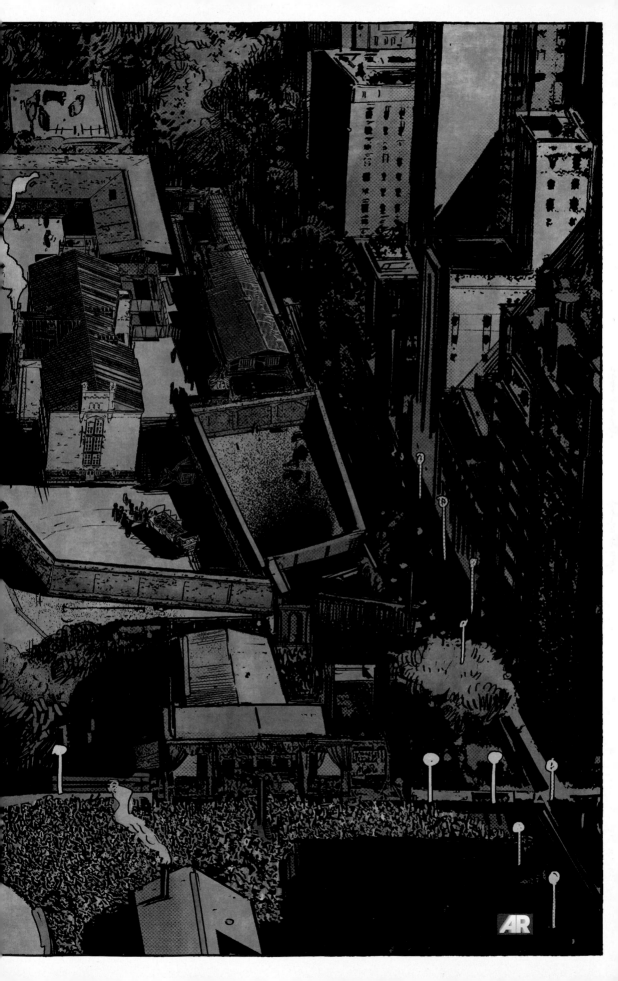

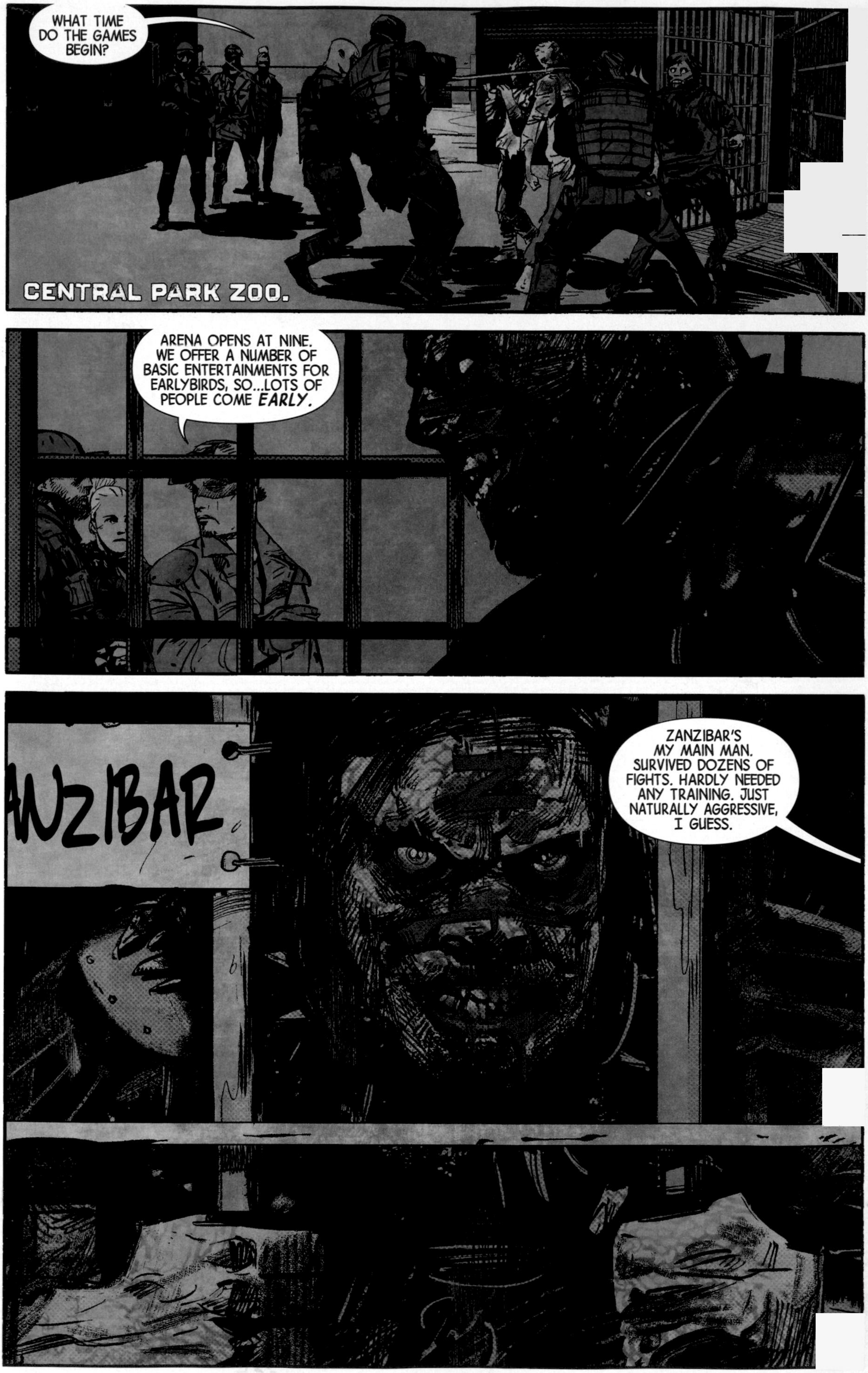
WHAT TIME DO THE GAMES BEGIN?
CENTRAL PARK ZOO.
ARENA OPENS AT NINE. WE OFFER A NUMBER OF BASIC ENTERTAINMENTS FOR EARLYBIRDS, SO...LOTS OF PEOPLE COME *EARLY*.
ANZIBAR
ZANZIBAR'S MY MAIN MAN. SURVIVED DOZENS OF FIGHTS. HARDLY NEEDED ANY TRAINING. JUST NATURALLY AGGRESSIVE, I GUESS.

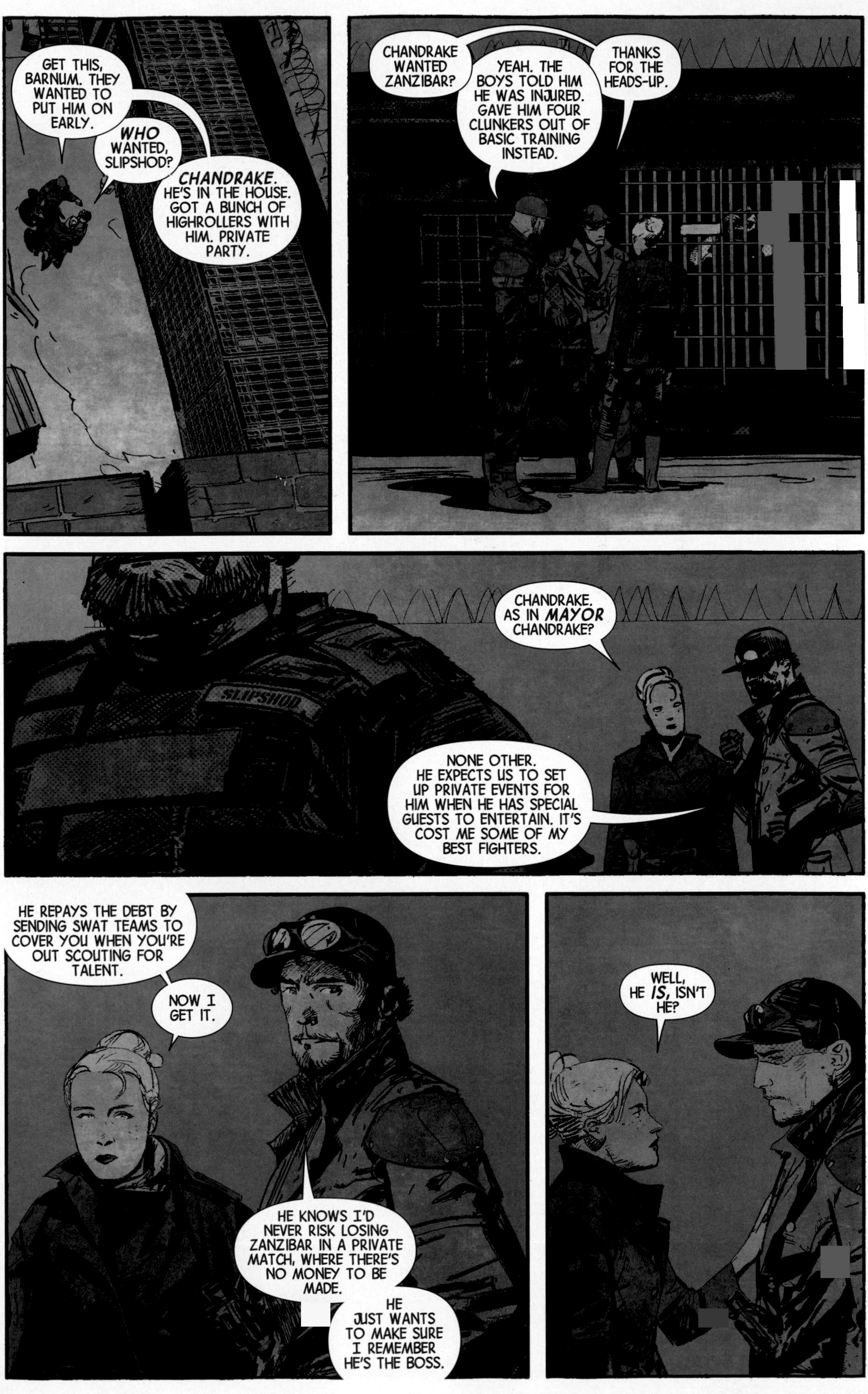
GET THIS, BARNUM. THEY WANTED TO PUT HIM ON EARLY.
WHO WANTED, SLIPSHOD?
CHANDRAKE. HE'S IN THE HOUSE. GOT A BUNCH OF HIGHROLLERS WITH HIM. PRIVATE PARTY.
CHANDRAKE WANTED ZANZIBAR?
YEAH. THE BOYS TOLD HIM HE WAS INJURED. GAVE HIM FOUR CLUNKERS OUT OF BASIC TRAINING INSTEAD.
THANKS FOR THE HEADS-UP.
SLIPSHOD
CHANDRAKE. AS IN MAYOR CHANDRAKE?
NONE OTHER. HE EXPECTS US TO SET UP PRIVATE EVENTS FOR HIM WHEN HE HAS SPECIAL GUESTS TO ENTERTAIN. IT'S COST ME SOME OF MY BEST FIGHTERS.
HE REPAYS THE DEBT BY SENDING SWAT TEAMS TO COVER YOU WHEN YOU'RE OUT SCOUTING FOR TALENT.
NOW I GET IT.
HE KNOWS I'D NEVER RISK LOSING ZANZIBAR IN A PRIVATE MATCH, WHERE THERE'S NO MONEY TO BE MADE.
HE JUST WANTS TO MAKE SURE I REMEMBER HE'S THE BOSS.
WELL, HE IS, ISN'T HE?

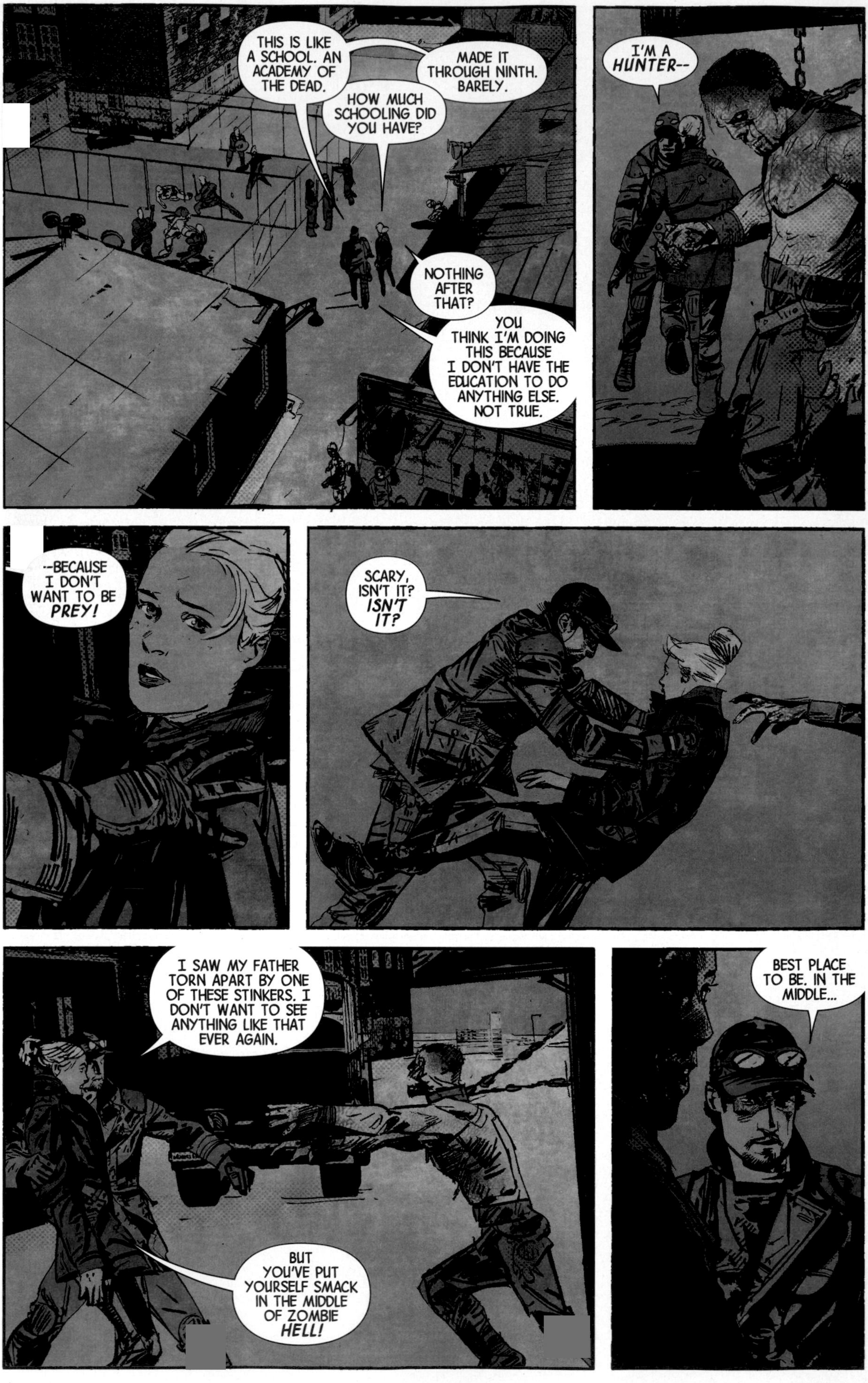
THIS IS LIKE A SCHOOL. AN ACADEMY OF THE DEAD.
MADE IT THROUGH NINTH. BARELY.
HOW MUCH SCHOOLING DID YOU HAVE?
NOTHING AFTER THAT?
YOU THINK I'M DOING THIS BECAUSE I DON'T HAVE THE EDUCATION TO DO ANYTHING ELSE. NOT TRUE.
I'M A HUNTER--
--BECAUSE I DON'T WANT TO BE PREY!
SCARY, ISN'T IT? ISN'T IT?
I SAW MY FATHER TORN APART BY ONE OF THESE STINKERS. I DON'T WANT TO SEE ANYTHING LIKE THAT EVER AGAIN.
BUT YOU'VE PUT YOURSELF SMACK IN THE MIDDLE OF ZOMBIE HELL!
BEST PLACE TO BE. IN THE MIDDLE...

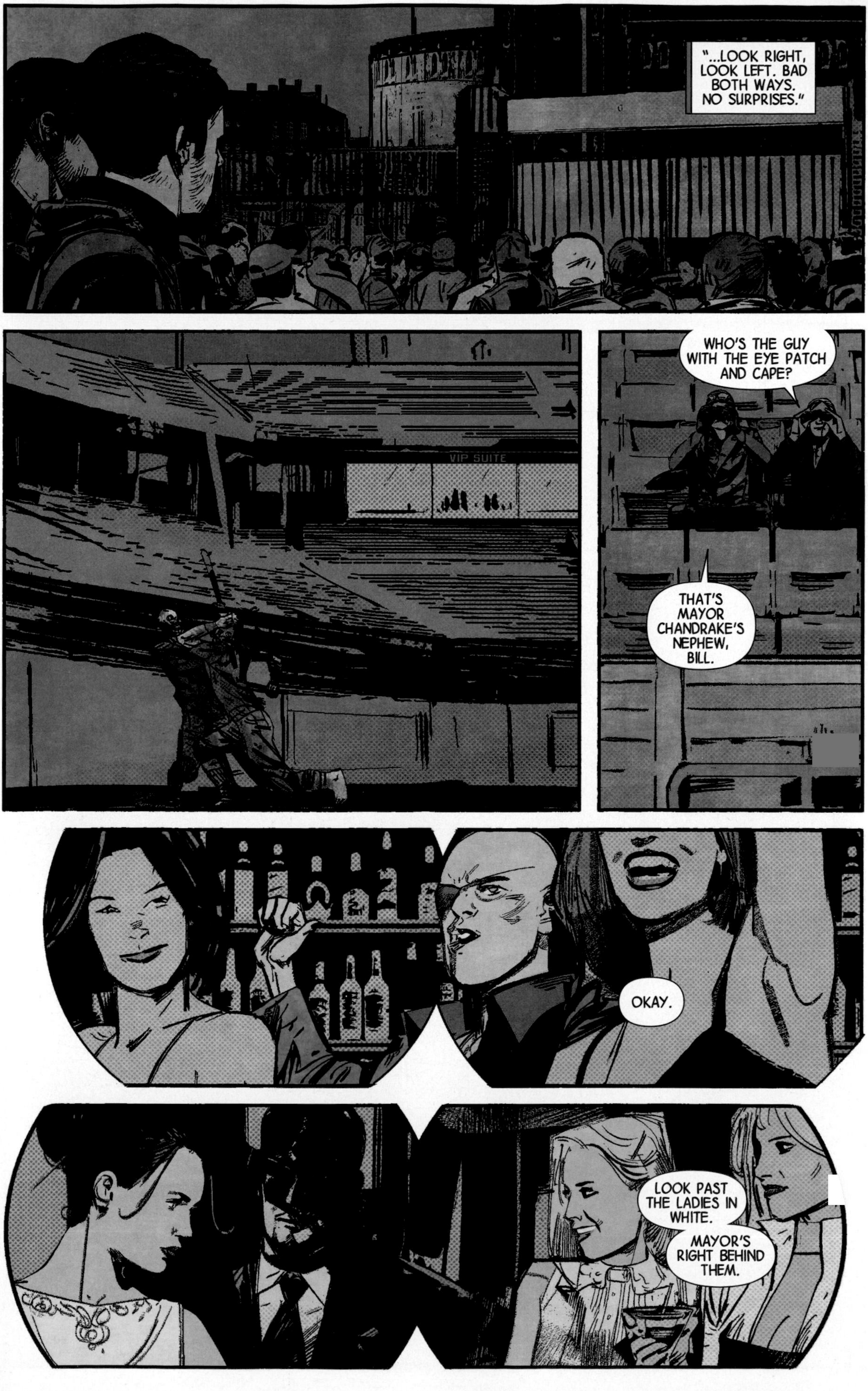
"...LOOK RIGHT, LOOK LEFT. BAD BOTH WAYS. NO SURPRISES."
VIP SUITE
WHO'S THE GUY WITH THE EYE PATCH AND CAPE?
THAT'S MAYOR CHANDRAKE'S NEPHEW, BILL.
OKAY.
LOOK PAST THE LADIES IN WHITE.
MAYOR'S RIGHT BEHIND THEM.

YOU SEE HIM?

OH YEAH.

HOW DO YOU GET THEM TO FIGHT?

FOOD.

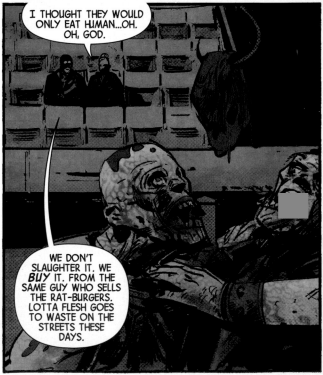

I THOUGHT THEY WOULD ONLY EAT HUMAN...OH. OH, GOD.

WE DON'T SLAUGHTER IT. WE *BUY* IT. FROM THE SAME GUY WHO SELLS THE RAT-BURGERS. LOTTA FLESH GOES TO WASTE ON THE STREETS THESE DAYS.

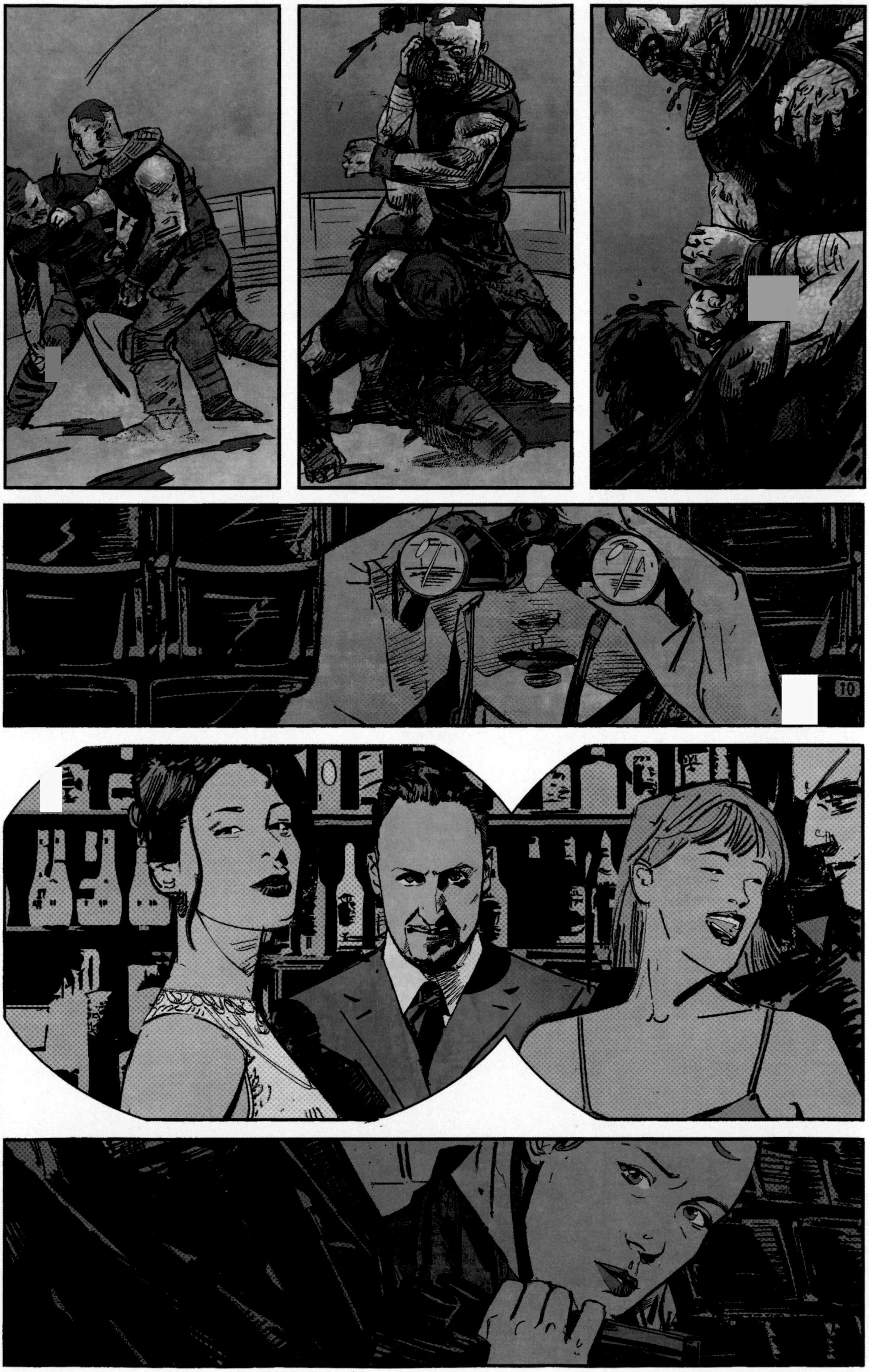
10

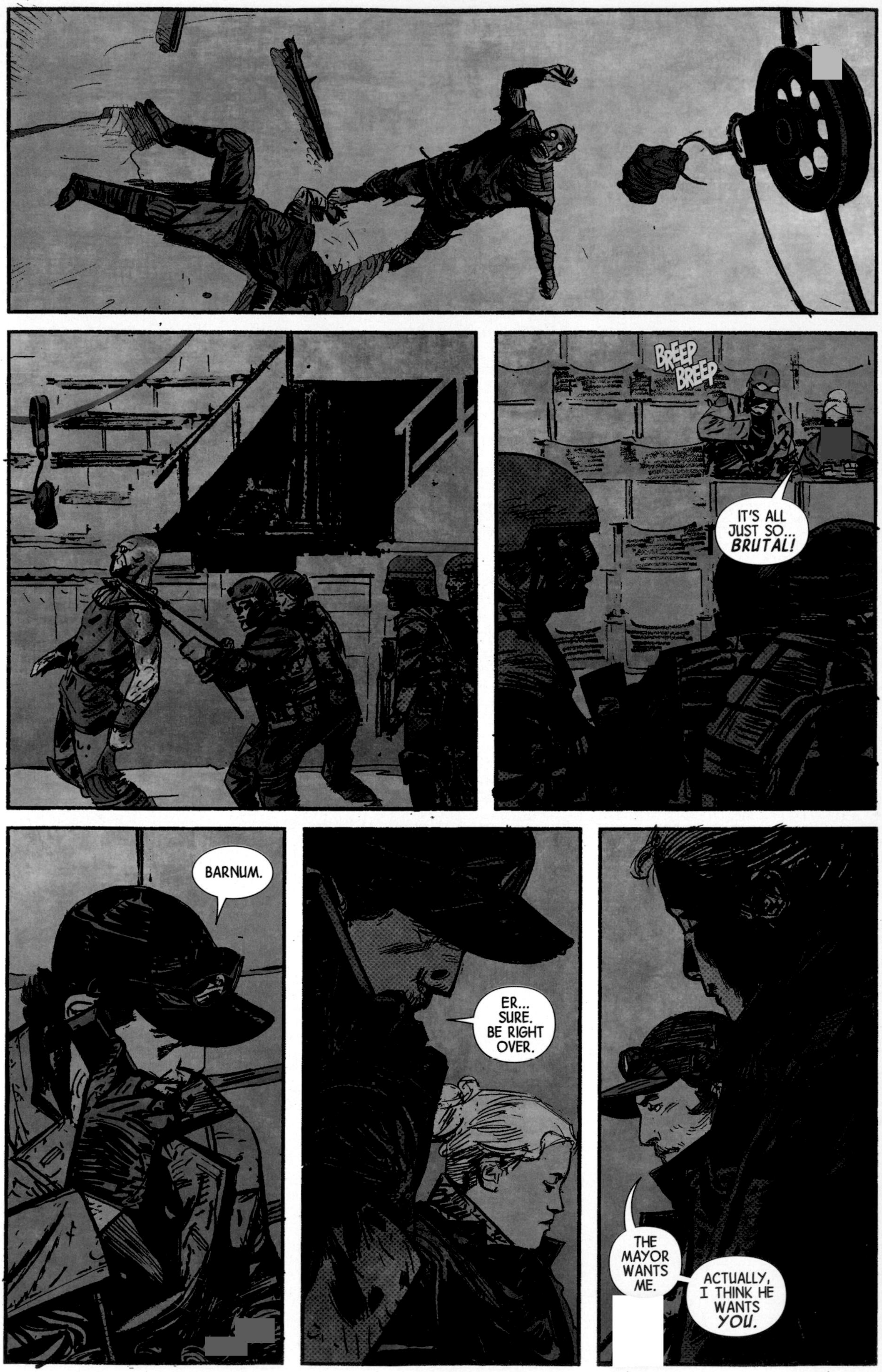
BREEP
BREEP
IT'S ALL JUST SO... BRUTAL!
BARNUM.
ER... SURE. BE RIGHT OVER.
THE MAYOR WANTS ME.
ACTUALLY, I THINK HE WANTS YOU.

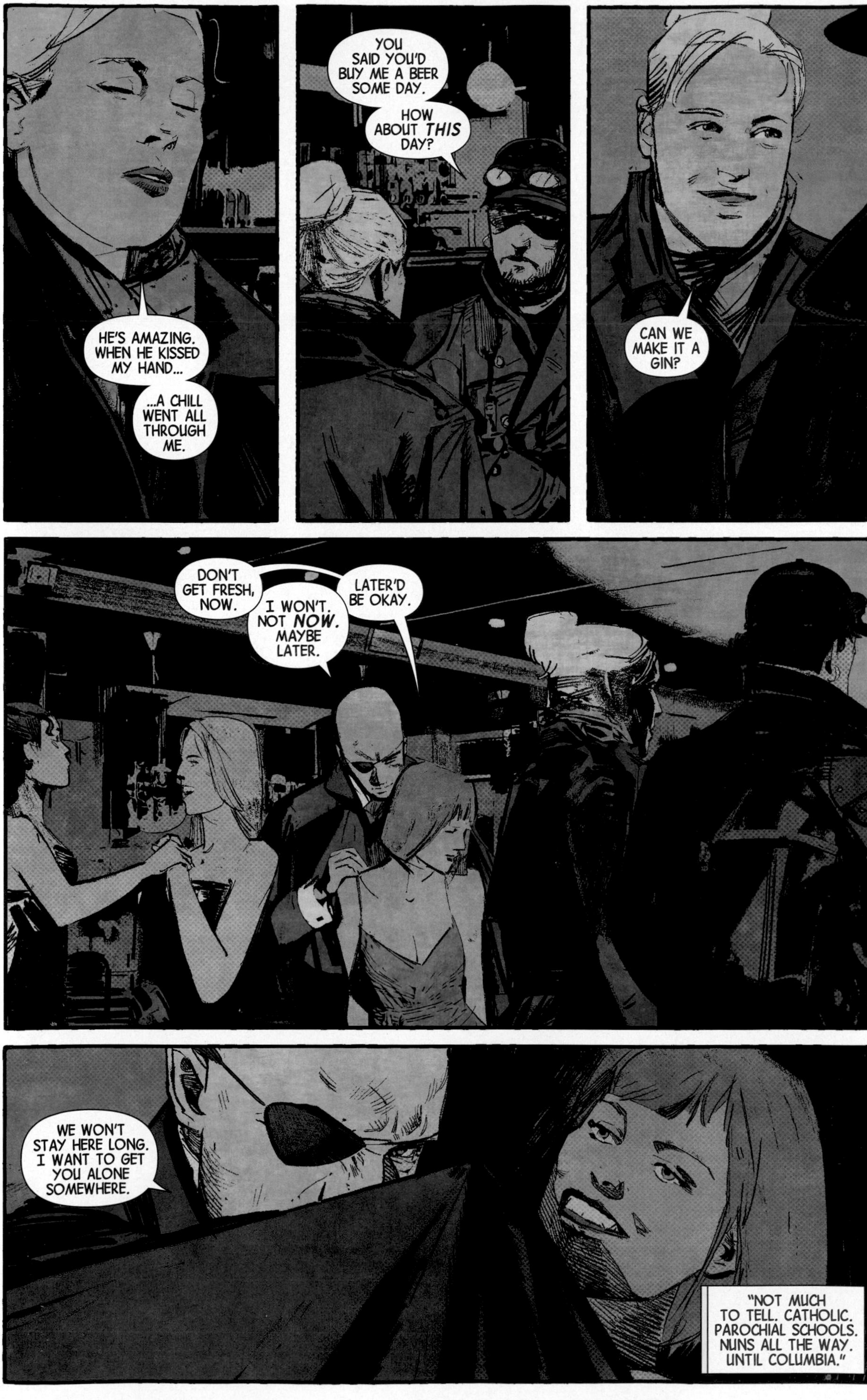
HE'S AMAZING. WHEN HE KISSED MY HAND...
...A CHILL WENT ALL THROUGH ME.
YOU SAID YOU'D BUY ME A BEER SOME DAY.
HOW ABOUT *THIS* DAY?
CAN WE MAKE IT A GIN?
DON'T GET FRESH, NOW.
LATER'D BE OKAY.
I WON'T. NOT *NOW.* MAYBE LATER.
WE WON'T STAY HERE LONG. I WANT TO GET YOU ALONE SOMEWHERE.
"NOT MUCH TO TELL. CATHOLIC. PAROCHIAL SCHOOLS. NUNS ALL THE WAY. UNTIL COLUMBIA."

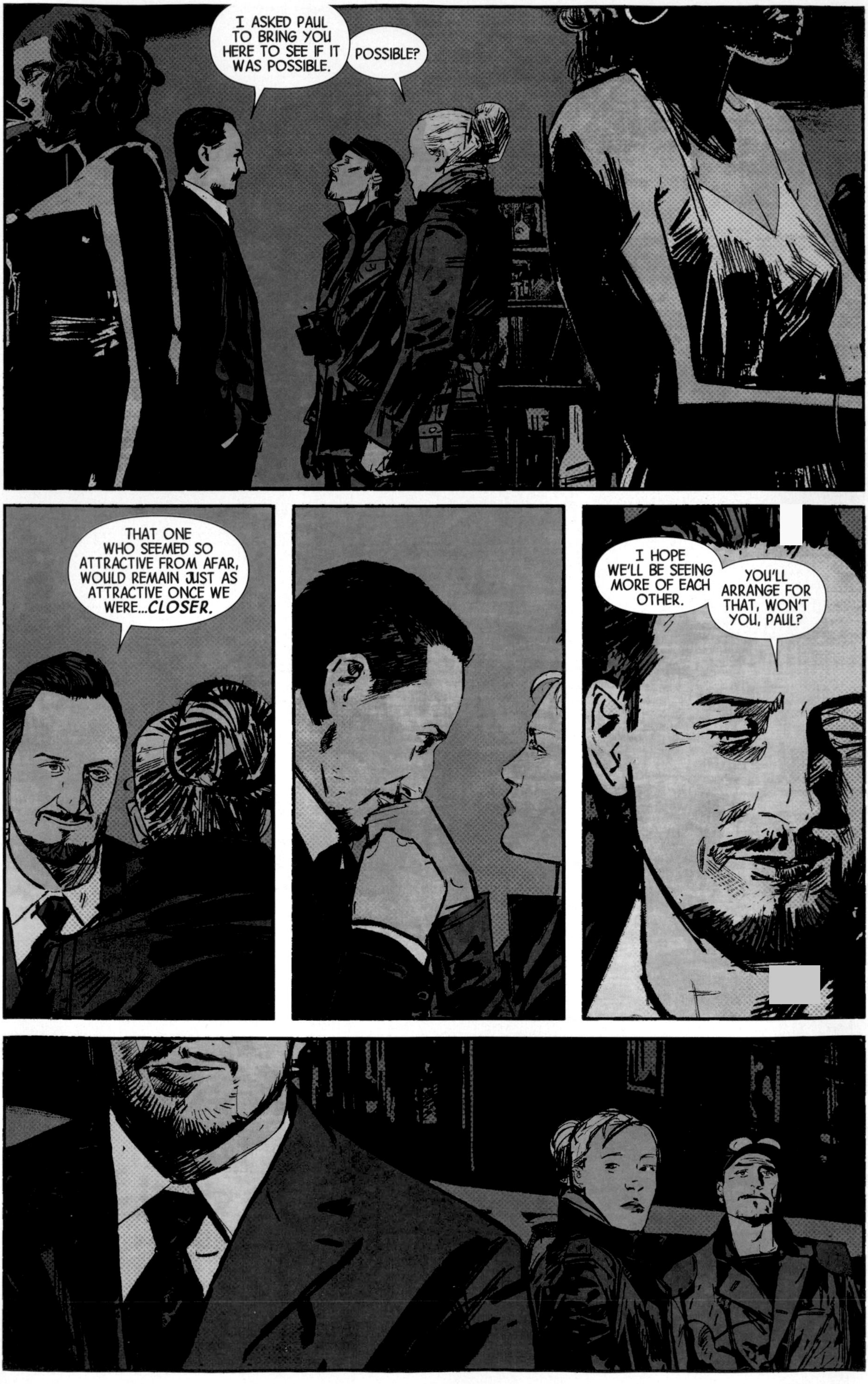
I ASKED PAUL TO BRING YOU HERE TO SEE IF IT WAS POSSIBLE.
POSSIBLE?
THAT ONE WHO SEEMED SO ATTRACTIVE FROM AFAR, WOULD REMAIN JUST AS ATTRACTIVE ONCE WE WERE...*CLOSER.*
I HOPE WE'LL BE SEEING MORE OF EACH OTHER.
YOU'LL ARRANGE FOR THAT, WON'T YOU, PAUL?

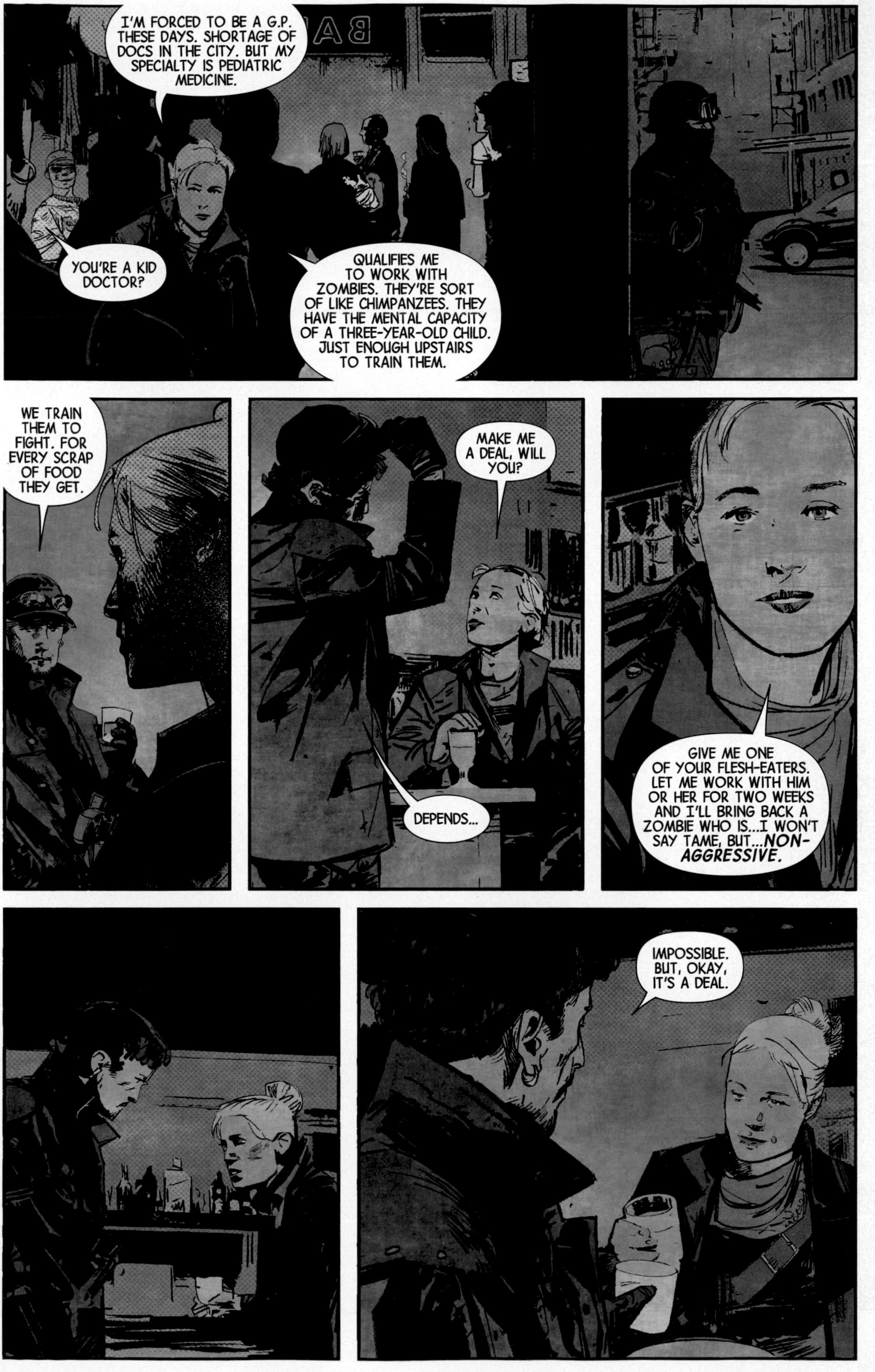
I'M FORCED TO BE A G.P. THESE DAYS. SHORTAGE OF DOCS IN THE CITY. BUT MY SPECIALTY IS PEDIATRIC MEDICINE.
YOU'RE A KID DOCTOR?
QUALIFIES ME TO WORK WITH ZOMBIES. THEY'RE SORT OF LIKE CHIMPANZEES. THEY HAVE THE MENTAL CAPACITY OF A THREE-YEAR-OLD CHILD. JUST ENOUGH UPSTAIRS TO TRAIN THEM.
WE TRAIN THEM TO FIGHT. FOR EVERY SCRAP OF FOOD THEY GET.
MAKE ME A DEAL, WILL YOU?
DEPENDS...
GIVE ME ONE OF YOUR FLESH-EATERS. LET ME WORK WITH HIM OR HER FOR TWO WEEKS AND I'LL BRING BACK A ZOMBIE WHO IS...I WON'T SAY TAME, BUT...*NON-AGGRESSIVE.*
IMPOSSIBLE. BUT, OKAY, IT'S A DEAL.

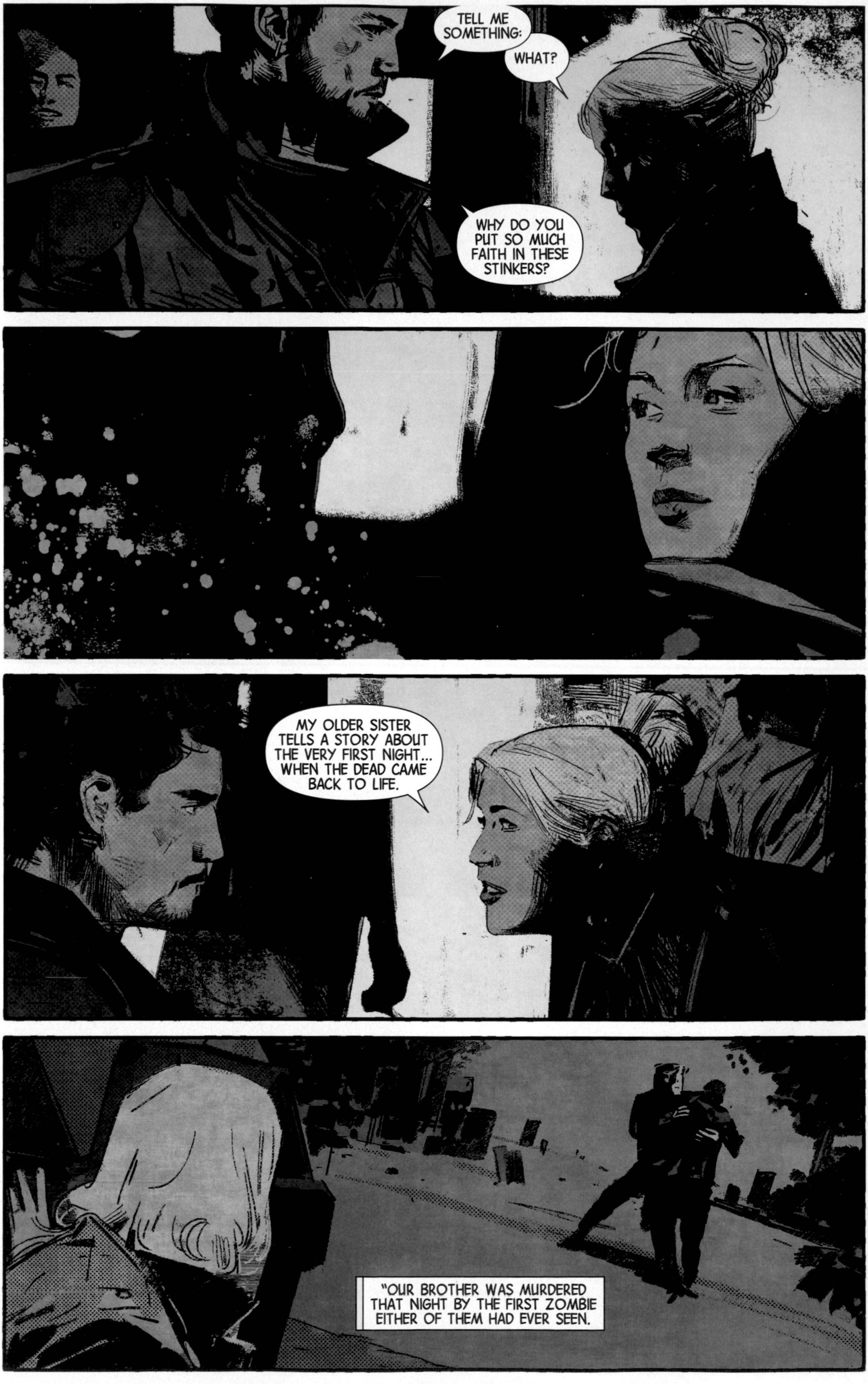
TELL ME SOMETHING:
WHAT?
WHY DO YOU PUT SO MUCH FAITH IN THESE STINKERS?
MY OLDER SISTER TELLS A STORY ABOUT THE VERY FIRST NIGHT... WHEN THE DEAD CAME BACK TO LIFE.
"OUR BROTHER WAS MURDERED THAT NIGHT BY THE FIRST ZOMBIE EITHER OF THEM HAD EVER SEEN.

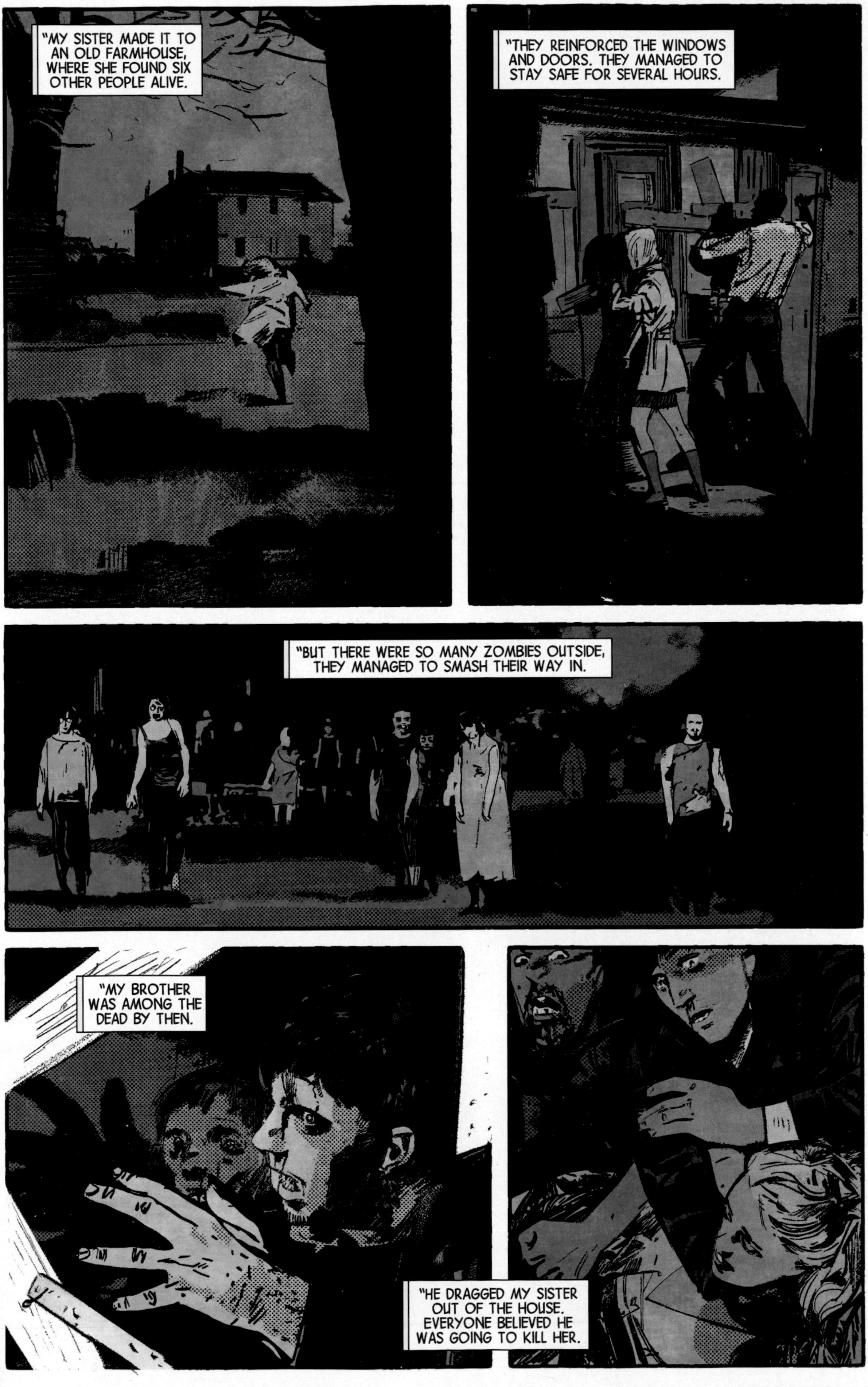
"MY SISTER MADE IT TO AN OLD FARMHOUSE, WHERE SHE FOUND SIX OTHER PEOPLE ALIVE.
"THEY REINFORCED THE WINDOWS AND DOORS. THEY MANAGED TO STAY SAFE FOR SEVERAL HOURS.
"BUT THERE WERE SO MANY ZOMBIES OUTSIDE, THEY MANAGED TO SMASH THEIR WAY IN.
"MY BROTHER WAS AMONG THE DEAD BY THEN.
"HE DRAGGED MY SISTER OUT OF THE HOUSE. EVERYONE BELIEVED HE WAS GOING TO KILL HER.

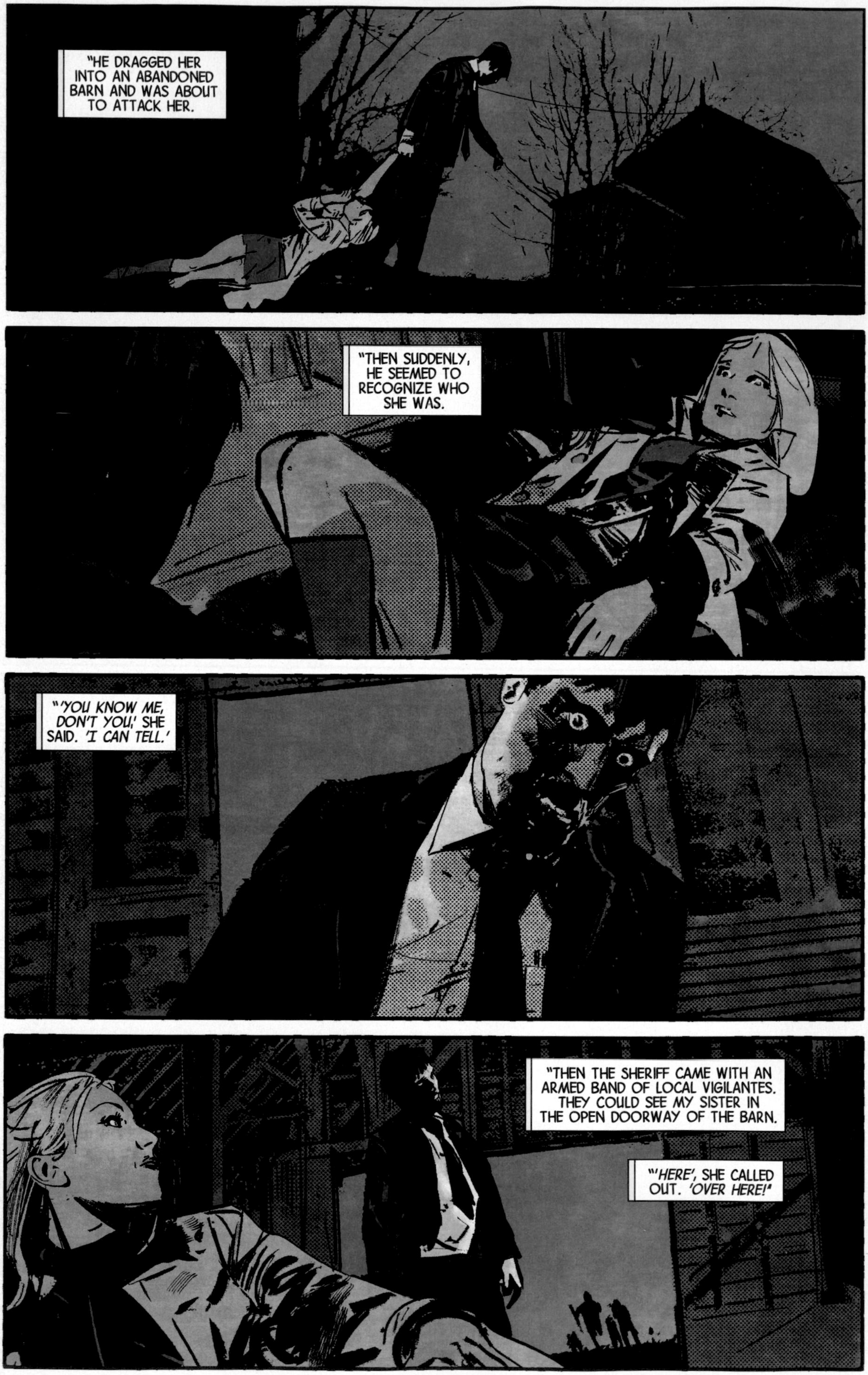
"HE DRAGGED HER INTO AN ABANDONED BARN AND WAS ABOUT TO ATTACK HER.
"THEN SUDDENLY, HE SEEMED TO RECOGNIZE WHO SHE WAS.
"'YOU KNOW ME, DON'T YOU,' SHE SAID. 'I CAN TELL.'
"THEN THE SHERIFF CAME WITH AN ARMED BAND OF LOCAL VIGILANTES. THEY COULD SEE MY SISTER IN THE OPEN DOORWAY OF THE BARN.
"'HERE', SHE CALLED OUT. 'OVER HERE!'

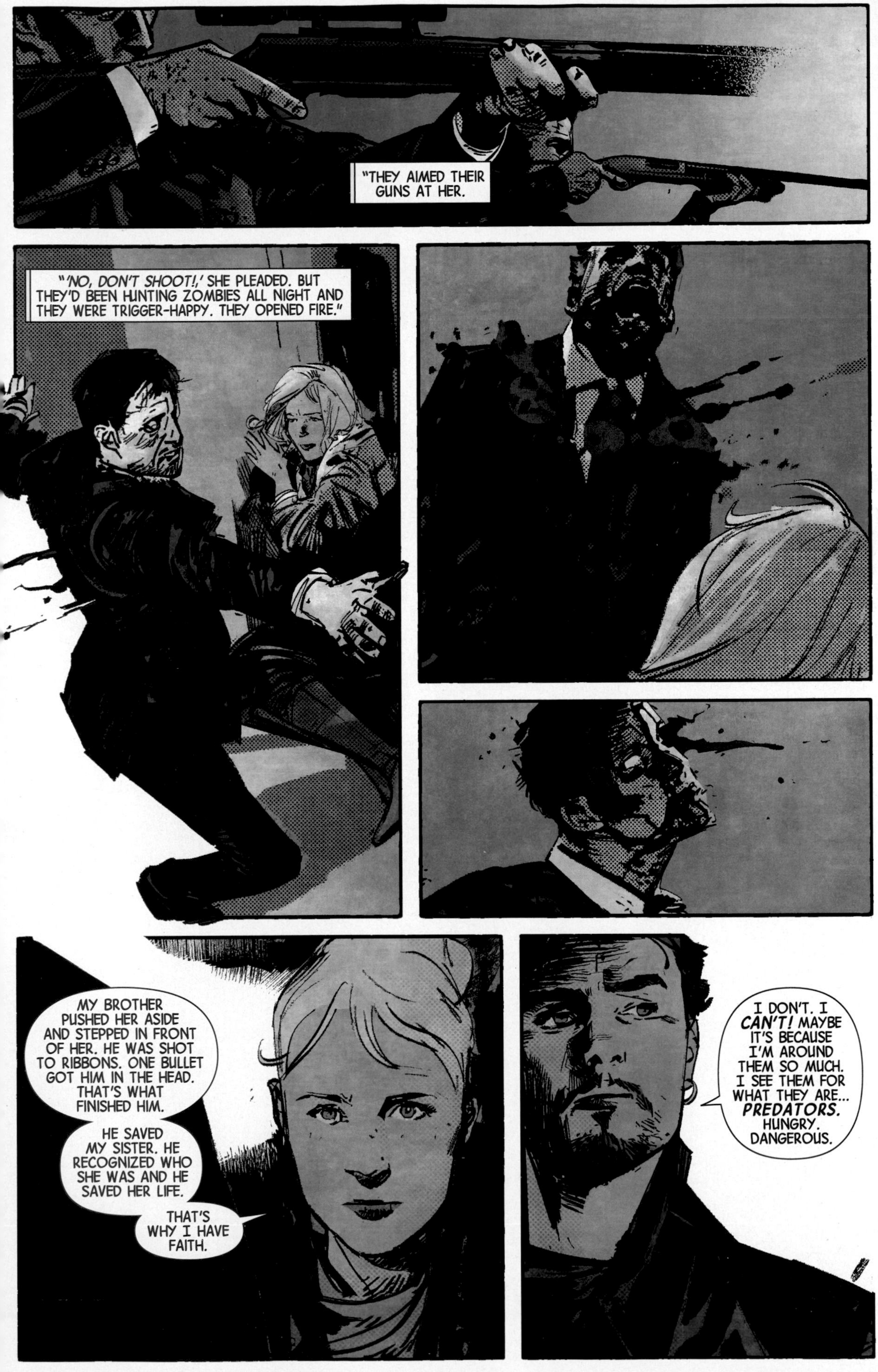
"THEY AIMED THEIR GUNS AT HER.
"'NO, DON'T SHOOT!,' SHE PLEADED. BUT THEY'D BEEN HUNTING ZOMBIES ALL NIGHT AND THEY WERE TRIGGER-HAPPY. THEY OPENED FIRE."
MY BROTHER PUSHED HER ASIDE AND STEPPED IN FRONT OF HER. HE WAS SHOT TO RIBBONS. ONE BULLET GOT HIM IN THE HEAD. THAT'S WHAT FINISHED HIM.
HE SAVED MY SISTER. HE RECOGNIZED WHO SHE WAS AND HE SAVED HER LIFE.
THAT'S WHY I HAVE FAITH.
I DON'T. I CAN'T! MAYBE IT'S BECAUSE I'M AROUND THEM SO MUCH. I SEE THEM FOR WHAT THEY ARE... PREDATORS. HUNGRY. DANGEROUS.

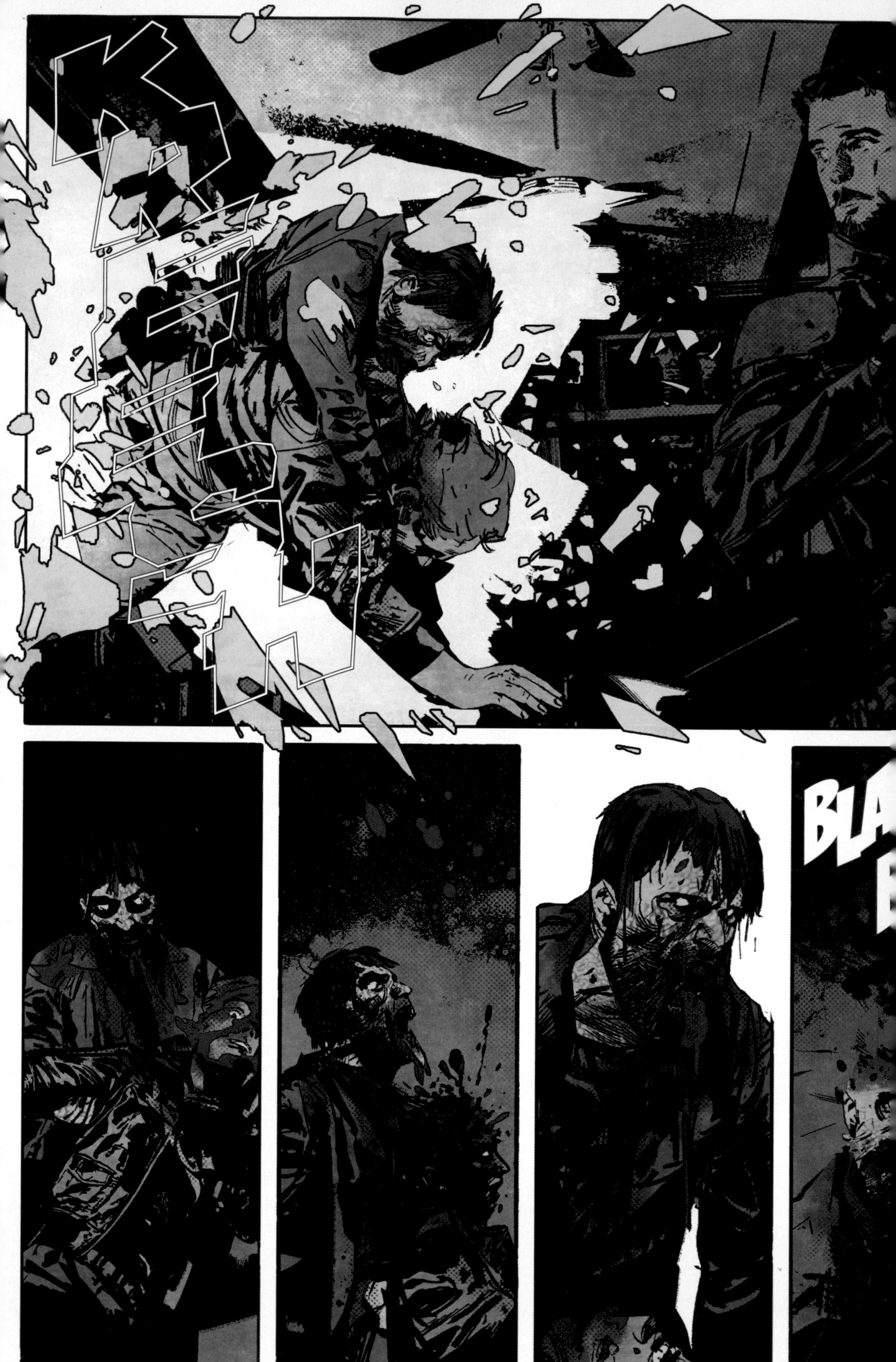

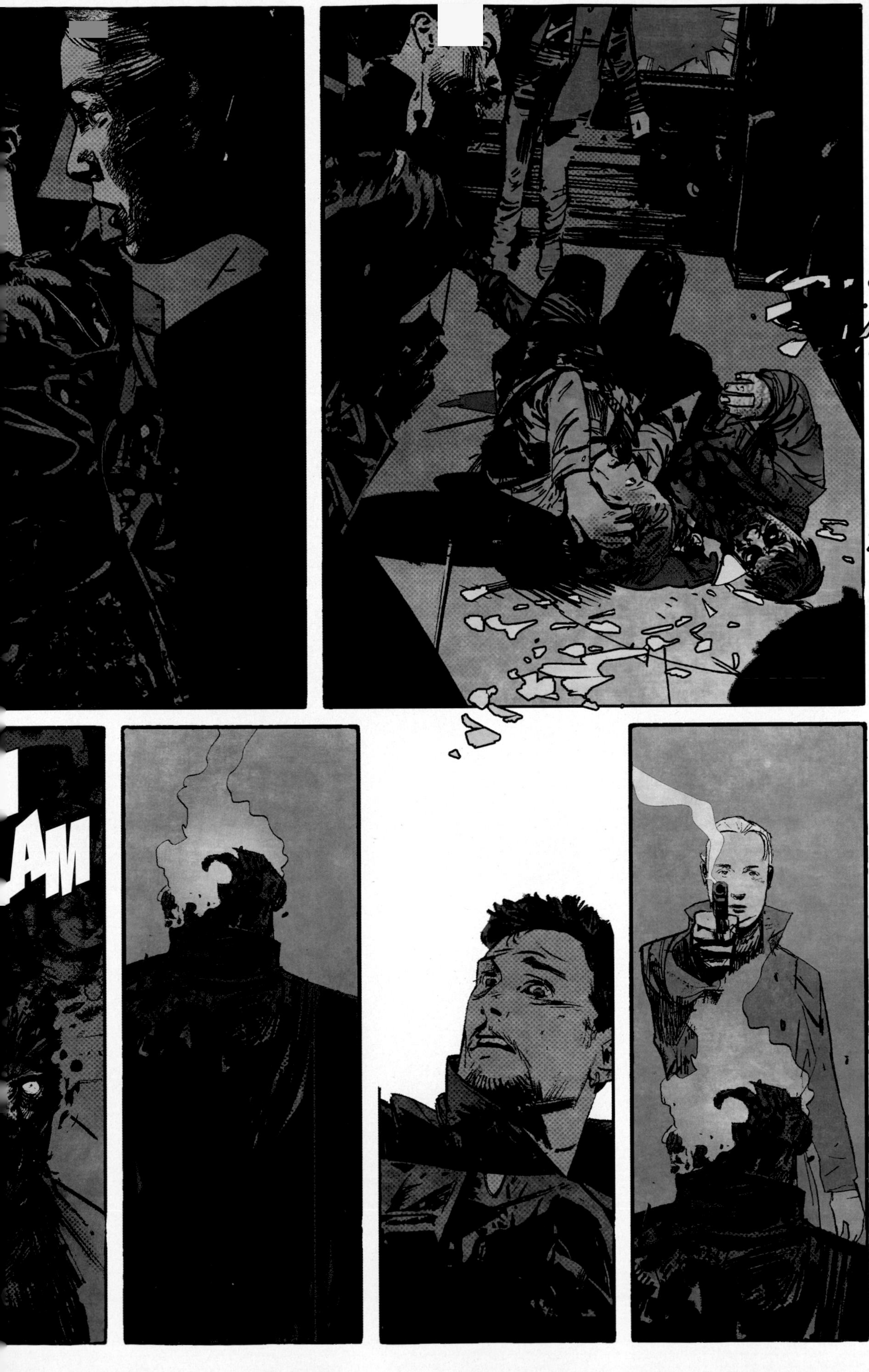
AM

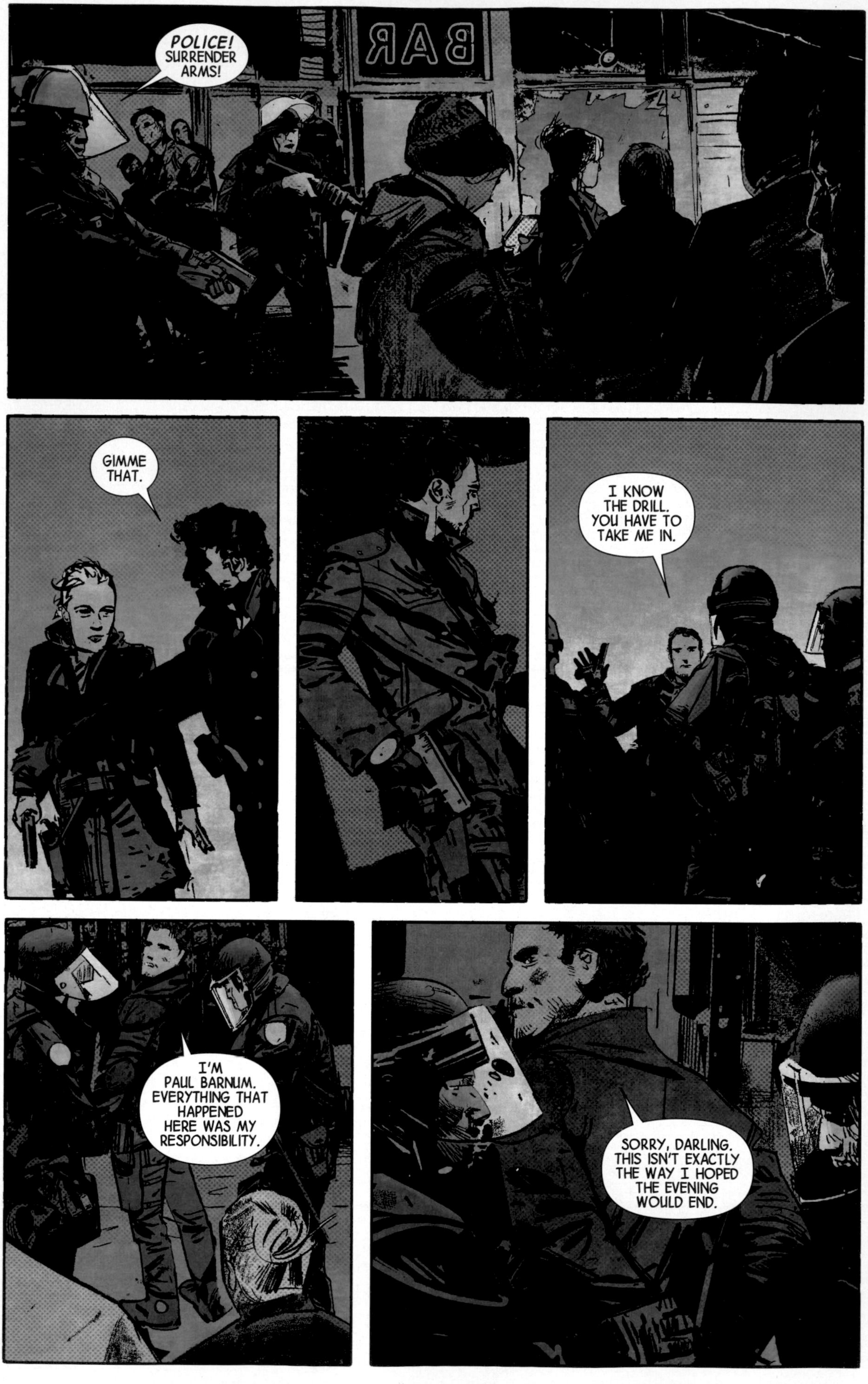
BAR
POLICE! SURRENDER ARMS!
GIMME THAT.
I KNOW THE DRILL. YOU HAVE TO TAKE ME IN.
I'M PAUL BARNUM. EVERYTHING THAT HAPPENED HERE WAS MY RESPONSIBILITY.
SORRY, DARLING. THIS ISN'T EXACTLY THE WAY I HOPED THE EVENING WOULD END.

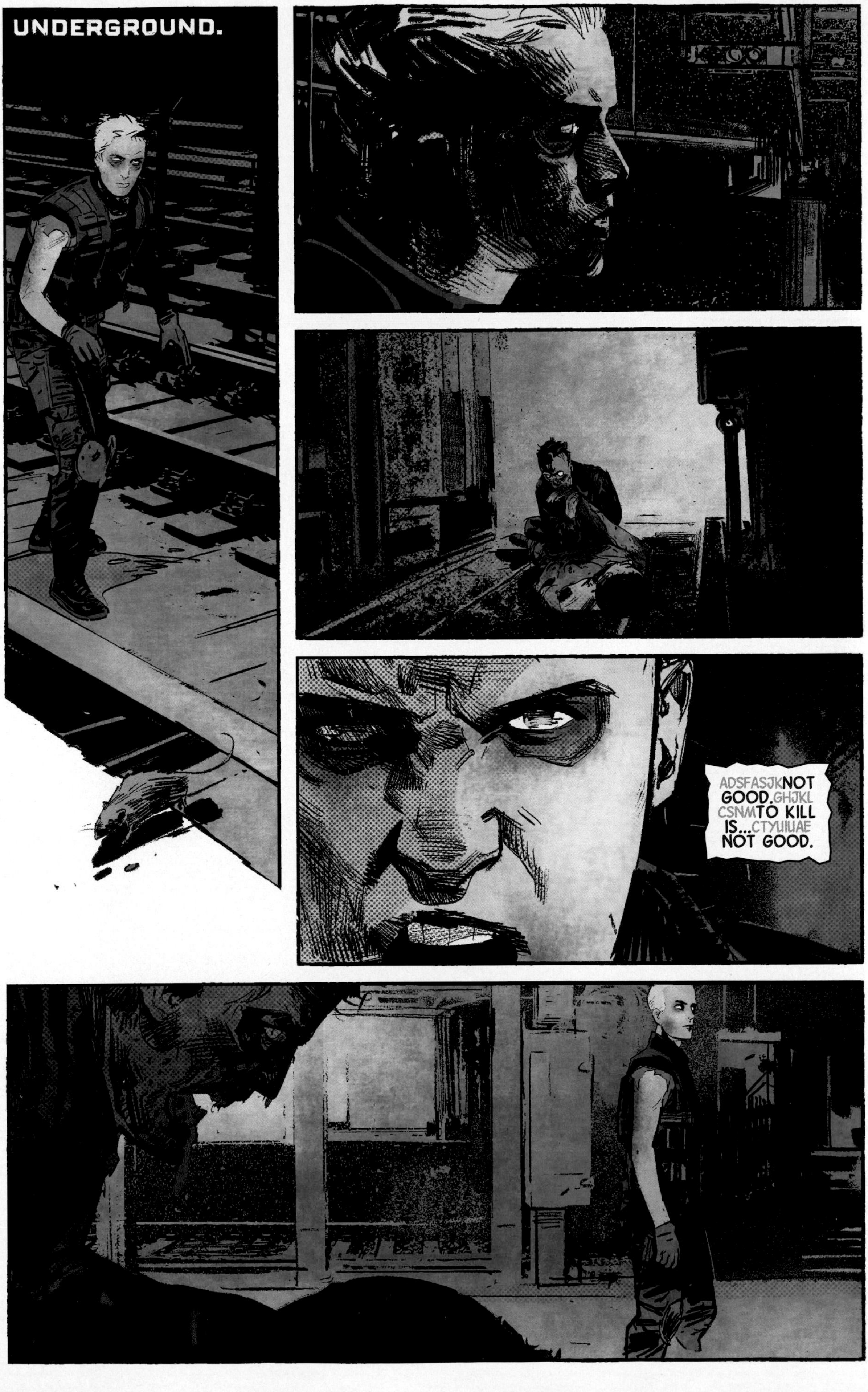
UNDERGROUND.
ADSFASJKNOT GOOD.GHJKL CSNMTO KILL IS...СТУИШАЕ NOT GOOD.

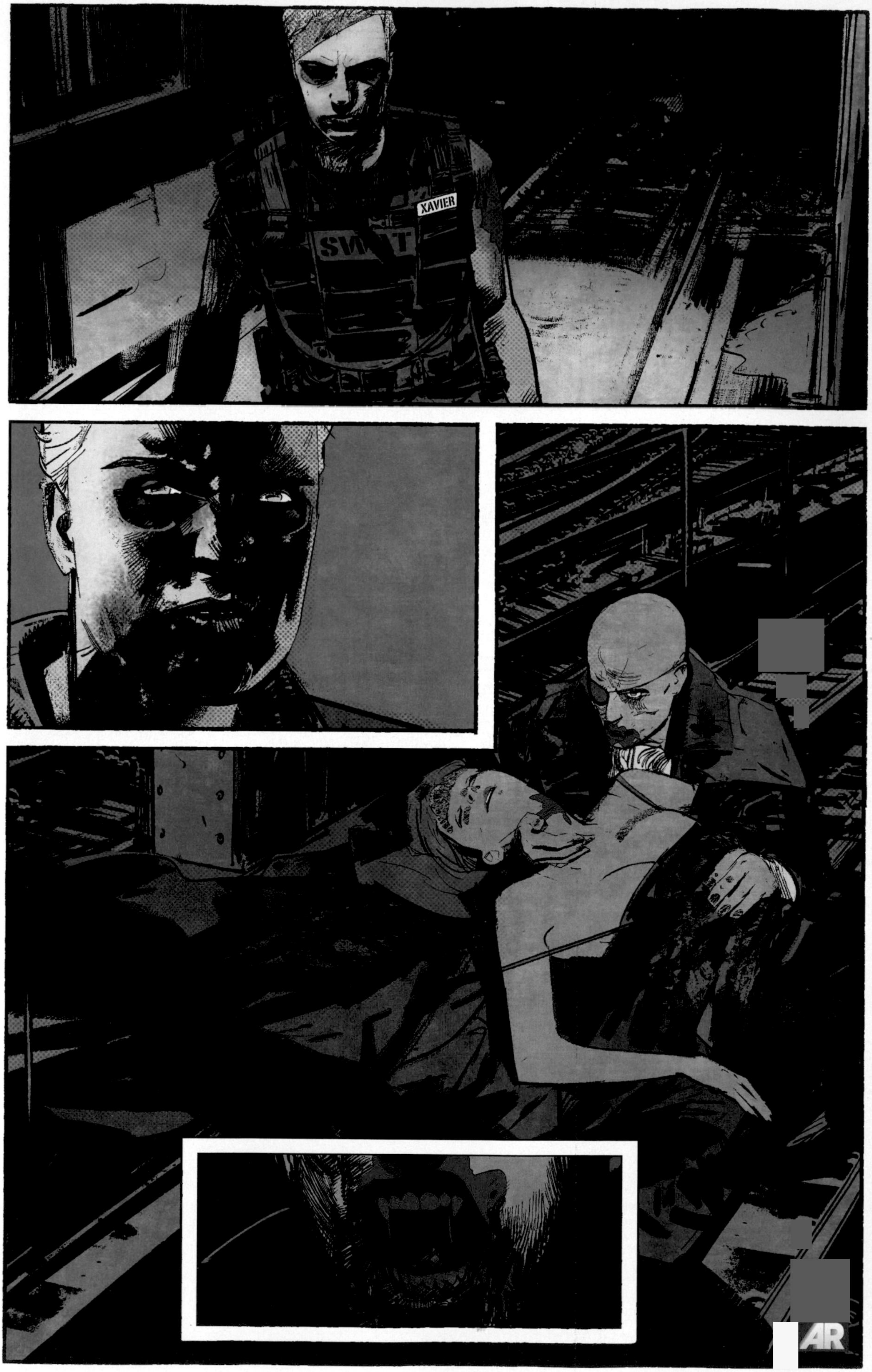
XAVIER
SWAT

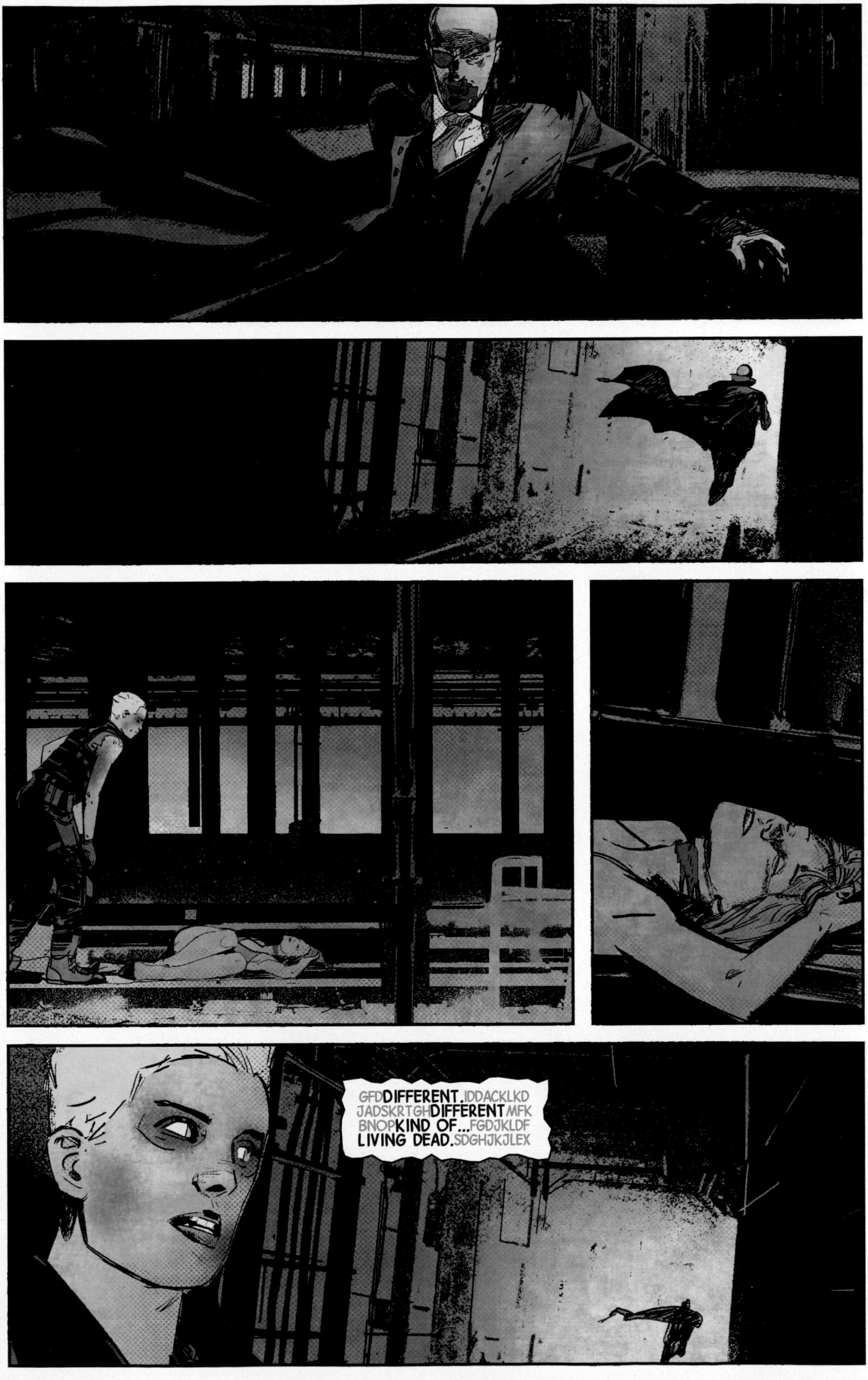
GFDDIFFERENT.IDDACKLKD
JADSKRTGHDIFFERENTMFK
BNOPKIND OF...FGDJKLDF
LIVING DEAD.SDGHJKJLEX

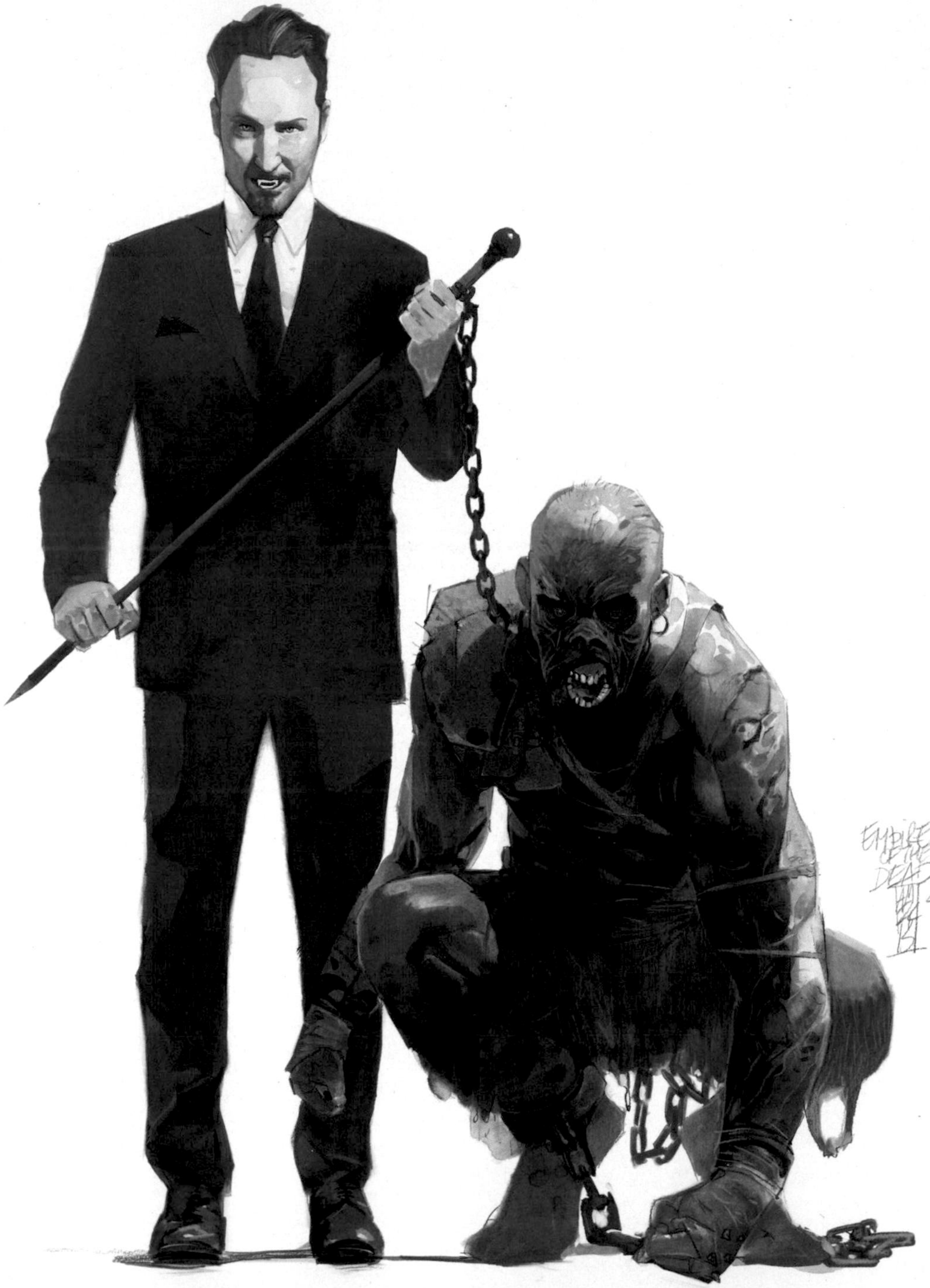
EMPIRE OF THE DEAD 2

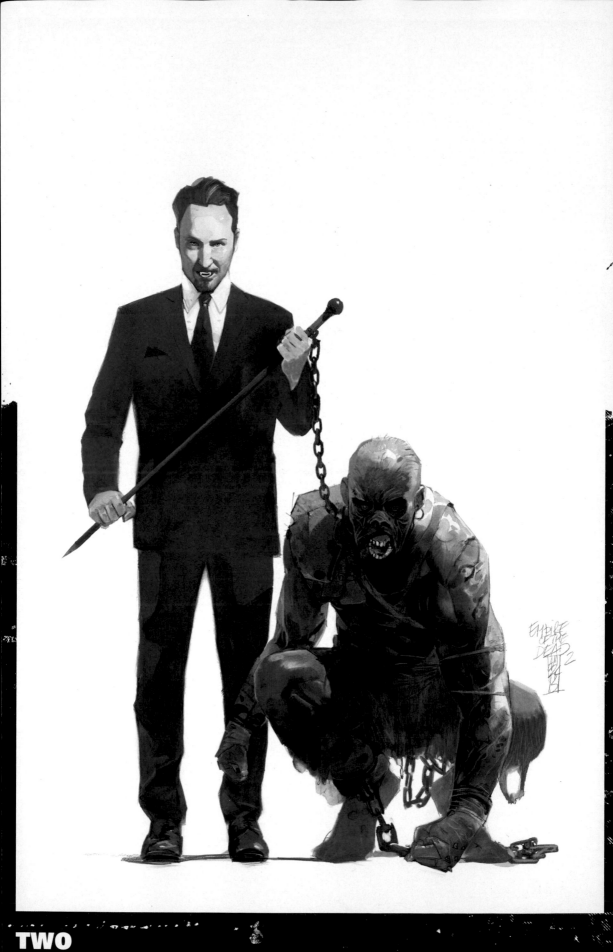

TWO

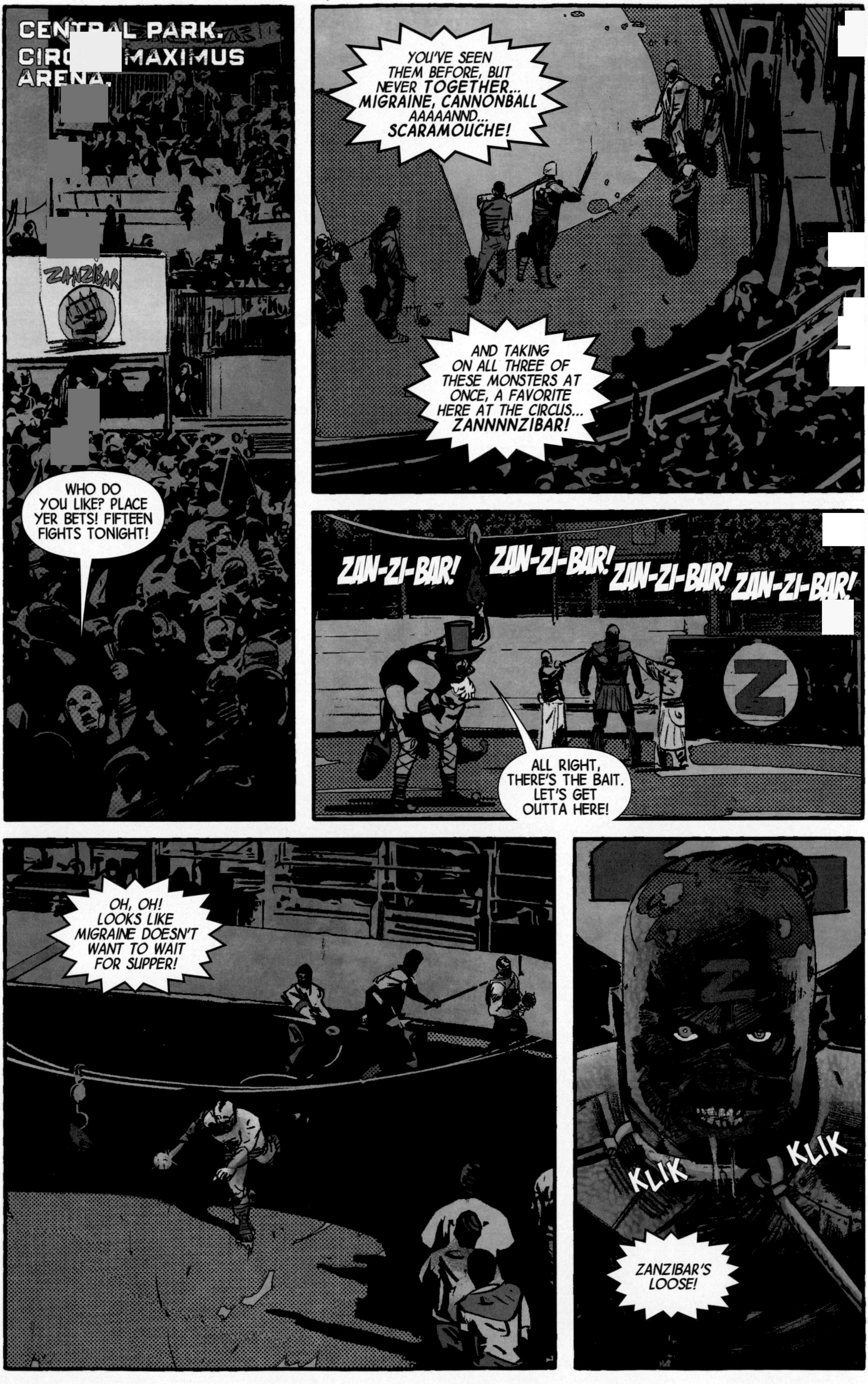
CENTRAL PARK.
CIRC MAXIMUS
ARENA.
WHO DO YOU LIKE? PLACE YER BETS! FIFTEEN FIGHTS TONIGHT!
YOU'VE SEEN THEM BEFORE, BUT NEVER TOGETHER... MIGRAINE, CANNONBALL AAAAAND... SCARAMOUCHE!
AND TAKING ON ALL THREE OF THESE MONSTERS AT ONCE, A FAVORITE HERE AT THE CIRCUS... ZANNNNZIBAR!
ZAN-ZI-BAR! ZAN-ZI-BAR! ZAN-ZI-BAR! ZAN-ZI-BAR!
ZANZIBAR
Z
ALL RIGHT, THERE'S THE BAIT. LET'S GET OUTTA HERE!
OH, OH! LOOKS LIKE MIGRAINE DOESN'T WANT TO WAIT FOR SUPPER!
KLIK
KLIK
ZANZIBAR'S LOOSE!

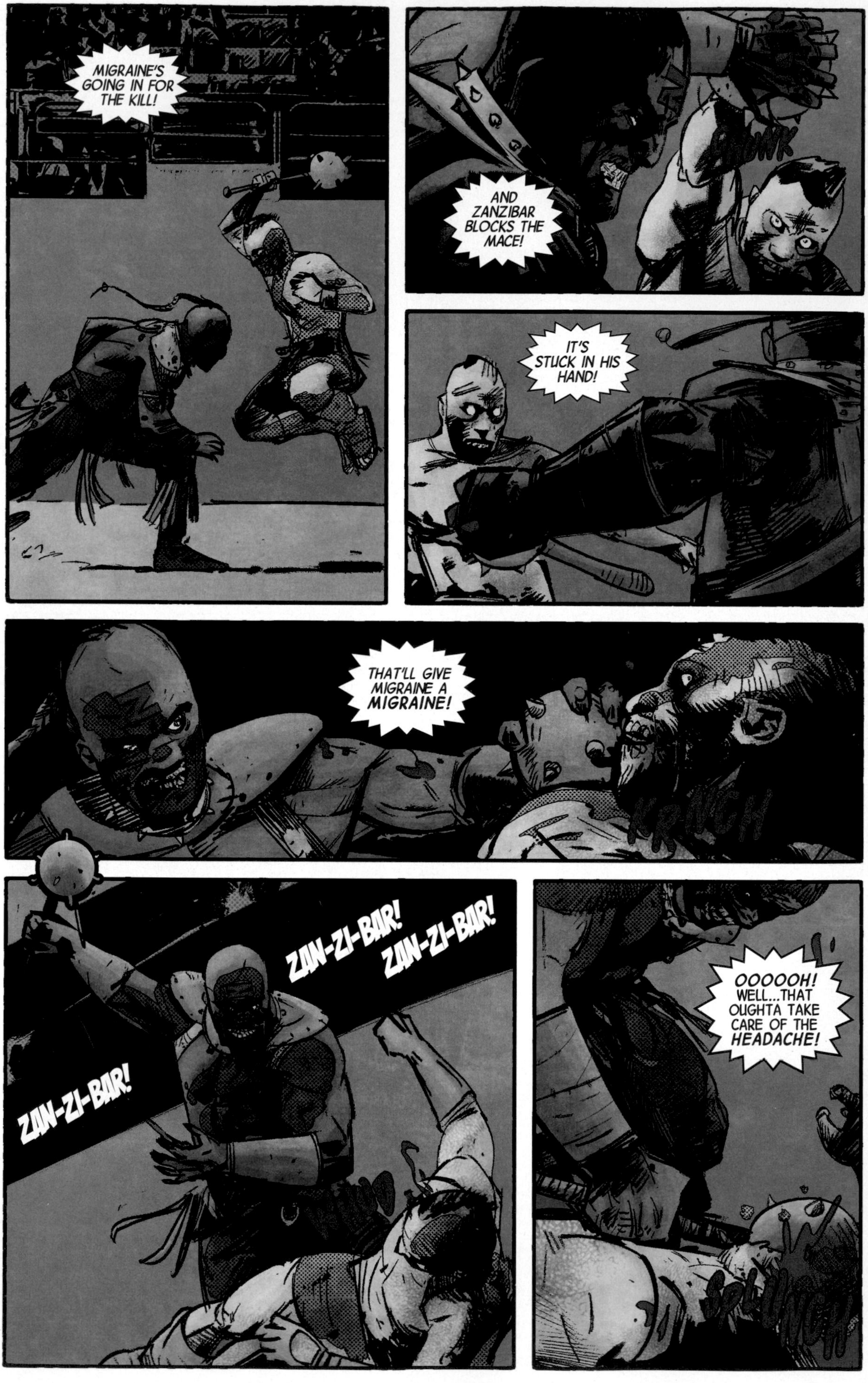
MIGRAINE'S GOING IN FOR THE KILL!
AND ZANZIBAR BLOCKS THE MACE!
IT'S STUCK IN HIS HAND!
THAT'LL GIVE MIGRAINE A MIGRAINE!
ZAN-ZI-BAR! ZAN-ZI-BAR!
ZAN-ZI-BAR!
OOOOOH! WELL...THAT OUGHTA TAKE CARE OF THE HEADACHE!

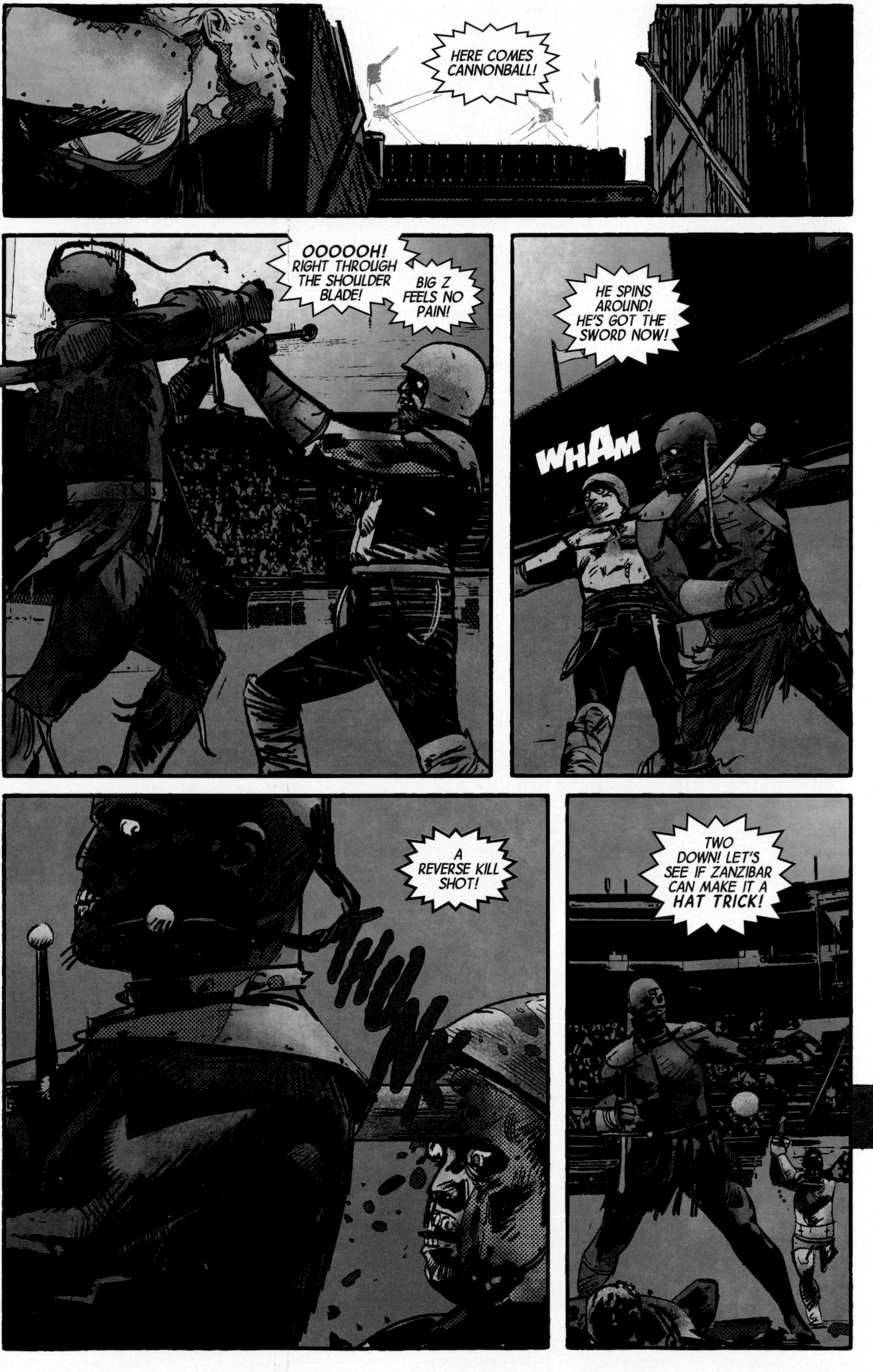
HERE COMES CANNONBALL!
OOOOOH! RIGHT THROUGH THE SHOULDER BLADE!
BIG Z FEELS NO PAIN!
HE SPINS AROUND! HE'S GOT THE SWORD NOW!
WHAM
A REVERSE KILL SHOT!
THUNK
TWO DOWN! LET'S SEE IF ZANZIBAR CAN MAKE IT A HAT TRICK!

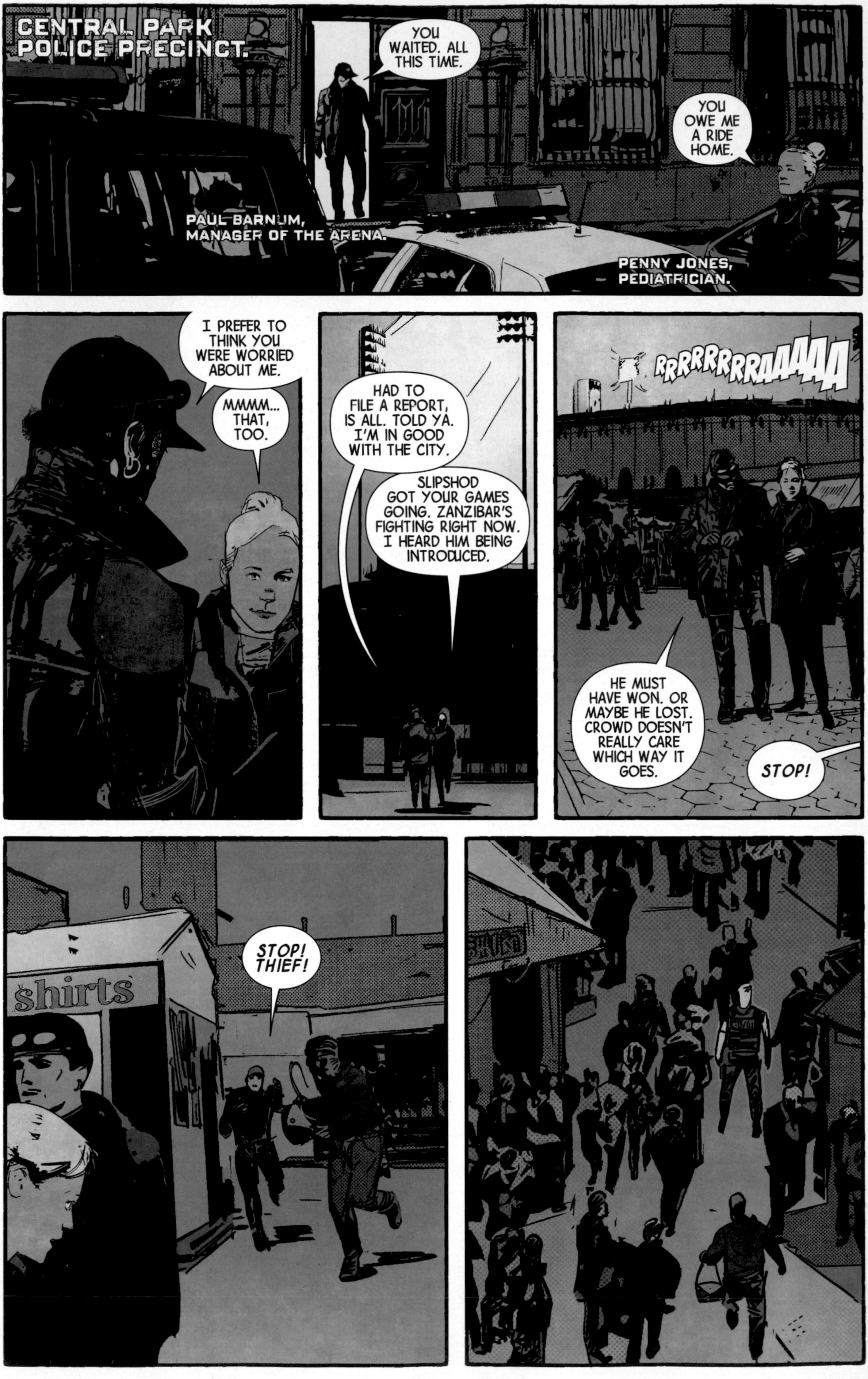
CENTRAL PARK POLICE PRECINCT.
YOU WAITED. ALL THIS TIME.
YOU OWE ME A RIDE HOME.
PAUL BARNUM, MANAGER OF THE ARENA.
PENNY JONES, PEDIATRICIAN.
I PREFER TO THINK YOU WERE WORRIED ABOUT ME.
MMMM... THAT, TOO.
HAD TO FILE A REPORT, IS ALL. TOLD YA. I'M IN GOOD WITH THE CITY.
SLIPSHOD GOT YOUR GAMES GOING. ZANZIBAR'S FIGHTING RIGHT NOW. I HEARD HIM BEING INTRODUCED.
RRRRRRRRAAAAAA
HE MUST HAVE WON. OR MAYBE HE LOST. CROWD DOESN'T REALLY CARE WHICH WAY IT GOES.
STOP!
shirts
STOP! THIEF!

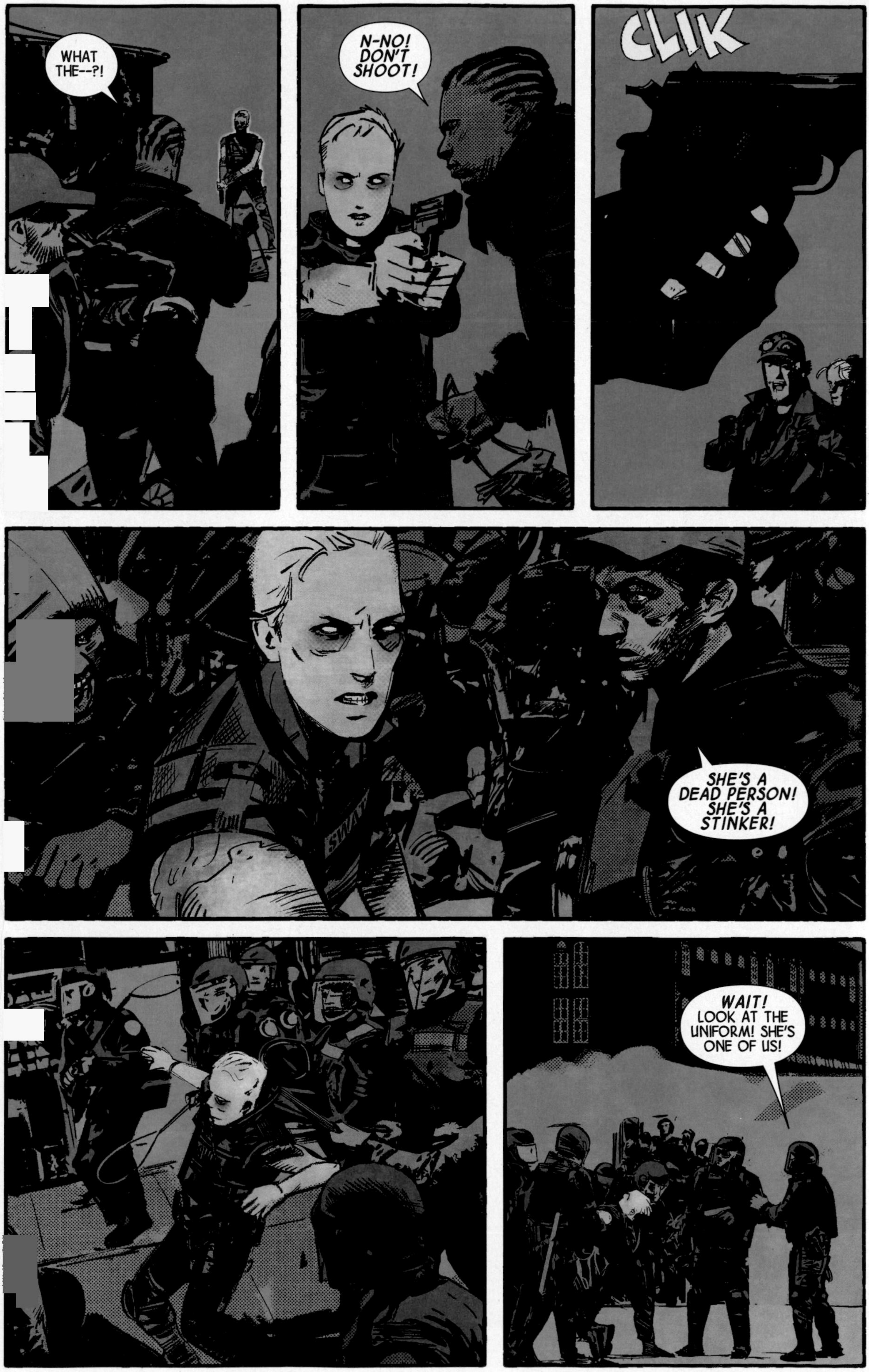
WHAT THE--?!
N-NO! DON'T SHOOT!
CLIK
SHE'S A DEAD PERSON! SHE'S A STINKER!
WAIT! LOOK AT THE UNIFORM! SHE'S ONE OF US!

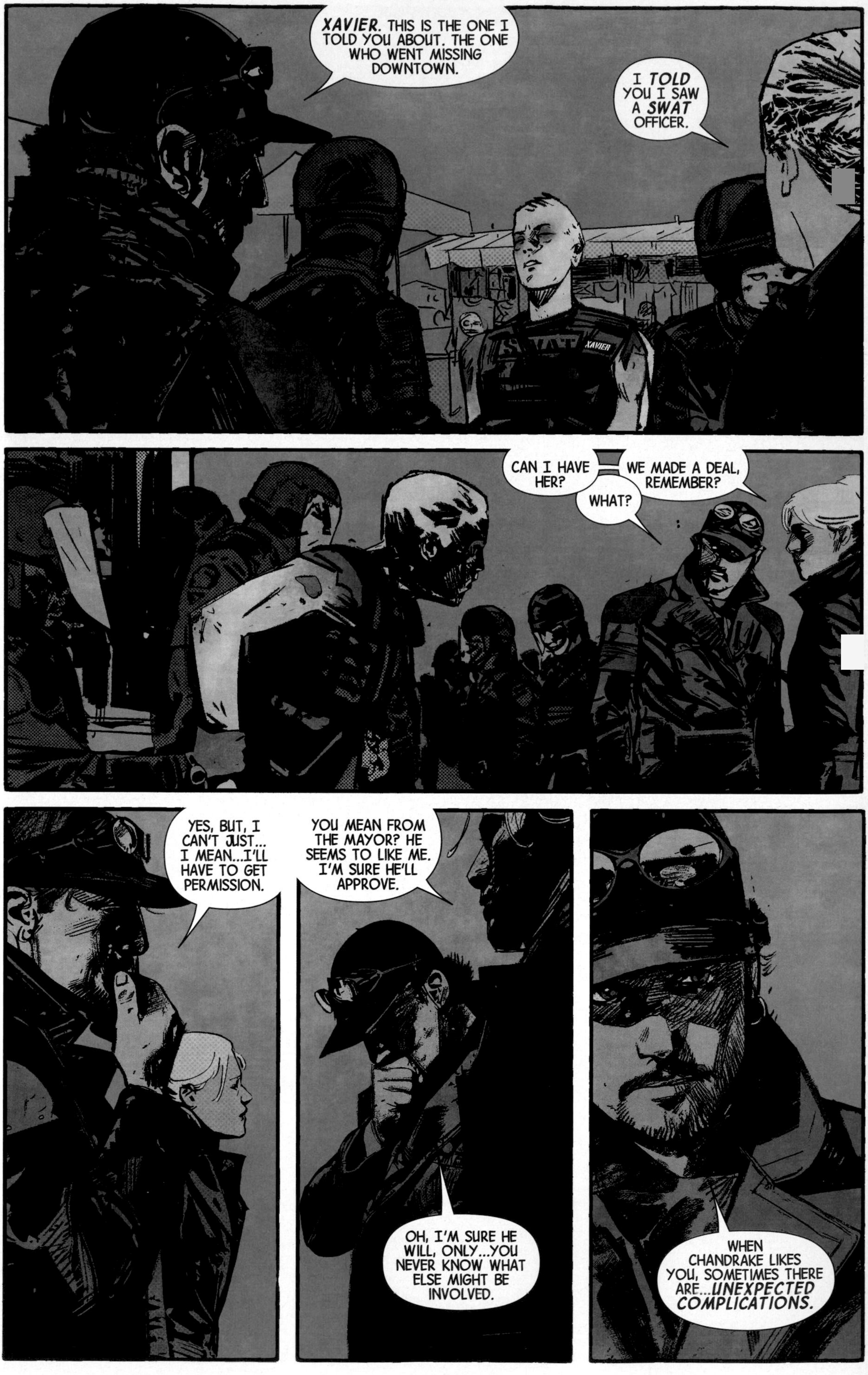
XAVIER. THIS IS THE ONE I TOLD YOU ABOUT. THE ONE WHO WENT MISSING DOWNTOWN.
I TOLD YOU I SAW A SWAT OFFICER.
XAVIER
CAN I HAVE HER?
WHAT?
WE MADE A DEAL, REMEMBER?
YES, BUT, I CAN'T JUST... I MEAN...I'LL HAVE TO GET PERMISSION.
YOU MEAN FROM THE MAYOR? HE SEEMS TO LIKE ME. I'M SURE HE'LL APPROVE.
OH, I'M SURE HE WILL, ONLY...YOU NEVER KNOW WHAT ELSE MIGHT BE INVOLVED.
WHEN CHANDRAKE LIKES YOU, SOMETIMES THERE ARE...UNEXPECTED COMPLICATIONS.

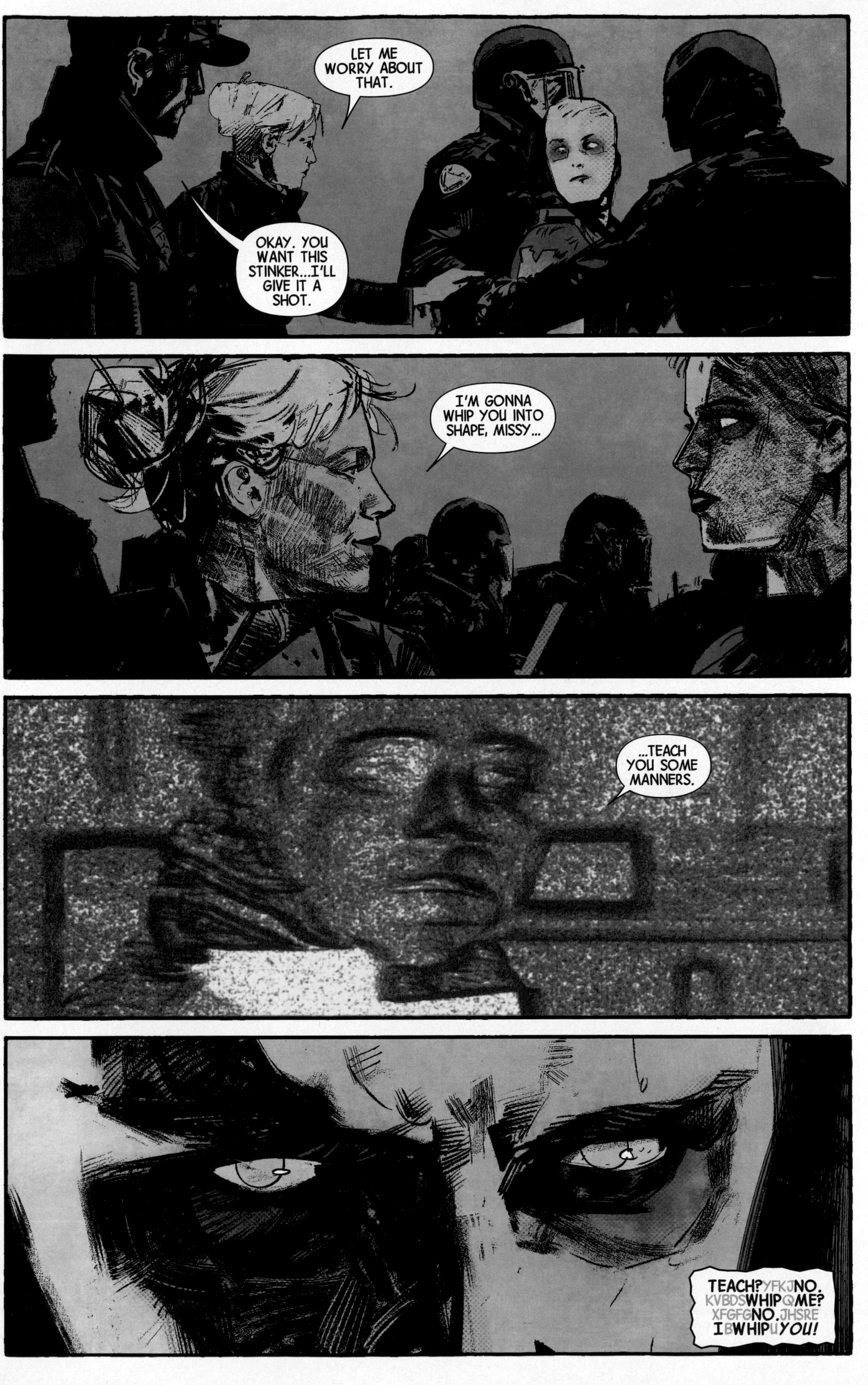
LET ME WORRY ABOUT THAT.
OKAY. YOU WANT THIS STINKER...I'LL GIVE IT A SHOT.
I'M GONNA WHIP YOU INTO SHAPE, MISSY...
...TEACH YOU SOME MANNERS.
TEACH?YFKJNO. KVBDSWHIPQME? XFGFGNO.JHSRE IBWHIPUYOU!

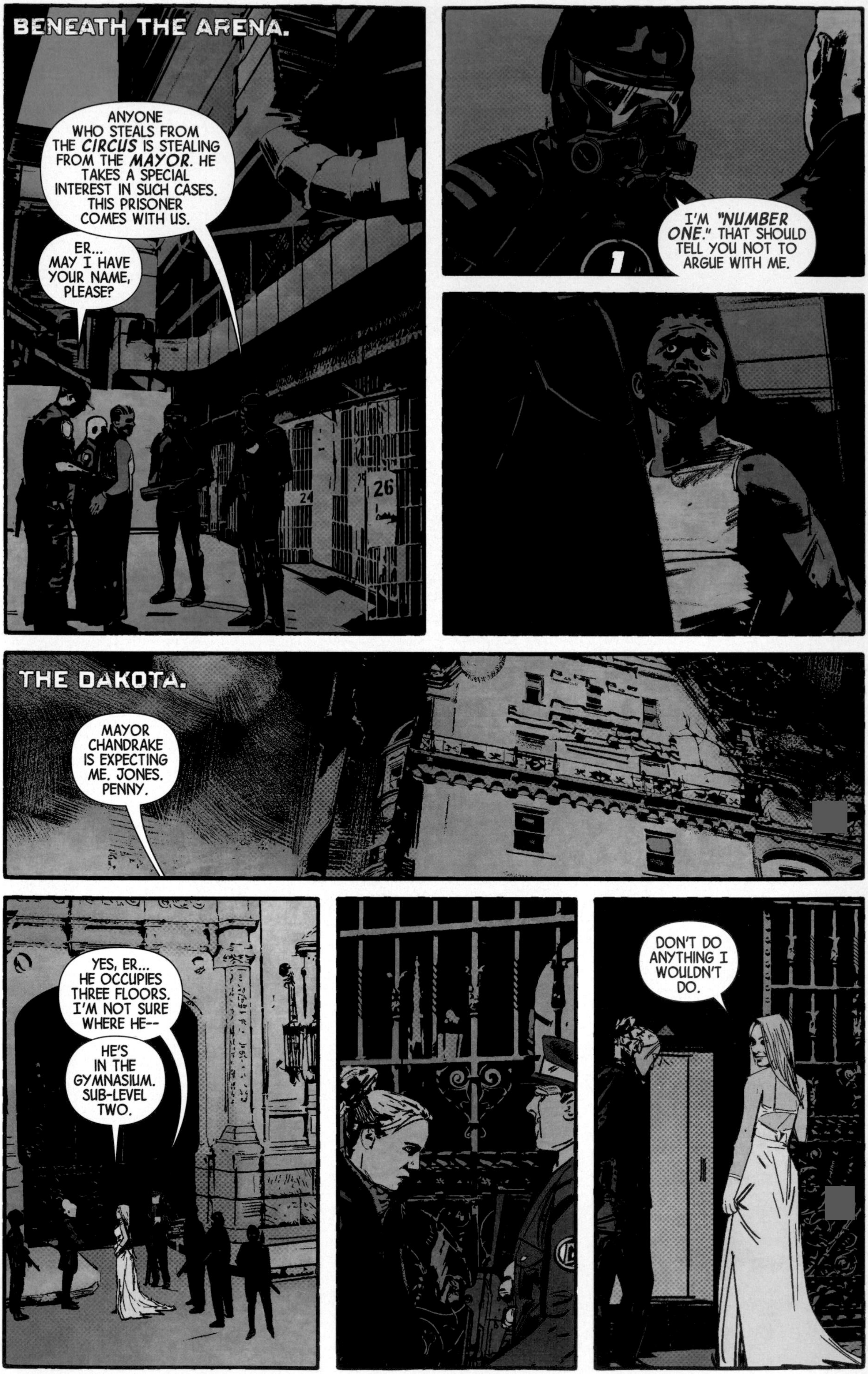
BENEATH THE ARENA.
ANYONE WHO STEALS FROM THE *CIRCUS* IS STEALING FROM THE *MAYOR*. HE TAKES A SPECIAL INTEREST IN SUCH CASES. THIS PRISONER COMES WITH US.
ER... MAY I HAVE YOUR NAME, PLEASE?
I'M *"NUMBER ONE."* THAT SHOULD TELL YOU NOT TO ARGUE WITH ME.
THE DAKOTA.
MAYOR CHANDRAKE IS EXPECTING ME. JONES. PENNY.
YES, ER... HE OCCUPIES THREE FLOORS. I'M NOT SURE WHERE HE--
HE'S IN THE GYMNASIUM. SUB-LEVEL TWO.
DON'T DO ANYTHING I WOULDN'T DO.

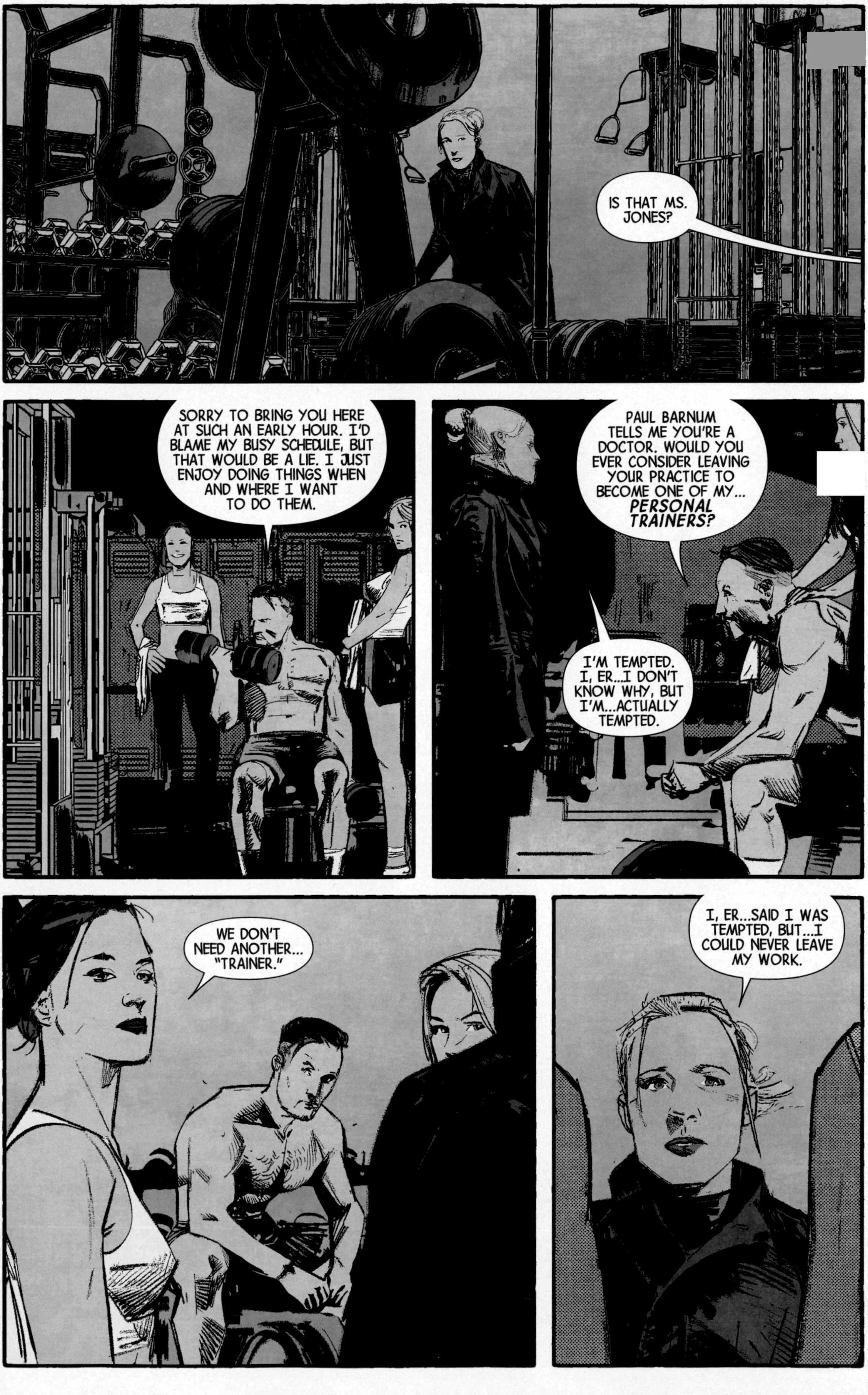
IS THAT MS. JONES?
SORRY TO BRING YOU HERE AT SUCH AN EARLY HOUR. I'D BLAME MY BUSY SCHEDULE, BUT THAT WOULD BE A LIE. I JUST ENJOY DOING THINGS WHEN AND WHERE I WANT TO DO THEM.
PAUL BARNUM TELLS ME YOU'RE A DOCTOR. WOULD YOU EVER CONSIDER LEAVING YOUR PRACTICE TO BECOME ONE OF MY... *PERSONAL TRAINERS?*
I'M TEMPTED. I, ER...I DON'T KNOW WHY, BUT I'M...ACTUALLY TEMPTED.
WE DON'T NEED ANOTHER... "TRAINER."
I, ER...SAID I WAS TEMPTED, BUT...I COULD NEVER LEAVE MY WORK.

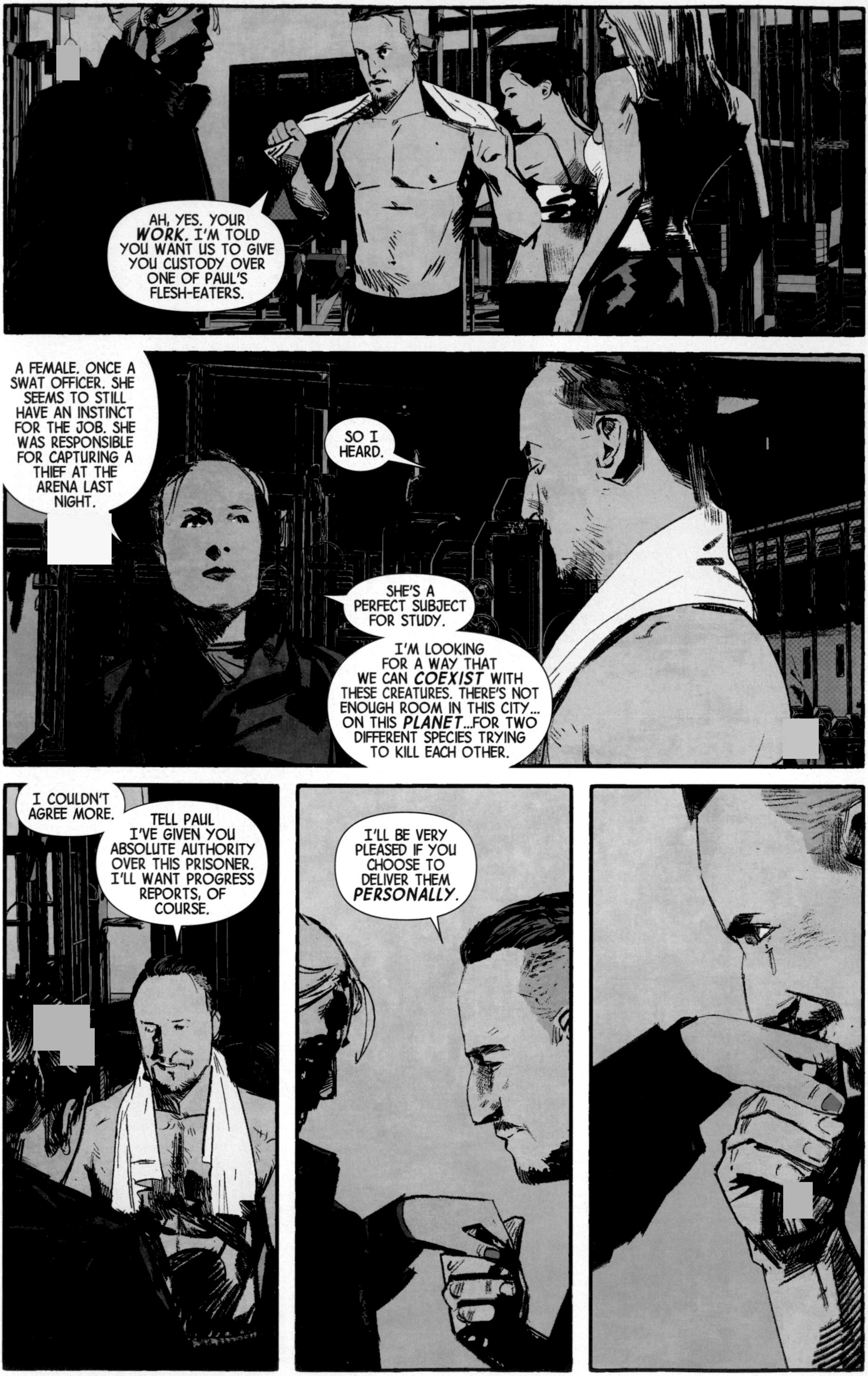
AH, YES. YOUR WORK. I'M TOLD YOU WANT US TO GIVE YOU CUSTODY OVER ONE OF PAUL'S FLESH-EATERS.
A FEMALE. ONCE A SWAT OFFICER. SHE SEEMS TO STILL HAVE AN INSTINCT FOR THE JOB. SHE WAS RESPONSIBLE FOR CAPTURING A THIEF AT THE ARENA LAST NIGHT.
SO I HEARD.
SHE'S A PERFECT SUBJECT FOR STUDY.
I'M LOOKING FOR A WAY THAT WE CAN COEXIST WITH THESE CREATURES. THERE'S NOT ENOUGH ROOM IN THIS CITY... ON THIS PLANET...FOR TWO DIFFERENT SPECIES TRYING TO KILL EACH OTHER.
I COULDN'T AGREE MORE.
TELL PAUL I'VE GIVEN YOU ABSOLUTE AUTHORITY OVER THIS PRISONER. I'LL WANT PROGRESS REPORTS, OF COURSE.
I'LL BE VERY PLEASED IF YOU CHOOSE TO DELIVER THEM PERSONALLY.

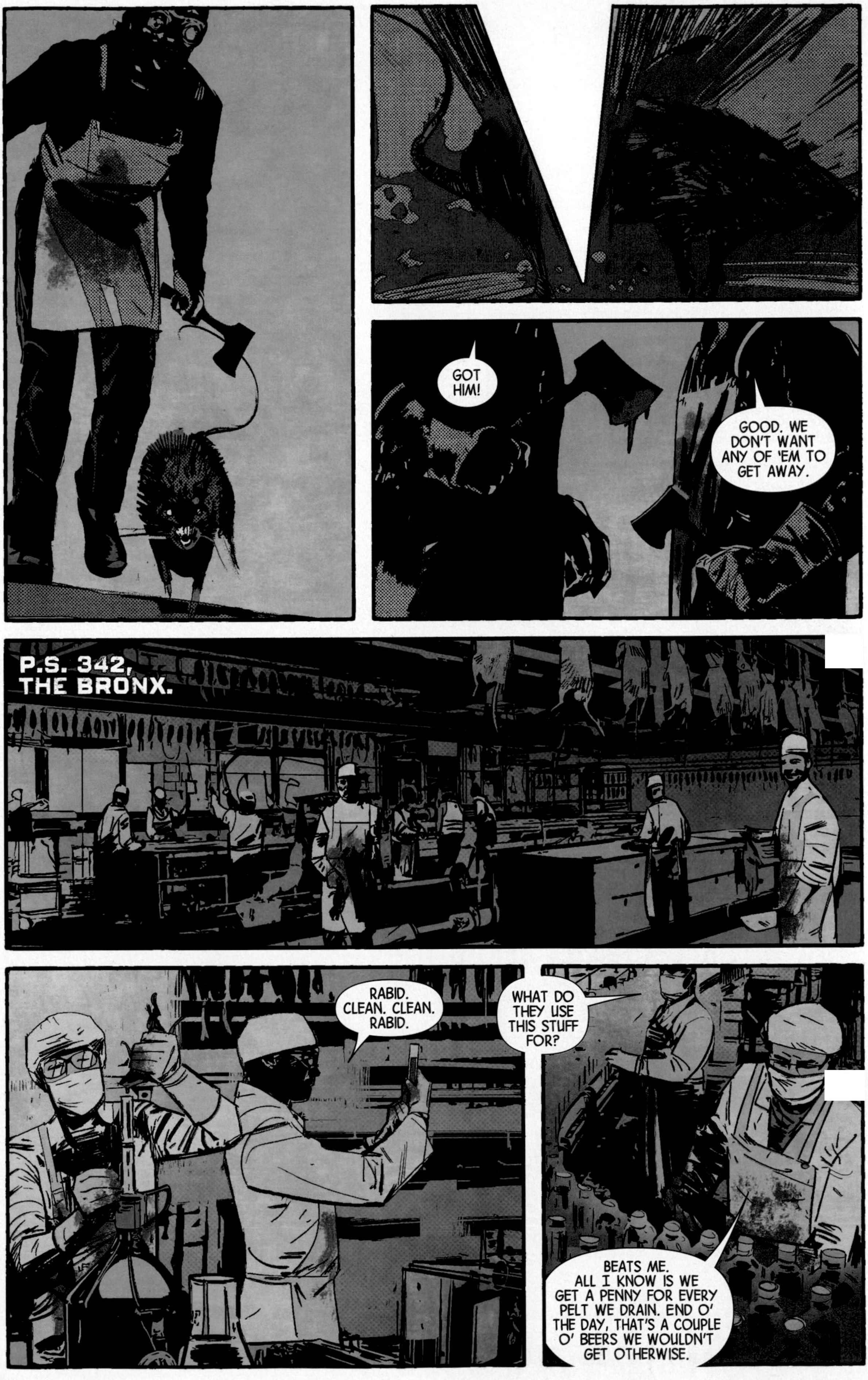
GOT HIM!
GOOD. WE DON'T WANT ANY OF 'EM TO GET AWAY.
P.S. 342, THE BRONX.
RABID. CLEAN. CLEAN. RABID.
WHAT DO THEY USE THIS STUFF FOR?
BEATS ME. ALL I KNOW IS WE GET A PENNY FOR EVERY PELT WE DRAIN. END O' THE DAY, THAT'S A COUPLE O' BEERS WE WOULDN'T GET OTHERWISE.

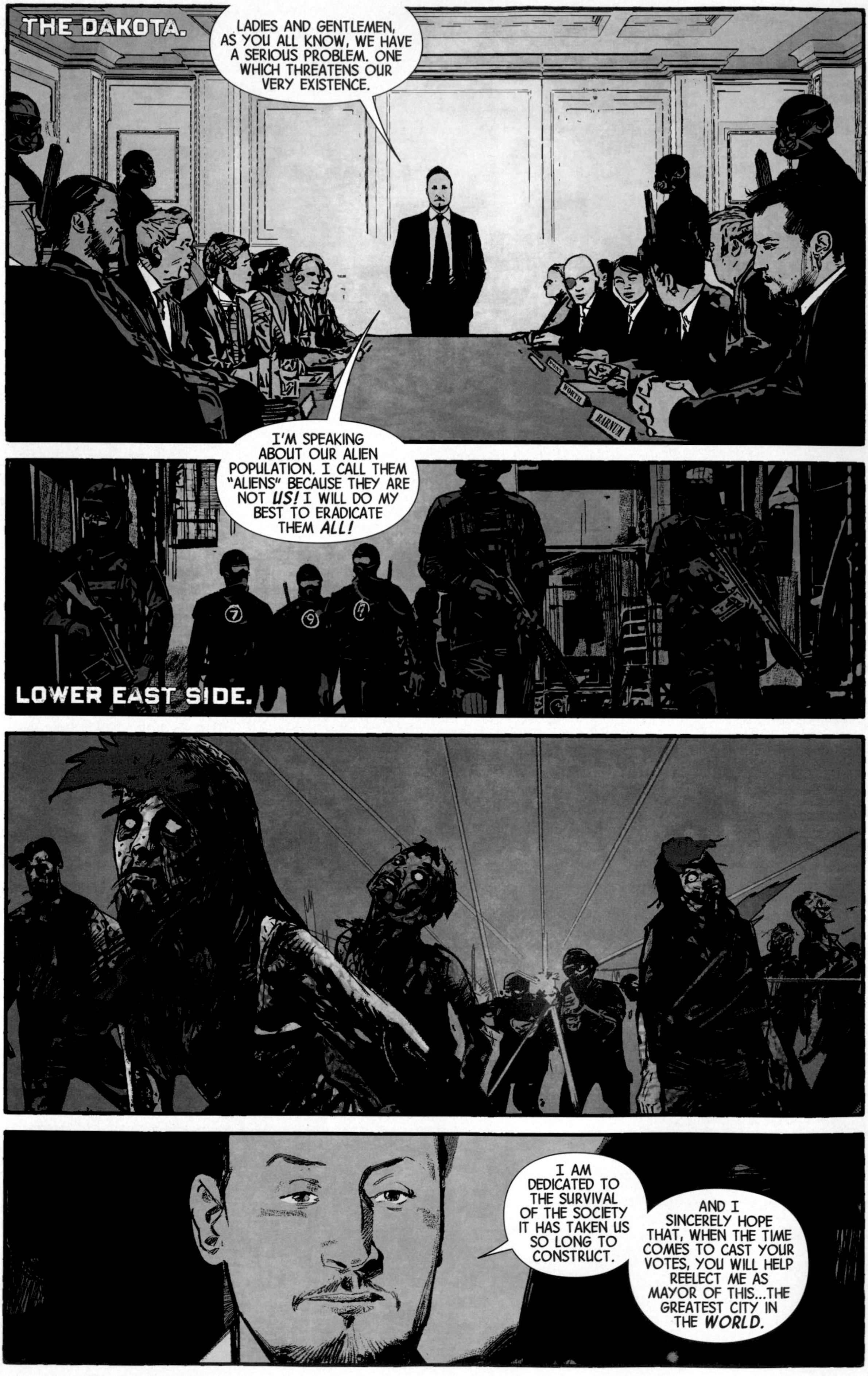
THE DAKOTA.
LADIES AND GENTLEMEN, AS YOU ALL KNOW, WE HAVE A SERIOUS PROBLEM. ONE WHICH THREATENS OUR VERY EXISTENCE.
PONT
WORTH
BARNUM
I'M SPEAKING ABOUT OUR ALIEN POPULATION. I CALL THEM "ALIENS" BECAUSE THEY ARE NOT US! I WILL DO MY BEST TO ERADICATE THEM ALL!
LOWER EAST SIDE.
I AM DEDICATED TO THE SURVIVAL OF THE SOCIETY IT HAS TAKEN US SO LONG TO CONSTRUCT.
AND I SINCERELY HOPE THAT, WHEN THE TIME COMES TO CAST YOUR VOTES, YOU WILL HELP REELECT ME AS MAYOR OF THIS...THE GREATEST CITY IN THE WORLD.

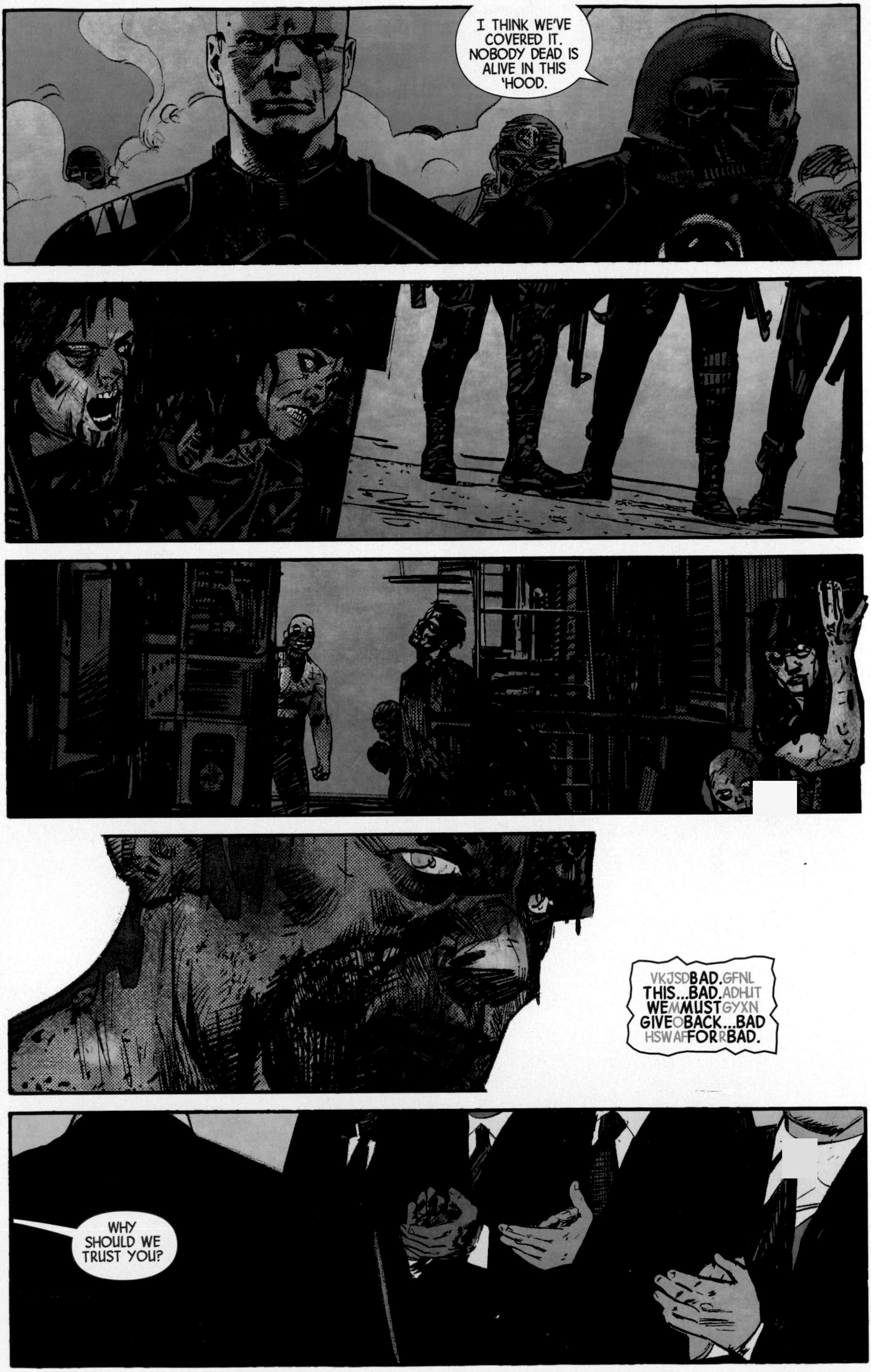
I THINK WE'VE COVERED IT. NOBODY DEAD IS ALIVE IN THIS 'HOOD.
VKJSDBAD.GFNL THIS...BAD.ADHJT WEMMUSTGYXN GIVEOBACK...BAD HSWAFFORRBAD.
WHY SHOULD WE TRUST YOU?

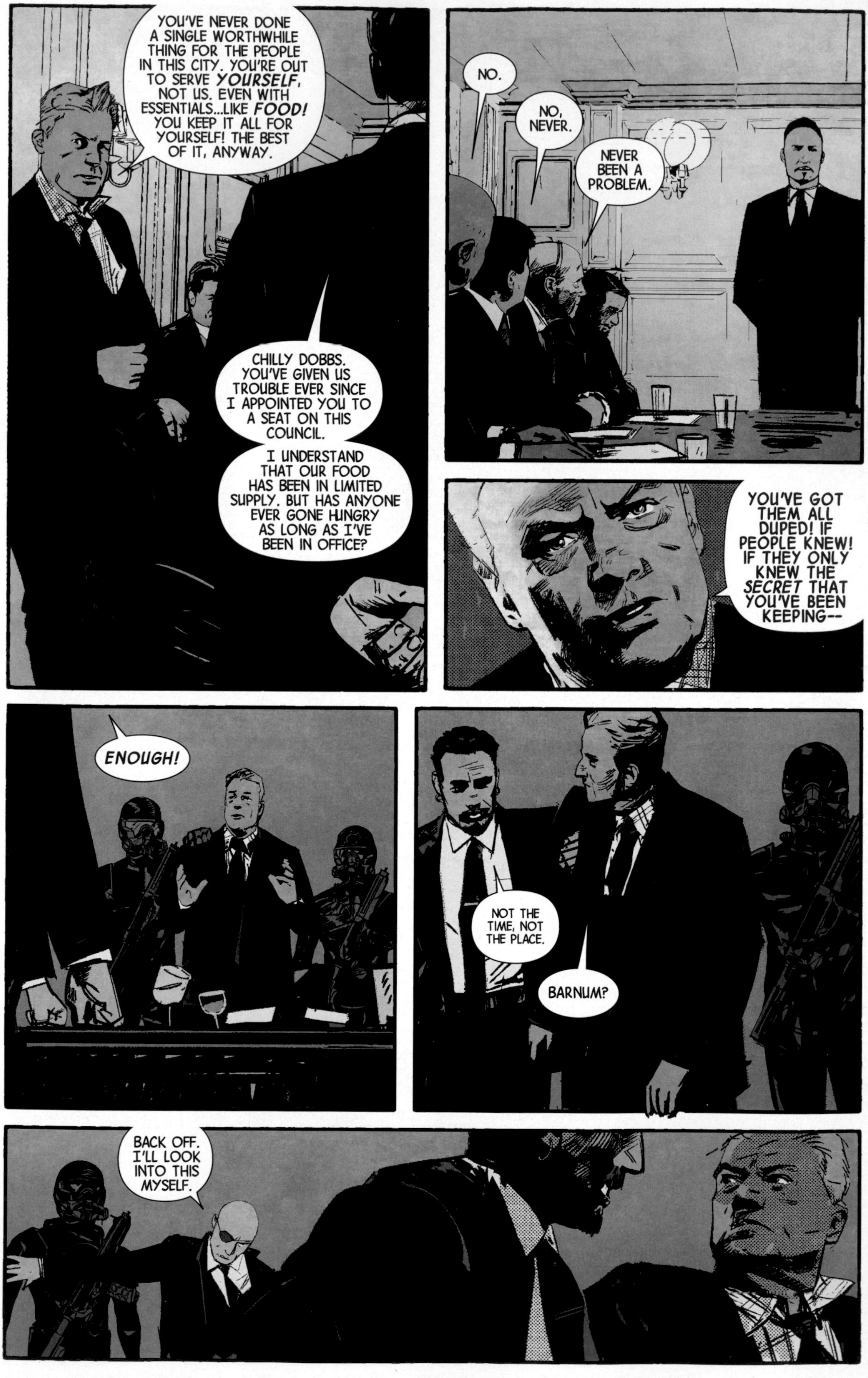
YOU'VE NEVER DONE A SINGLE WORTHWHILE THING FOR THE PEOPLE IN THIS CITY. YOU'RE OUT TO SERVE *YOURSELF*, NOT US. EVEN WITH ESSENTIALS...LIKE *FOOD!* YOU KEEP IT ALL FOR YOURSELF! THE BEST OF IT, ANYWAY.
CHILLY DOBBS. YOU'VE GIVEN US TROUBLE EVER SINCE I APPOINTED YOU TO A SEAT ON THIS COUNCIL.
I UNDERSTAND THAT OUR FOOD HAS BEEN IN LIMITED SUPPLY. BUT HAS ANYONE EVER GONE HUNGRY AS LONG AS I'VE BEEN IN OFFICE?
NO.
NO, NEVER.
NEVER BEEN A PROBLEM.
YOU'VE GOT THEM ALL DUPED! IF PEOPLE KNEW! IF THEY ONLY KNEW THE *SECRET* THAT YOU'VE BEEN KEEPING--
ENOUGH!
NOT THE TIME, NOT THE PLACE.
BARNUM?
BACK OFF. I'LL LOOK INTO THIS MYSELF.

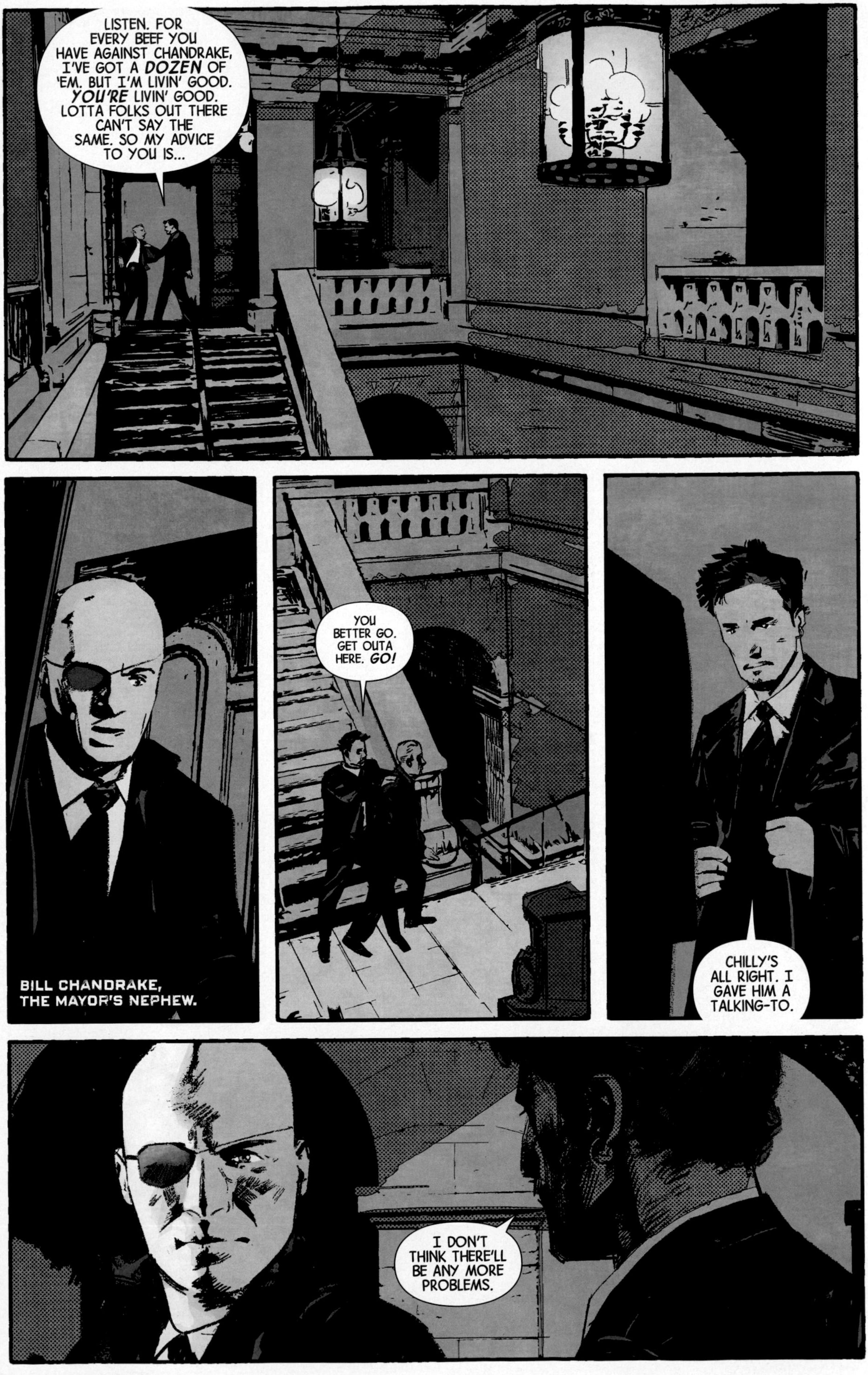
LISTEN. FOR EVERY BEEF YOU HAVE AGAINST CHANDRAKE, I'VE GOT A DOZEN OF 'EM. BUT I'M LIVIN' GOOD. YOU'RE LIVIN' GOOD. LOTTA FOLKS OUT THERE CAN'T SAY THE SAME. SO MY ADVICE TO YOU IS...
BILL CHANDRAKE, THE MAYOR'S NEPHEW.
YOU BETTER GO. GET OUTA HERE. GO!
CHILLY'S ALL RIGHT. I GAVE HIM A TALKING-TO.
I DON'T THINK THERE'LL BE ANY MORE PROBLEMS.

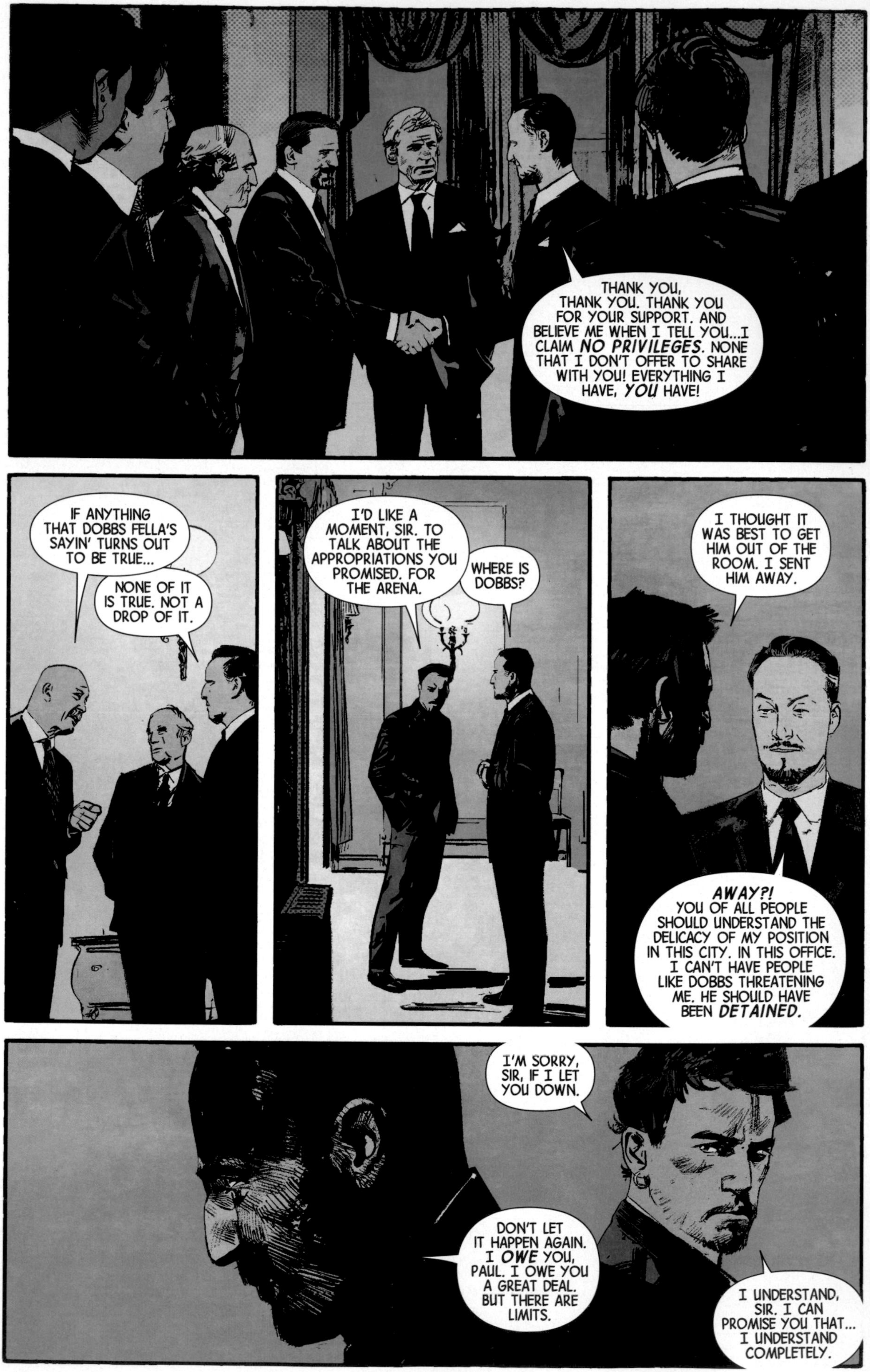
THANK YOU, THANK YOU. THANK YOU FOR YOUR SUPPORT. AND BELIEVE ME WHEN I TELL YOU...I CLAIM NO PRIVILEGES. NONE THAT I DON'T OFFER TO SHARE WITH YOU! EVERYTHING I HAVE, YOU HAVE!
IF ANYTHING THAT DOBBS FELLA'S SAYIN' TURNS OUT TO BE TRUE...
NONE OF IT IS TRUE. NOT A DROP OF IT.
I'D LIKE A MOMENT, SIR. TO TALK ABOUT THE APPROPRIATIONS YOU PROMISED. FOR THE ARENA.
WHERE IS DOBBS?
I THOUGHT IT WAS BEST TO GET HIM OUT OF THE ROOM. I SENT HIM AWAY.
AWAY?! YOU OF ALL PEOPLE SHOULD UNDERSTAND THE DELICACY OF MY POSITION IN THIS CITY. IN THIS OFFICE. I CAN'T HAVE PEOPLE LIKE DOBBS THREATENING ME. HE SHOULD HAVE BEEN DETAINED.
I'M SORRY, SIR, IF I LET YOU DOWN.
DON'T LET IT HAPPEN AGAIN. I OWE YOU, PAUL. I OWE YOU A GREAT DEAL. BUT THERE ARE LIMITS.
I UNDERSTAND, SIR. I CAN PROMISE YOU THAT... I UNDERSTAND COMPLETELY.

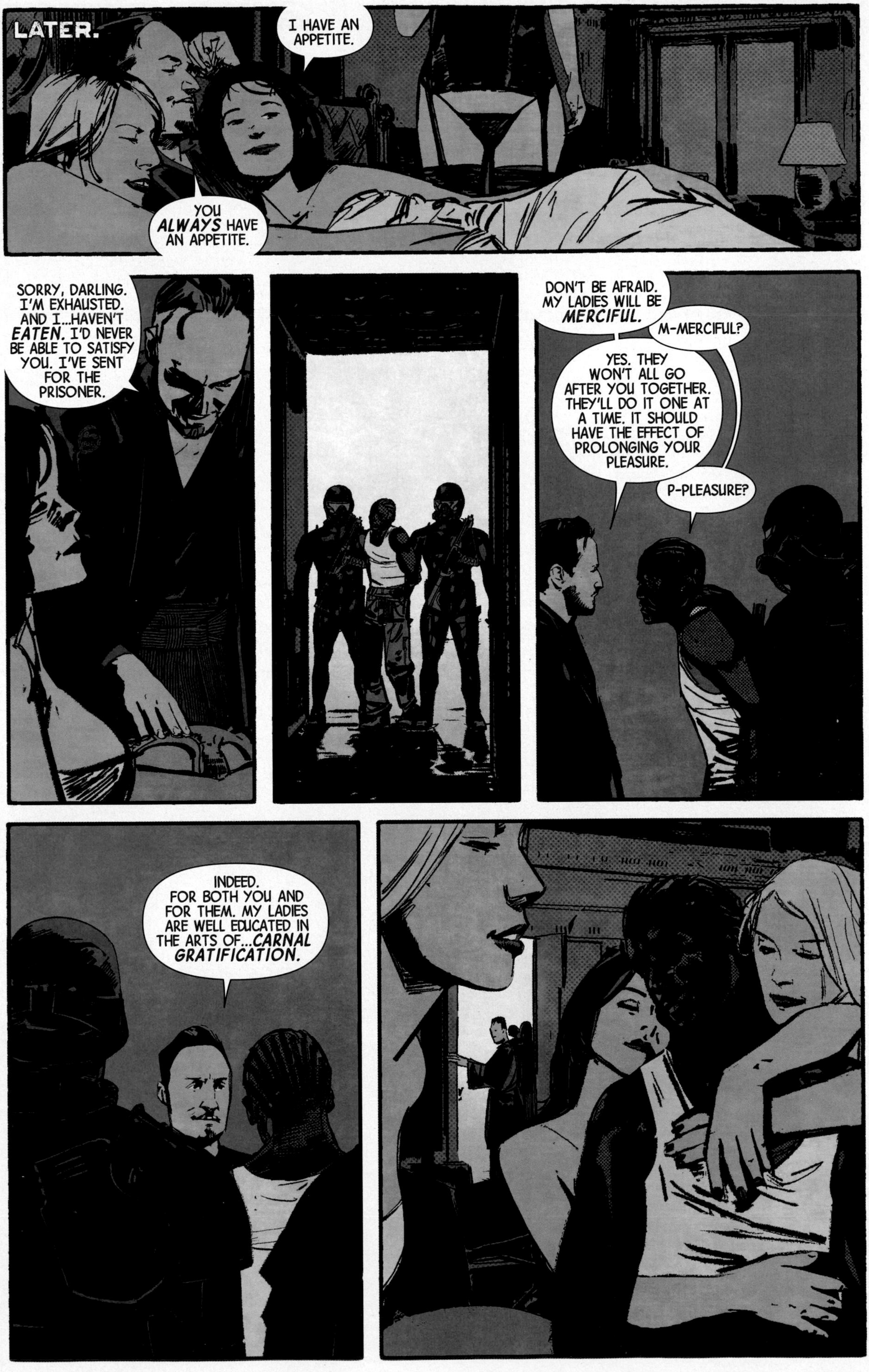
LATER.
I HAVE AN APPETITE.
YOU *ALWAYS* HAVE AN APPETITE.
SORRY, DARLING. I'M EXHAUSTED. AND I...HAVEN'T *EATEN.* I'D NEVER BE ABLE TO SATISFY YOU. I'VE SENT FOR THE PRISONER.
DON'T BE AFRAID. MY LADIES WILL BE *MERCIFUL.*
M-MERCIFUL?
YES. THEY WON'T ALL GO AFTER YOU TOGETHER. THEY'LL DO IT ONE AT A TIME. IT SHOULD HAVE THE EFFECT OF PROLONGING YOUR PLEASURE.
P-PLEASURE?
INDEED. FOR BOTH YOU AND FOR THEM. MY LADIES ARE WELL EDUCATED IN THE ARTS OF...*CARNAL GRATIFICATION.*

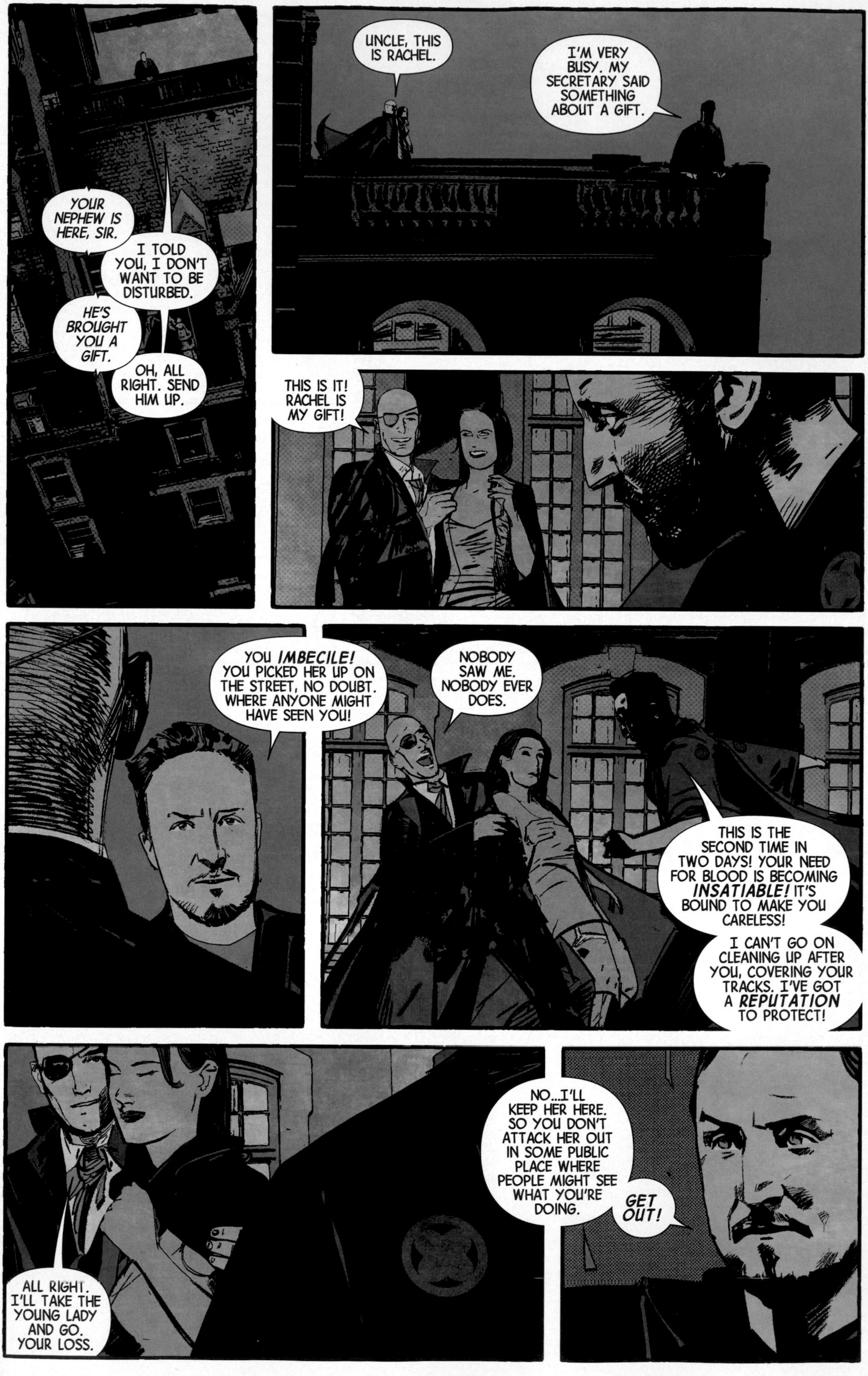
YOUR NEPHEW IS HERE, SIR.
I TOLD YOU, I DON'T WANT TO BE DISTURBED.
HE'S BROUGHT YOU A GIFT.
OH, ALL RIGHT. SEND HIM UP.
UNCLE, THIS IS RACHEL.
I'M VERY BUSY. MY SECRETARY SAID SOMETHING ABOUT A GIFT.
THIS IS IT! RACHEL IS MY GIFT!
YOU IMBECILE! YOU PICKED HER UP ON THE STREET, NO DOUBT. WHERE ANYONE MIGHT HAVE SEEN YOU!
NOBODY SAW ME. NOBODY EVER DOES.
THIS IS THE SECOND TIME IN TWO DAYS! YOUR NEED FOR BLOOD IS BECOMING INSATIABLE! IT'S BOUND TO MAKE YOU CARELESS!
I CAN'T GO ON CLEANING UP AFTER YOU, COVERING YOUR TRACKS. I'VE GOT A REPUTATION TO PROTECT!
ALL RIGHT. I'LL TAKE THE YOUNG LADY AND GO. YOUR LOSS.
NO...I'LL KEEP HER HERE. SO YOU DON'T ATTACK HER OUT IN SOME PUBLIC PLACE WHERE PEOPLE MIGHT SEE WHAT YOU'RE DOING.
GET OUT!

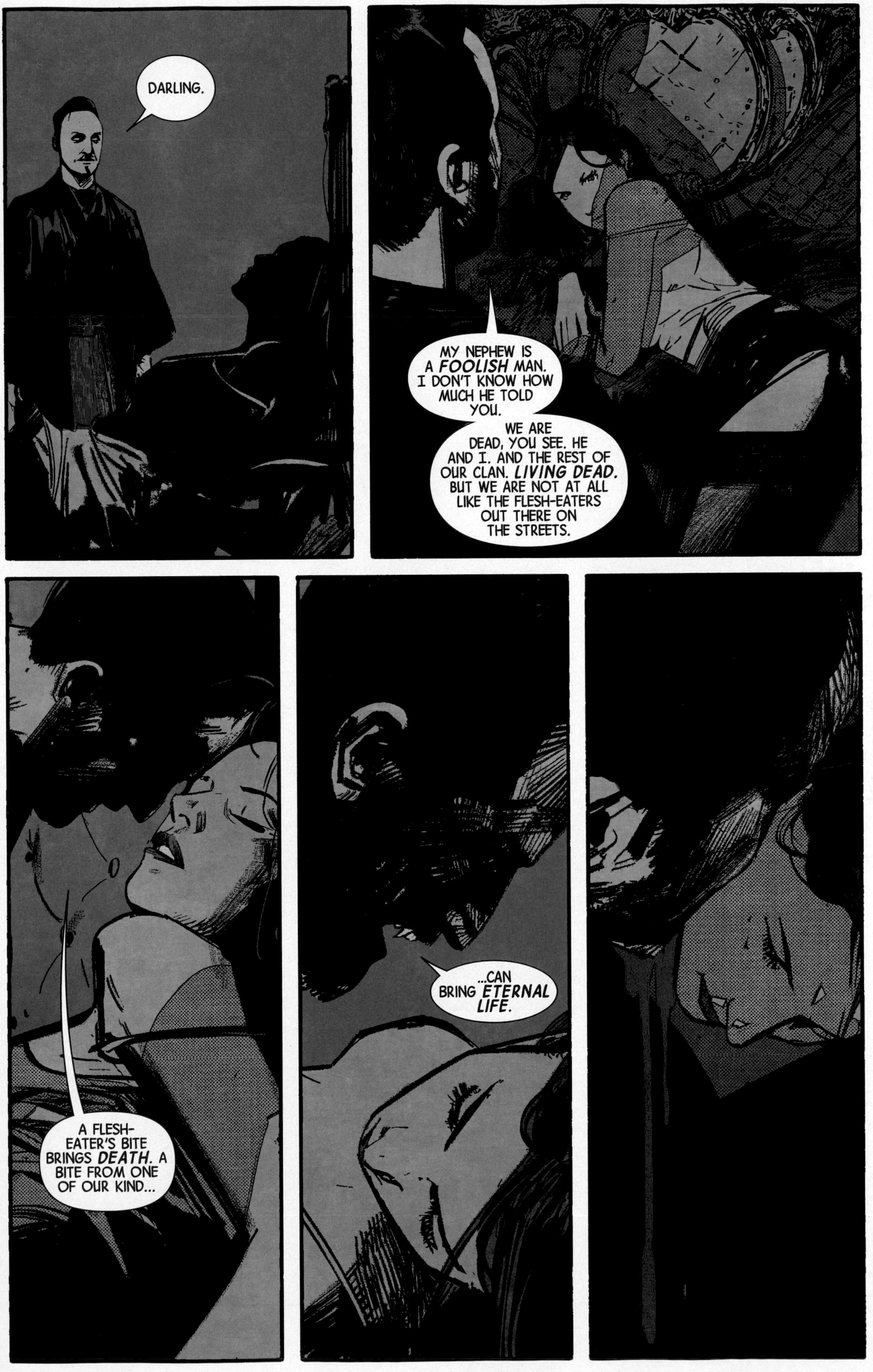
DARLING.
MY NEPHEW IS A FOOLISH MAN. I DON'T KNOW HOW MUCH HE TOLD YOU.
WE ARE DEAD, YOU SEE. HE AND I. AND THE REST OF OUR CLAN. LIVING DEAD. BUT WE ARE NOT AT ALL LIKE THE FLESH-EATERS OUT THERE ON THE STREETS.
A FLESH-EATER'S BITE BRINGS DEATH. A BITE FROM ONE OF OUR KIND...
...CAN BRING ETERNAL LIFE.

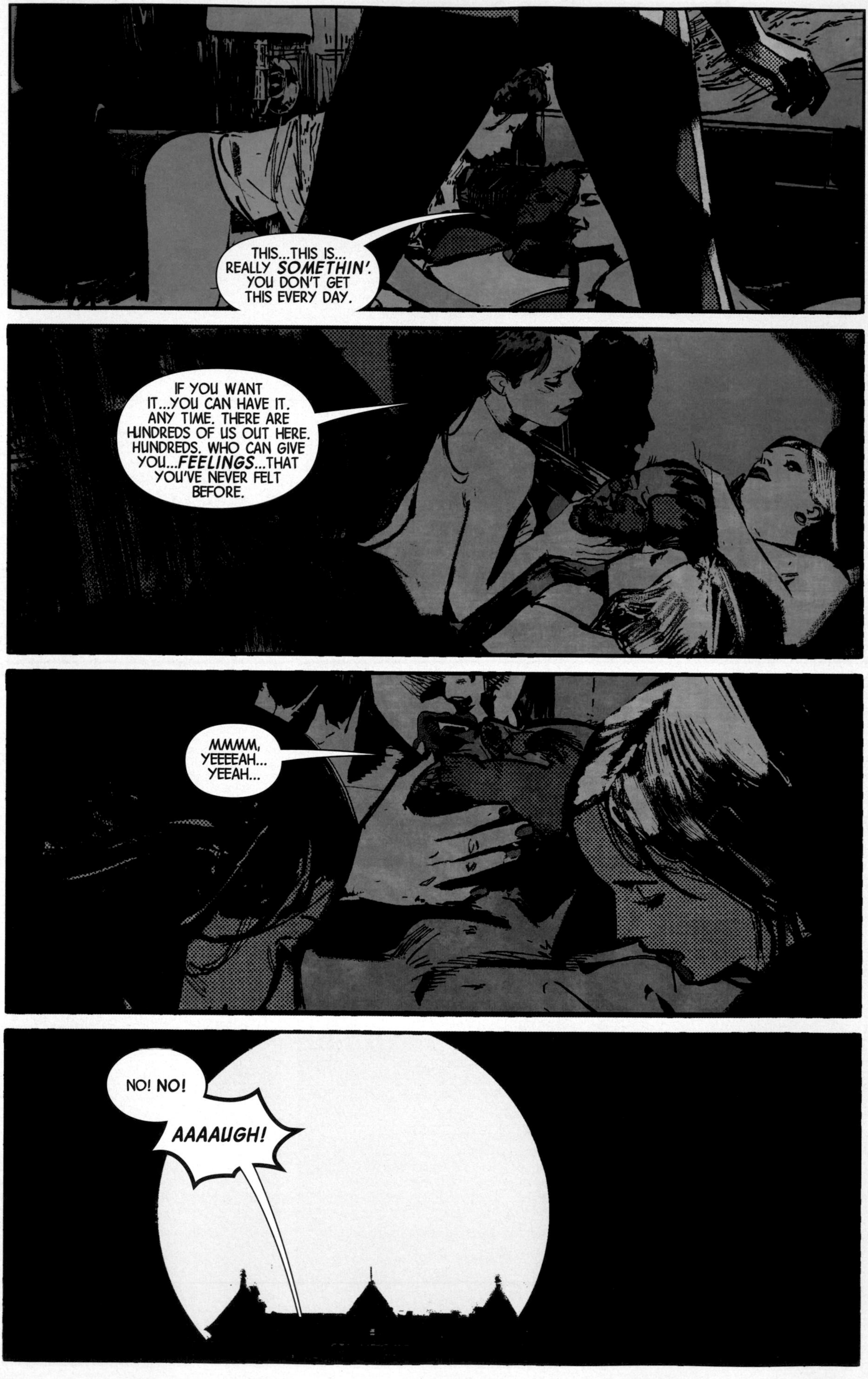
THIS...THIS IS... REALLY SOMETHIN'. YOU DON'T GET THIS EVERY DAY.
IF YOU WANT IT...YOU CAN HAVE IT. ANY TIME. THERE ARE HUNDREDS OF US OUT HERE. HUNDREDS. WHO CAN GIVE YOU...FEELINGS...THAT YOU'VE NEVER FELT BEFORE.
MMMM, YEEEEAH... YEEAH...
NO! NO!
AAAAUGH!

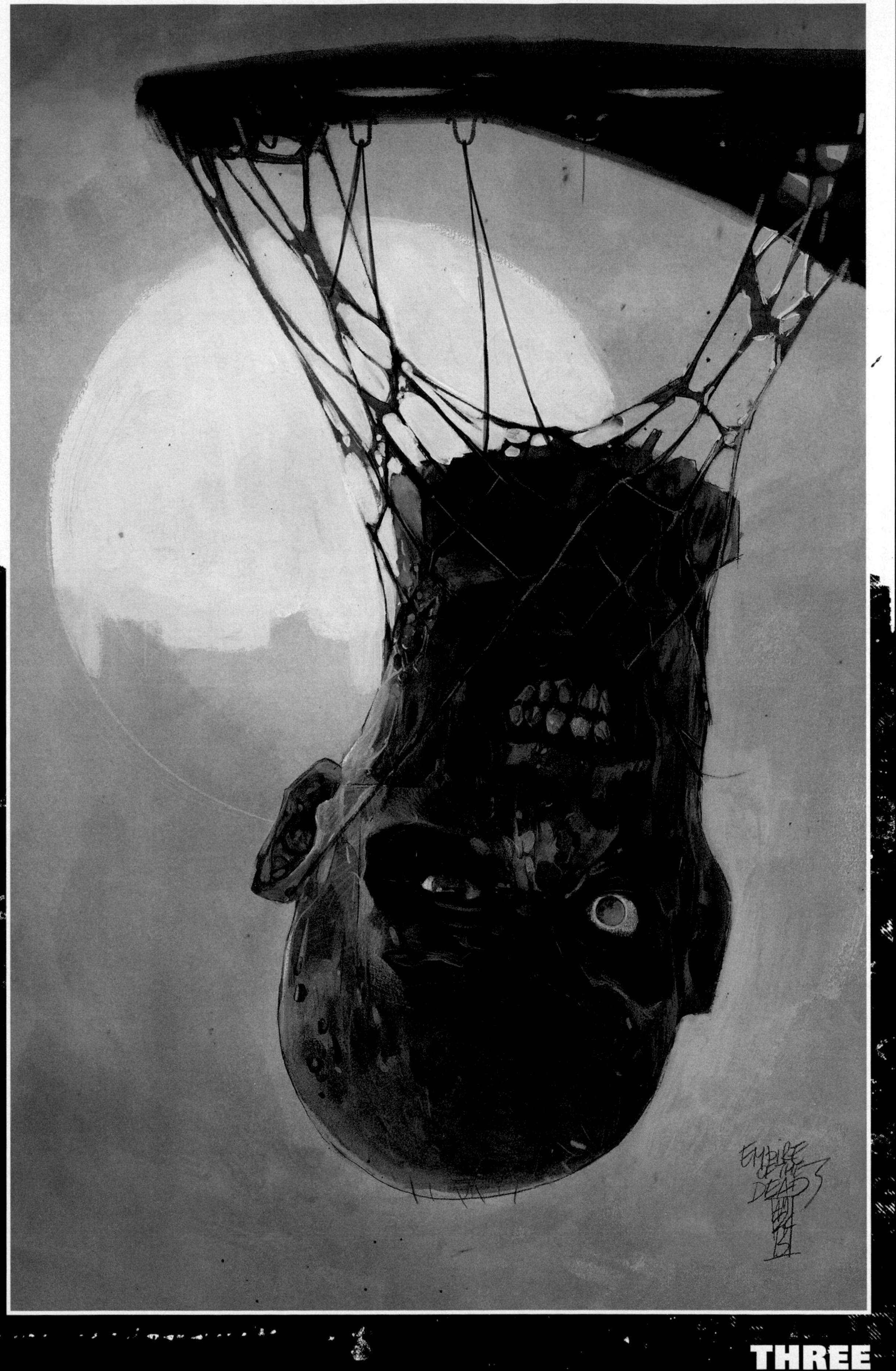
EMPIRE OF THE DEAD 3

THREE

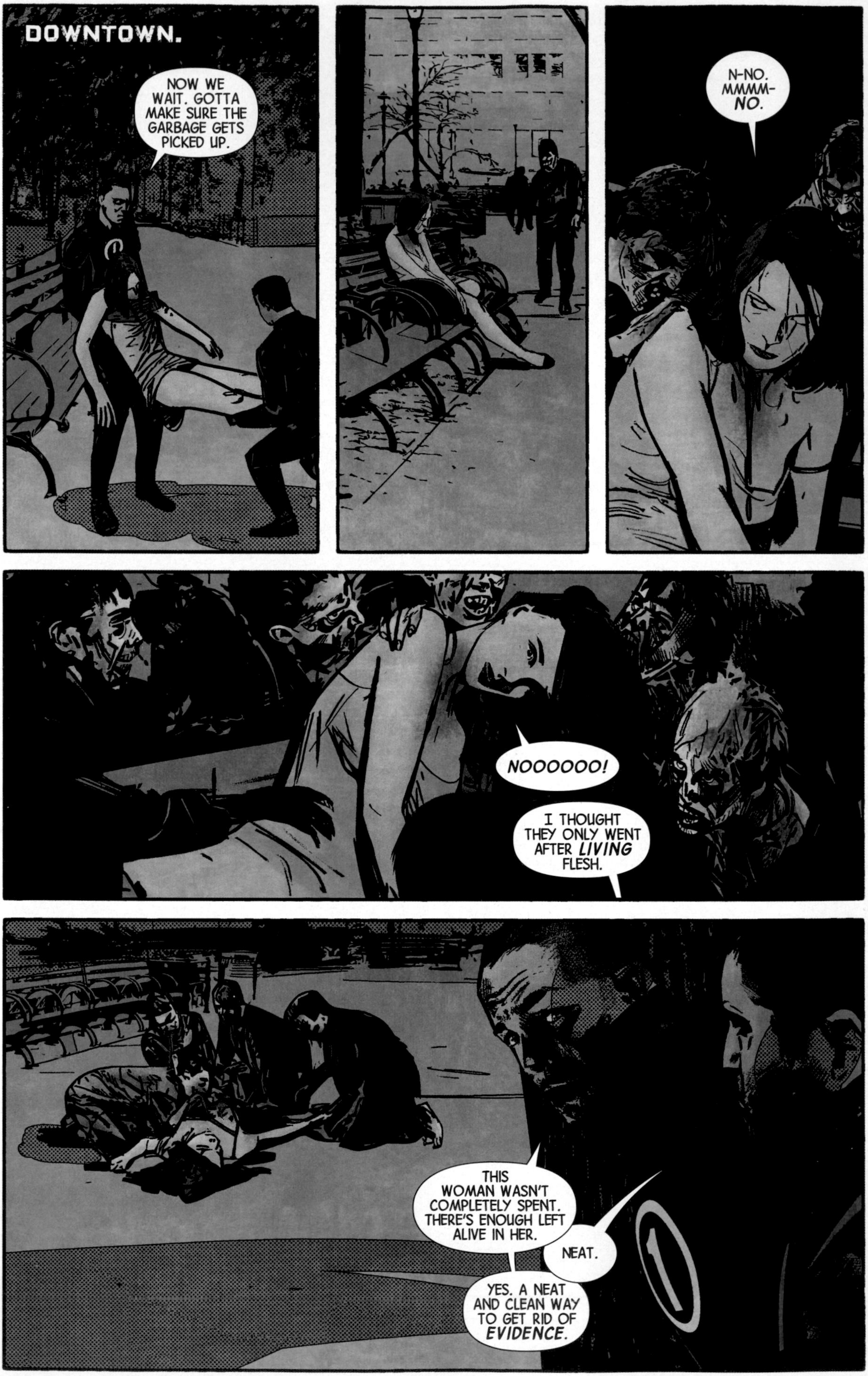
DOWNTOWN.
NOW WE WAIT. GOTTA MAKE SURE THE GARBAGE GETS PICKED UP.
N-NO. MMMM-NO.
NOOOOOO!
I THOUGHT THEY ONLY WENT AFTER LIVING FLESH.
THIS WOMAN WASN'T COMPLETELY SPENT. THERE'S ENOUGH LEFT ALIVE IN HER.
NEAT.
YES. A NEAT AND CLEAN WAY TO GET RID OF EVIDENCE.

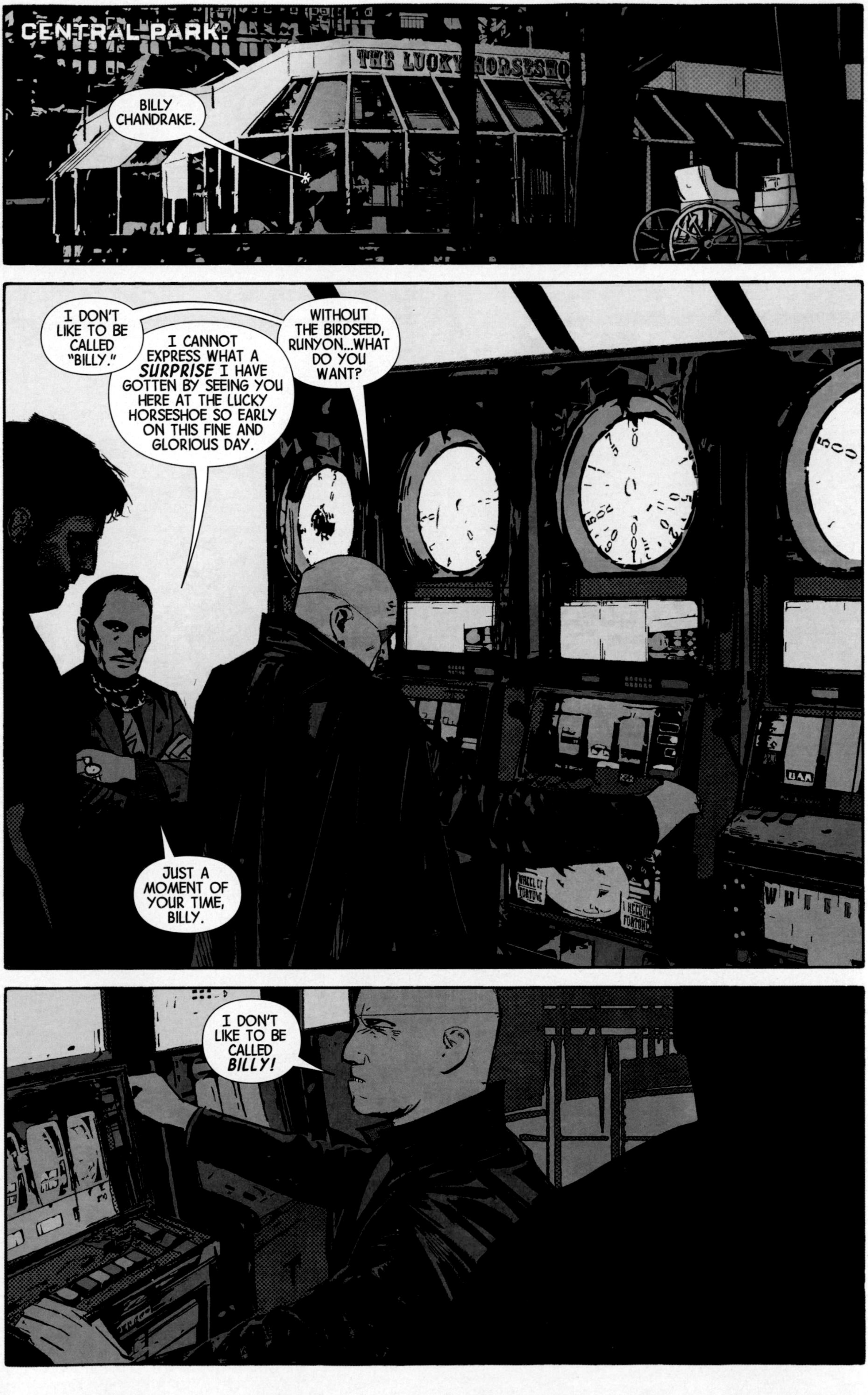
CENTRAL PARK.
THE LUCKY HORSESHO
BILLY CHANDRAKE.
I DON'T LIKE TO BE CALLED "BILLY."
I CANNOT EXPRESS WHAT A SURPRISE I HAVE GOTTEN BY SEEING YOU HERE AT THE LUCKY HORSESHOE SO EARLY ON THIS FINE AND GLORIOUS DAY.
WITHOUT THE BIRDSEED, RUNYON...WHAT DO YOU WANT?
JUST A MOMENT OF YOUR TIME, BILLY.
I DON'T LIKE TO BE CALLED BILLY!

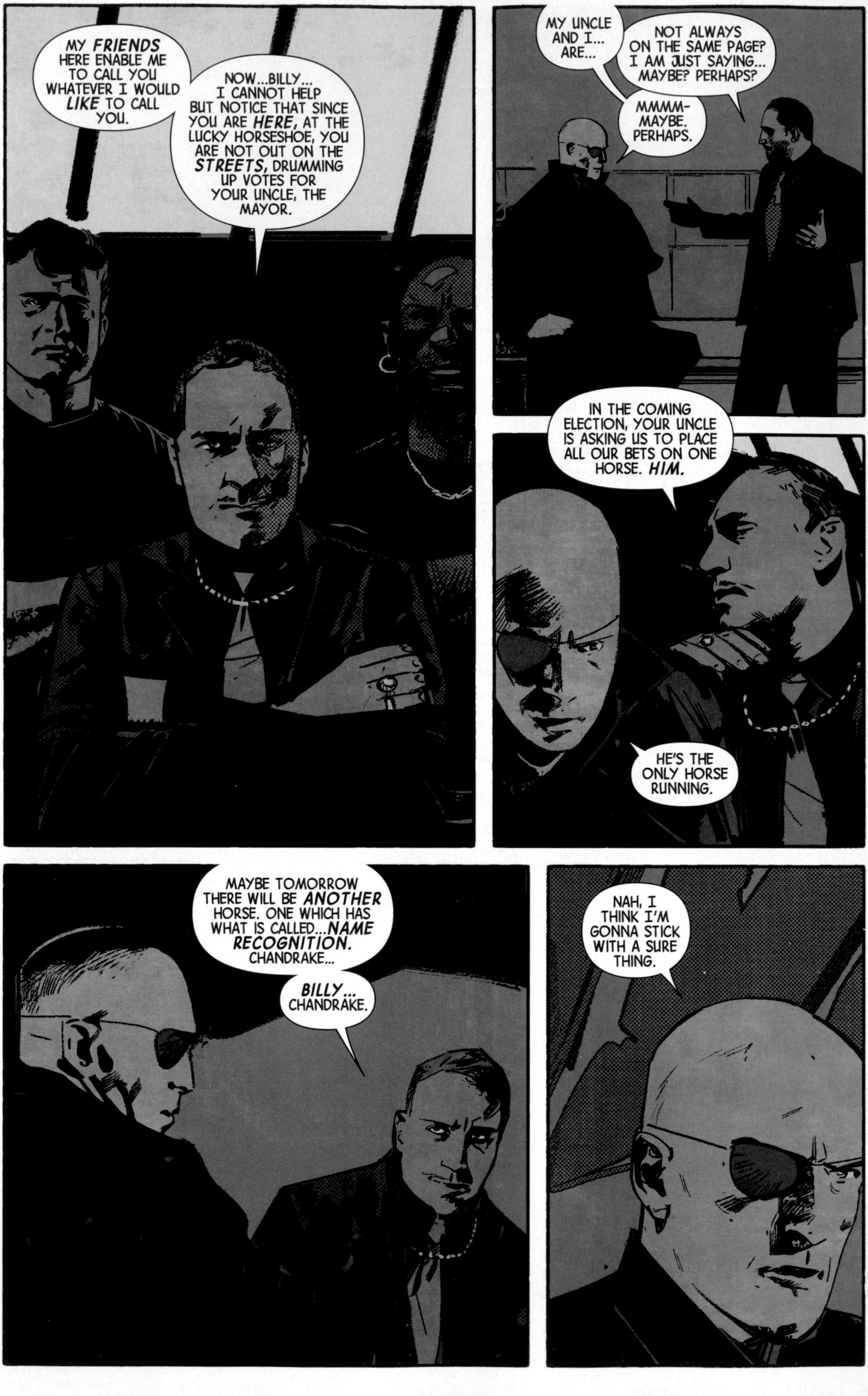

MY FRIENDS HERE ENABLE ME TO CALL YOU WHATEVER I WOULD LIKE TO CALL YOU.
NOW...BILLY... I CANNOT HELP BUT NOTICE THAT SINCE YOU ARE HERE, AT THE LUCKY HORSESHOE, YOU ARE NOT OUT ON THE STREETS, DRUMMING UP VOTES FOR YOUR UNCLE, THE MAYOR.
MY UNCLE AND I... ARE...
NOT ALWAYS ON THE SAME PAGE? I AM JUST SAYING... MAYBE? PERHAPS?
MMMM-MAYBE. PERHAPS.
IN THE COMING ELECTION, YOUR UNCLE IS ASKING US TO PLACE ALL OUR BETS ON ONE HORSE. HIM.
HE'S THE ONLY HORSE RUNNING.
MAYBE TOMORROW THERE WILL BE ANOTHER HORSE. ONE WHICH HAS WHAT IS CALLED...NAME RECOGNITION. CHANDRAKE...
BILLY... CHANDRAKE.
NAH, I THINK I'M GONNA STICK WITH A SURE THING.

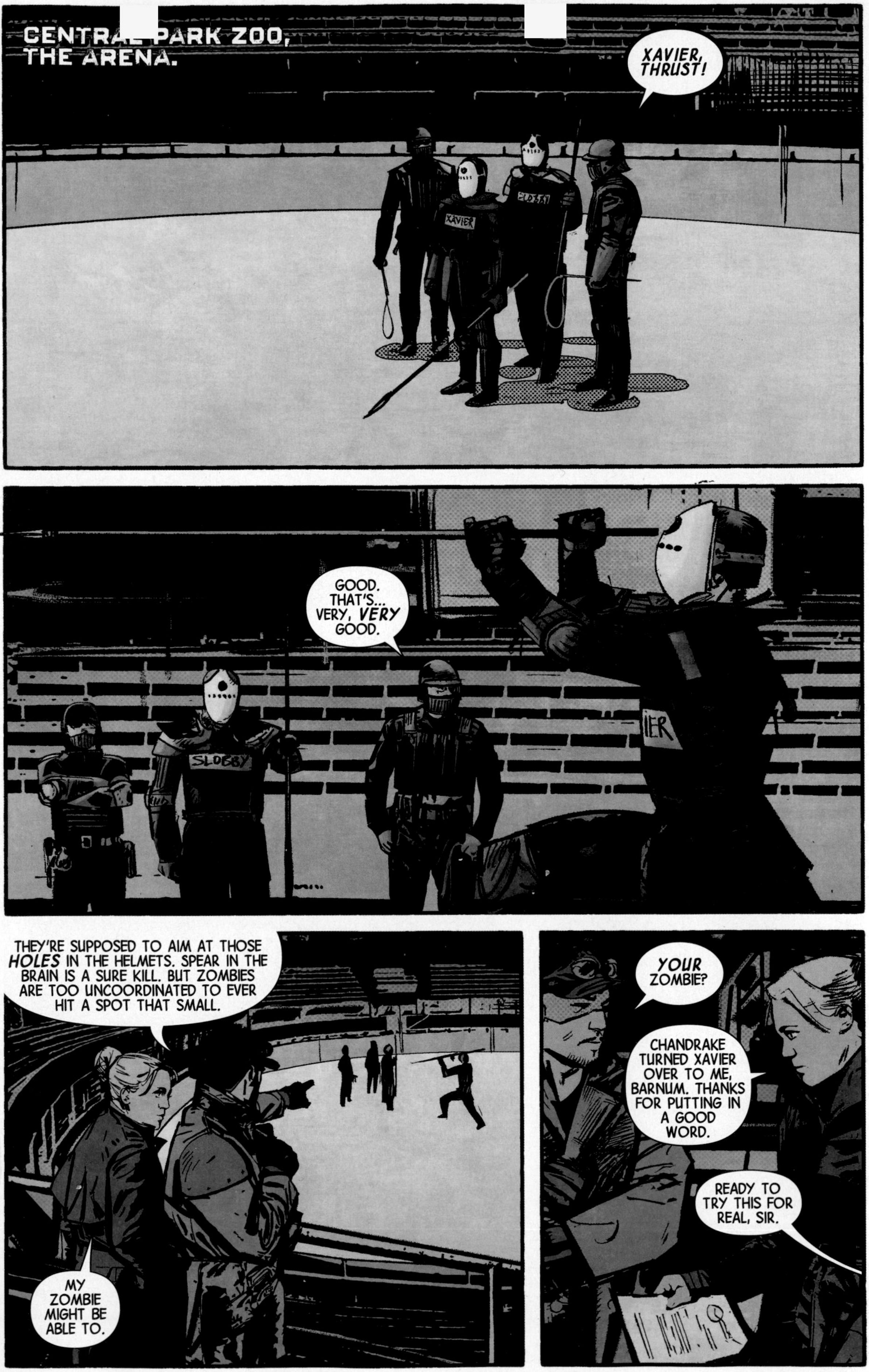
CENTRAL PARK ZOO, THE ARENA.
XAVIER, THRUST!
GOOD. THAT'S... VERY, VERY GOOD.
THEY'RE SUPPOSED TO AIM AT THOSE HOLES IN THE HELMETS. SPEAR IN THE BRAIN IS A SURE KILL. BUT ZOMBIES ARE TOO UNCOORDINATED TO EVER HIT A SPOT THAT SMALL.
MY ZOMBIE MIGHT BE ABLE TO.
YOUR ZOMBIE?
CHANDRAKE TURNED XAVIER OVER TO ME, BARNUM. THANKS FOR PUTTING IN A GOOD WORD.
READY TO TRY THIS FOR REAL, SIR.

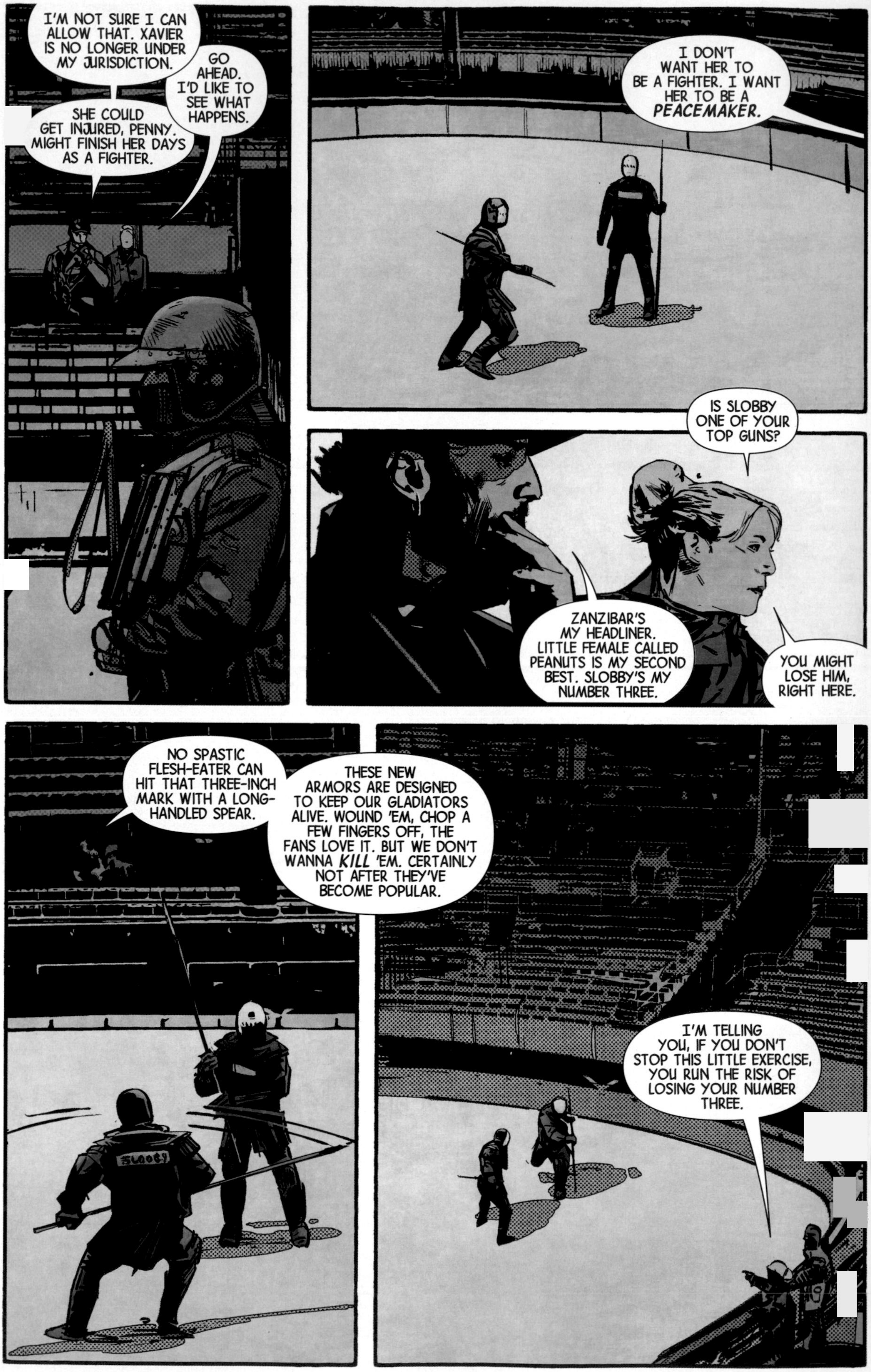
I'M NOT SURE I CAN ALLOW THAT. XAVIER IS NO LONGER UNDER MY JURISDICTION.
SHE COULD GET INJURED, PENNY. MIGHT FINISH HER DAYS AS A FIGHTER.
GO AHEAD. I'D LIKE TO SEE WHAT HAPPENS.
I DON'T WANT HER TO BE A FIGHTER. I WANT HER TO BE A *PEACEMAKER.*
IS SLOBBY ONE OF YOUR TOP GUNS?
ZANZIBAR'S MY HEADLINER. LITTLE FEMALE CALLED PEANUTS IS MY SECOND BEST. SLOBBY'S MY NUMBER THREE.
YOU MIGHT LOSE HIM, RIGHT HERE.
NO SPASTIC FLESH-EATER CAN HIT THAT THREE-INCH MARK WITH A LONG-HANDLED SPEAR.
THESE NEW ARMORS ARE DESIGNED TO KEEP OUR GLADIATORS ALIVE. WOUND 'EM, CHOP A FEW FINGERS OFF, THE FANS LOVE IT. BUT WE DON'T WANNA *KILL* 'EM. CERTAINLY NOT AFTER THEY'VE BECOME POPULAR.
SLOBBY
I'M TELLING YOU, IF YOU DON'T STOP THIS LITTLE EXERCISE, YOU RUN THE RISK OF LOSING YOUR NUMBER THREE.

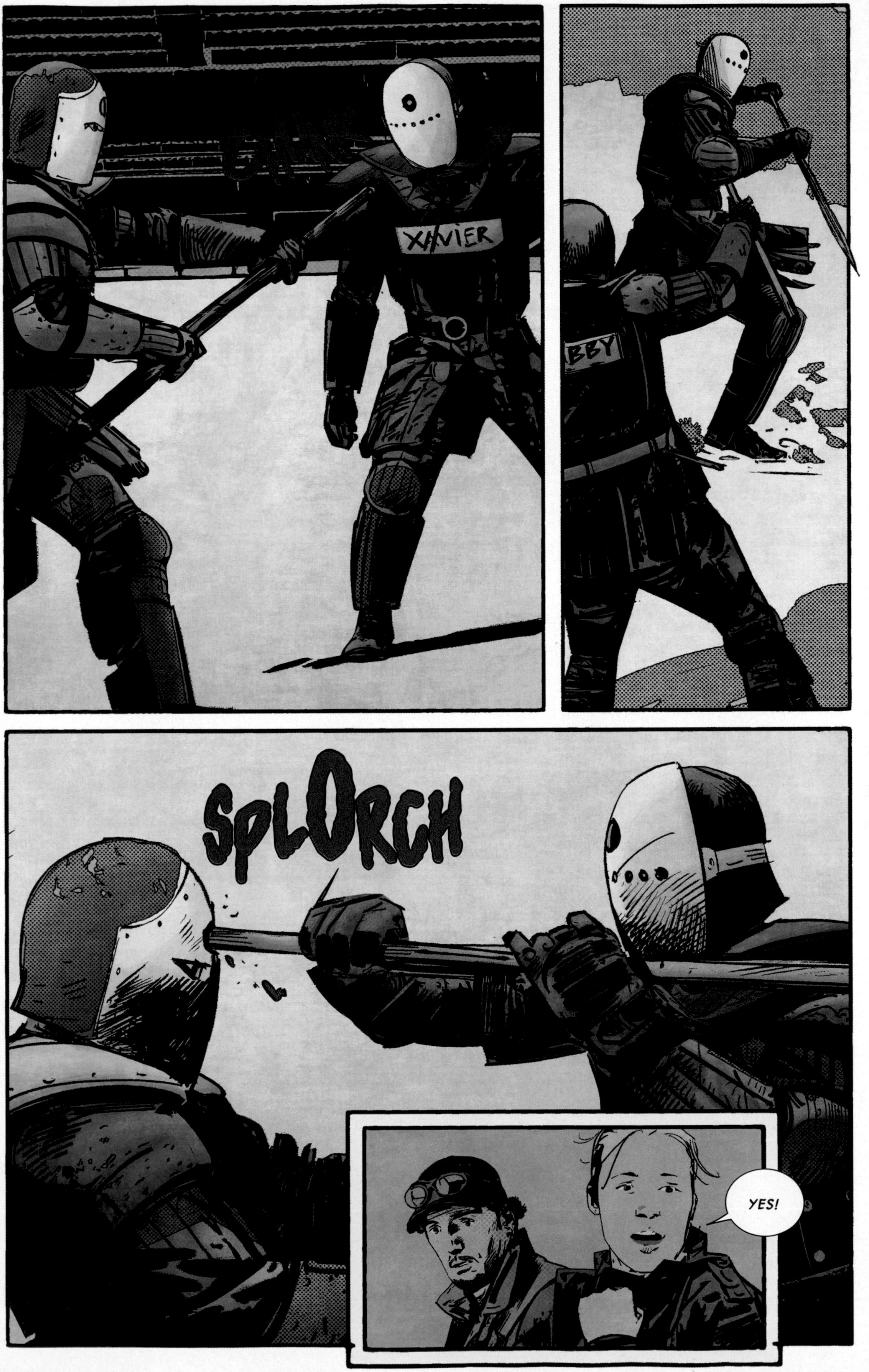
XAVIER
BBY
SPLORCH
YES!

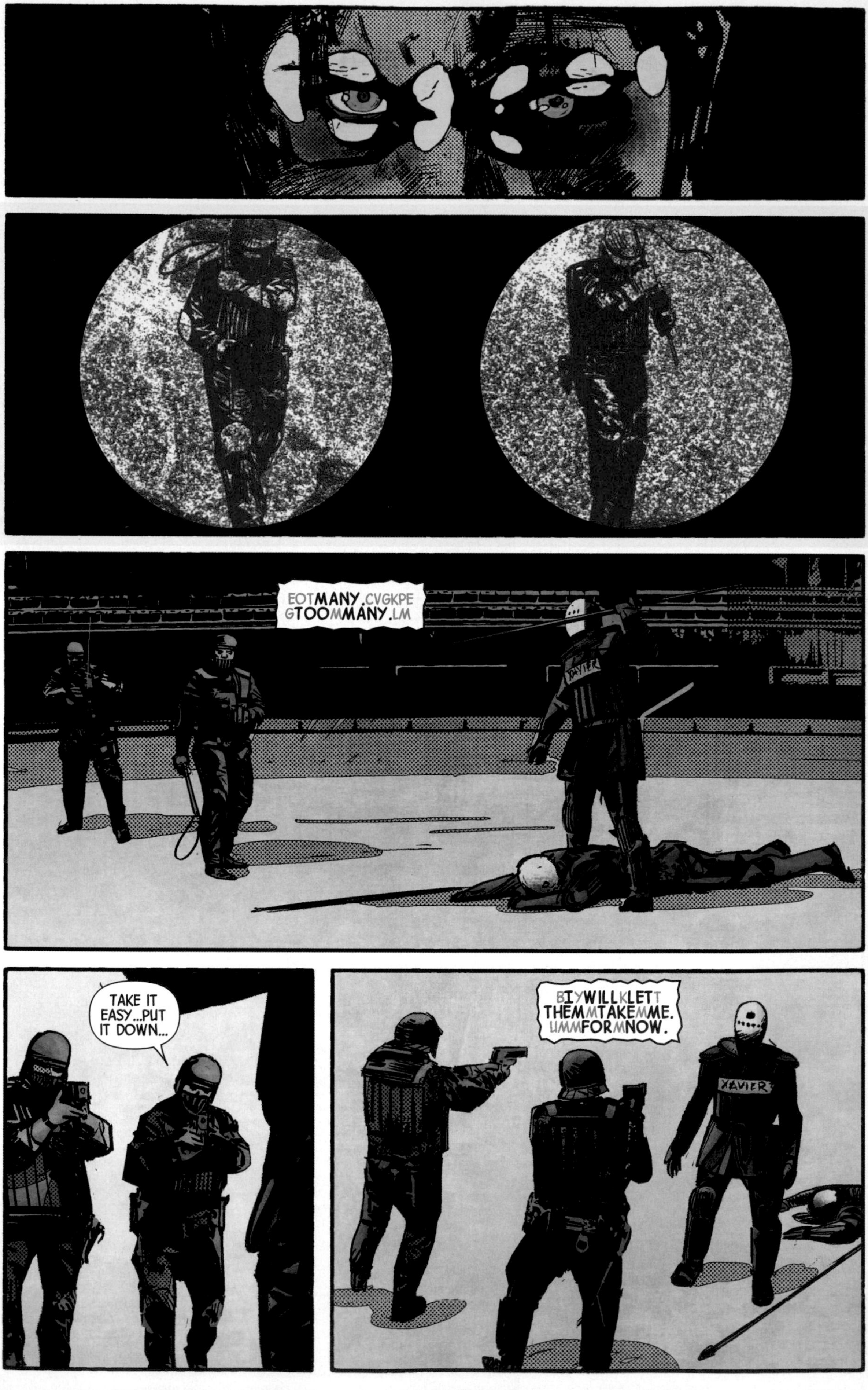
EOTMANY.CVGKPE GTOOMMANY.LM
TAKE IT EASY...PUT IT DOWN...
BIYWILLKLETT THEMMTAKEMME. UMMFORMNOW.

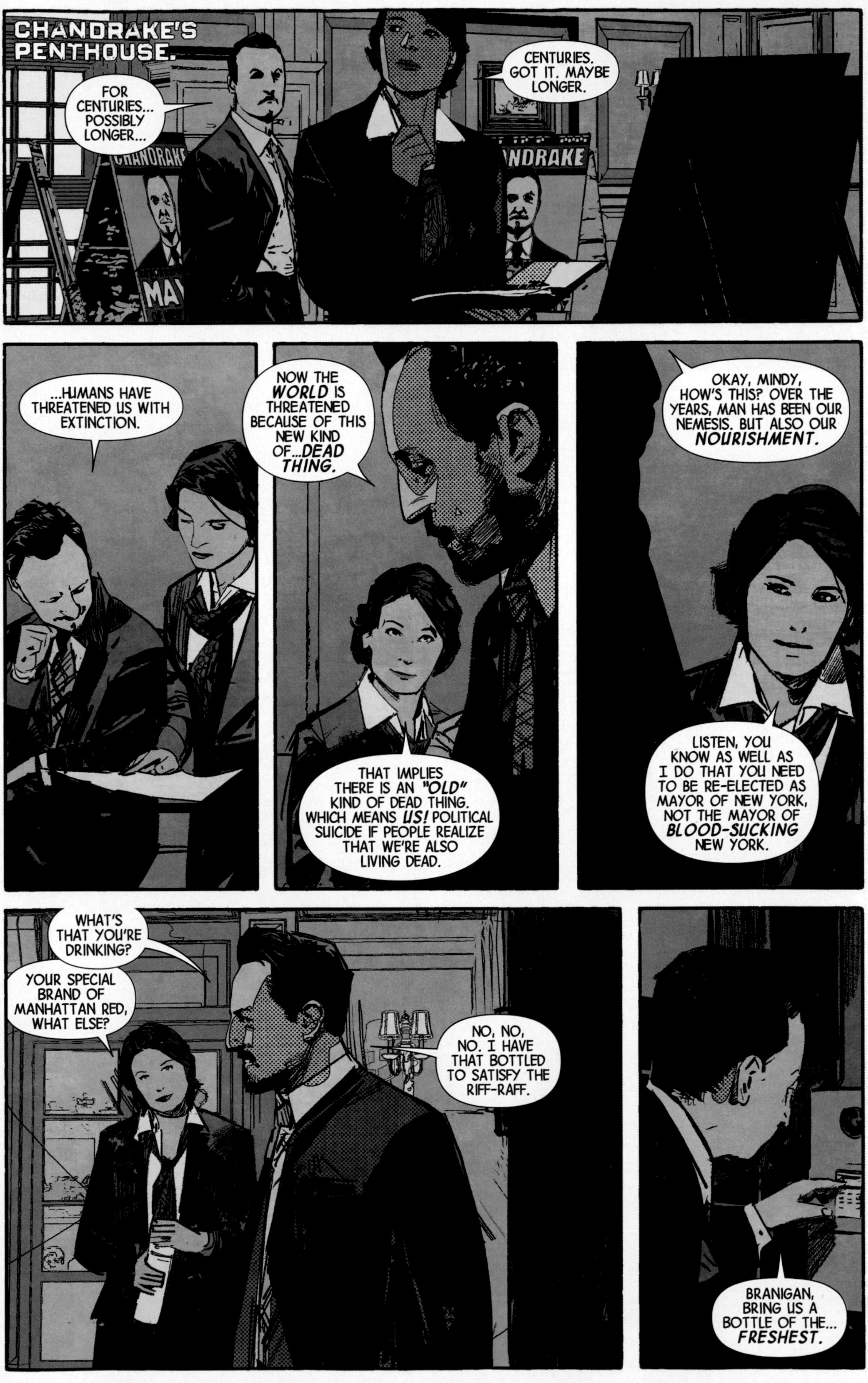
CHANDRAKE'S PENTHOUSE.
FOR CENTURIES... POSSIBLY LONGER...
CENTURIES. GOT IT. MAYBE LONGER.
CHANDRAKE
CHANDRAKE
MAY
...HUMANS HAVE THREATENED US WITH EXTINCTION.
NOW THE WORLD IS THREATENED BECAUSE OF THIS NEW KIND OF...DEAD THING.
THAT IMPLIES THERE IS AN "OLD" KIND OF DEAD THING. WHICH MEANS US! POLITICAL SUICIDE IF PEOPLE REALIZE THAT WE'RE ALSO LIVING DEAD.
OKAY, MINDY, HOW'S THIS? OVER THE YEARS, MAN HAS BEEN OUR NEMESIS. BUT ALSO OUR NOURISHMENT.
LISTEN, YOU KNOW AS WELL AS I DO THAT YOU NEED TO BE RE-ELECTED AS MAYOR OF NEW YORK, NOT THE MAYOR OF BLOOD-SUCKING NEW YORK.
WHAT'S THAT YOU'RE DRINKING?
YOUR SPECIAL BRAND OF MANHATTAN RED, WHAT ELSE?
NO, NO, NO. I HAVE THAT BOTTLED TO SATISFY THE RIFF-RAFF.
BRANIGAN, BRING US A BOTTLE OF THE... FRESHEST.

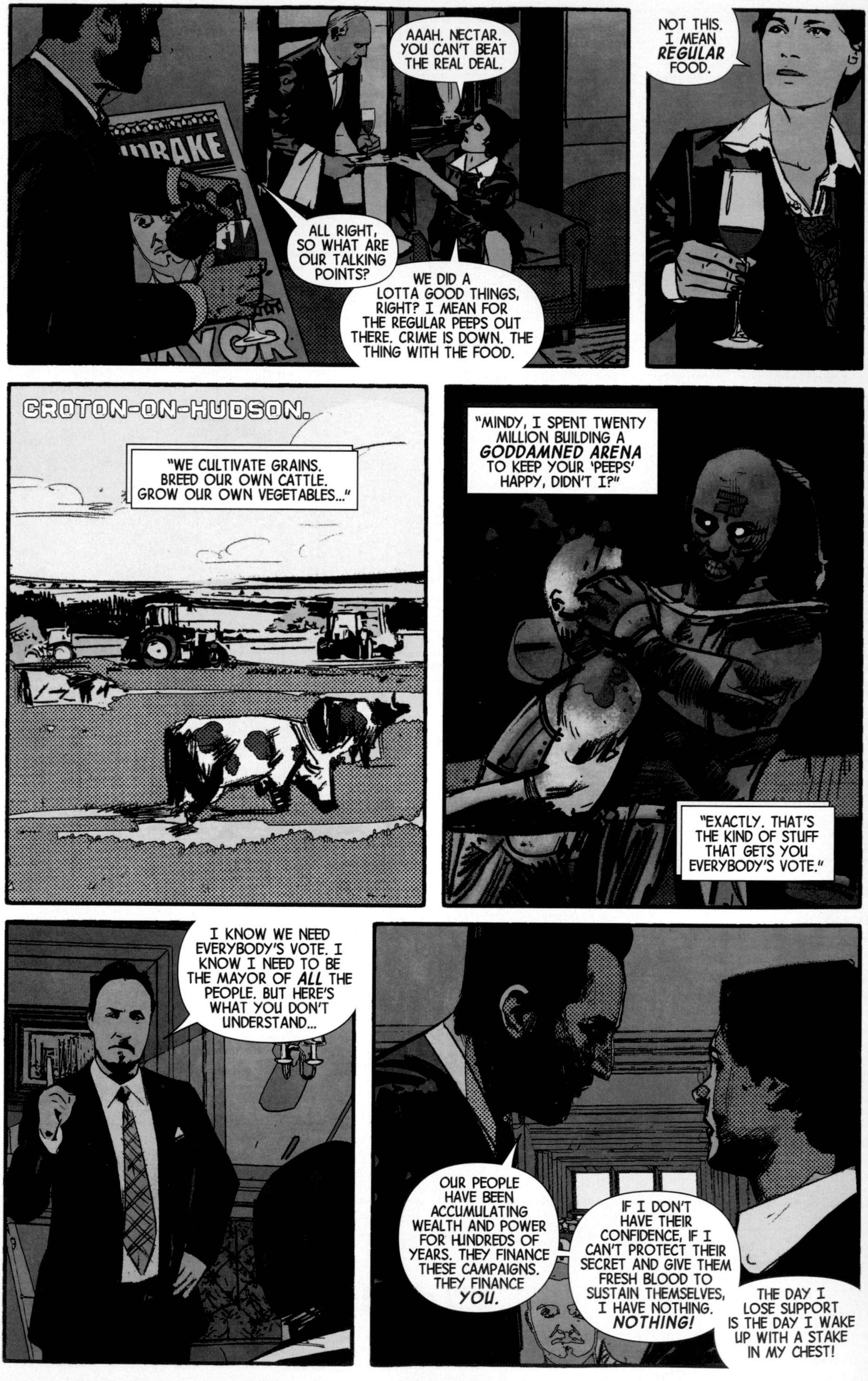
AAAH. NECTAR. YOU CAN'T BEAT THE REAL DEAL.
ALL RIGHT, SO WHAT ARE OUR TALKING POINTS?
WE DID A LOTTA GOOD THINGS, RIGHT? I MEAN FOR THE REGULAR PEEPS OUT THERE. CRIME IS DOWN. THE THING WITH THE FOOD.
NOT THIS. I MEAN REGULAR FOOD.
CROTON-ON-HUDSON.
"WE CULTIVATE GRAINS. BREED OUR OWN CATTLE. GROW OUR OWN VEGETABLES..."
"MINDY, I SPENT TWENTY MILLION BUILDING A GODDAMNED ARENA TO KEEP YOUR 'PEEPS' HAPPY, DIDN'T I?"
"EXACTLY. THAT'S THE KIND OF STUFF THAT GETS YOU EVERYBODY'S VOTE."
I KNOW WE NEED EVERYBODY'S VOTE. I KNOW I NEED TO BE THE MAYOR OF ALL THE PEOPLE. BUT HERE'S WHAT YOU DON'T UNDERSTAND...
OUR PEOPLE HAVE BEEN ACCUMULATING WEALTH AND POWER FOR HUNDREDS OF YEARS. THEY FINANCE THESE CAMPAIGNS. THEY FINANCE YOU.
IF I DON'T HAVE THEIR CONFIDENCE, IF I CAN'T PROTECT THEIR SECRET AND GIVE THEM FRESH BLOOD TO SUSTAIN THEMSELVES, I HAVE NOTHING. NOTHING!
THE DAY I LOSE SUPPORT IS THE DAY I WAKE UP WITH A STAKE IN MY CHEST!

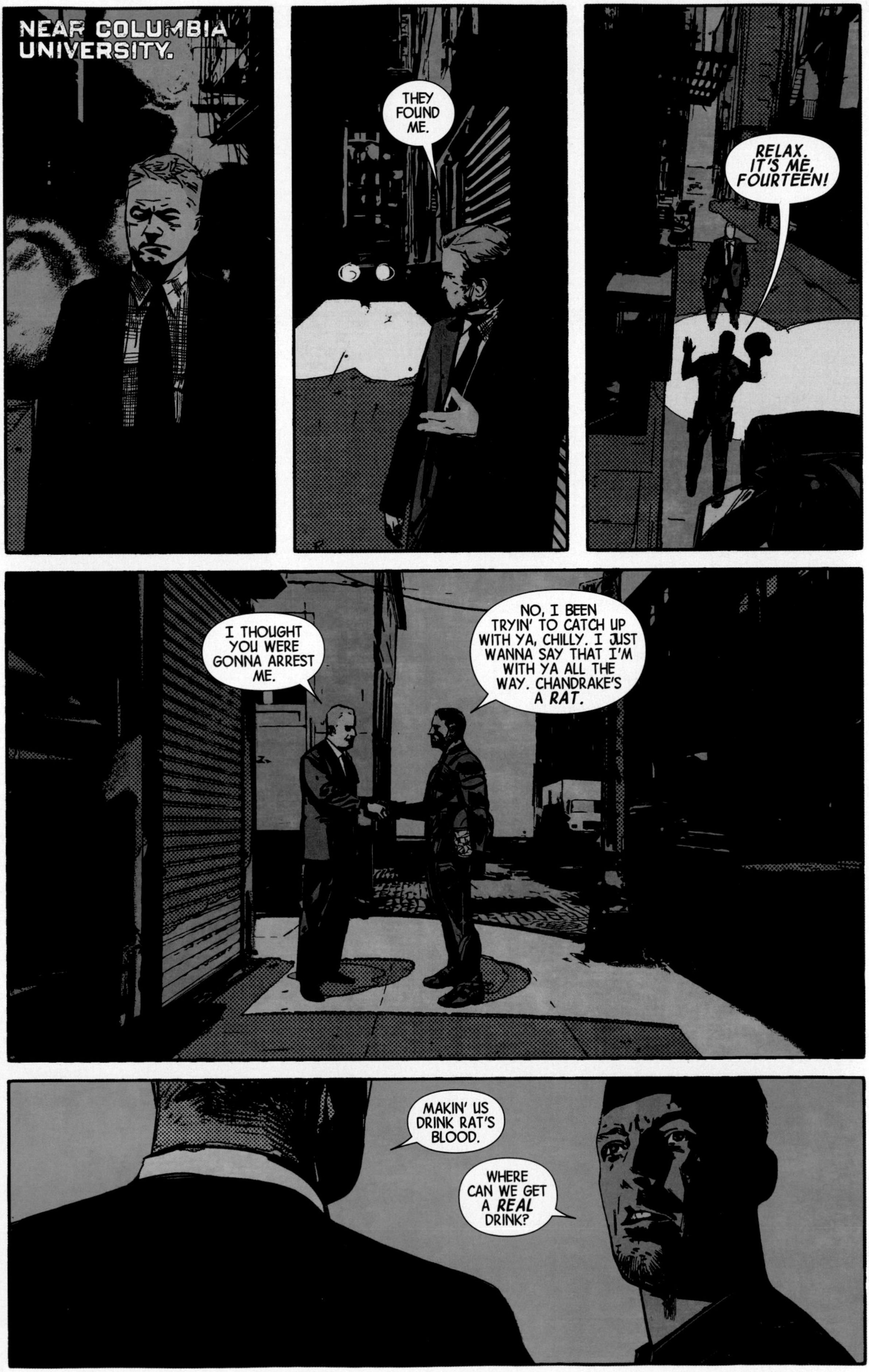
NEAR COLUMBIA UNIVERSITY.
THEY FOUND ME.
RELAX. IT'S ME, FOURTEEN!
I THOUGHT YOU WERE GONNA ARREST ME.
NO, I BEEN TRYIN' TO CATCH UP WITH YA, CHILLY. I JUST WANNA SAY THAT I'M WITH YA ALL THE WAY. CHANDRAKE'S A *RAT.*
MAKIN' US DRINK RAT'S BLOOD.
WHERE CAN WE GET A *REAL* DRINK?

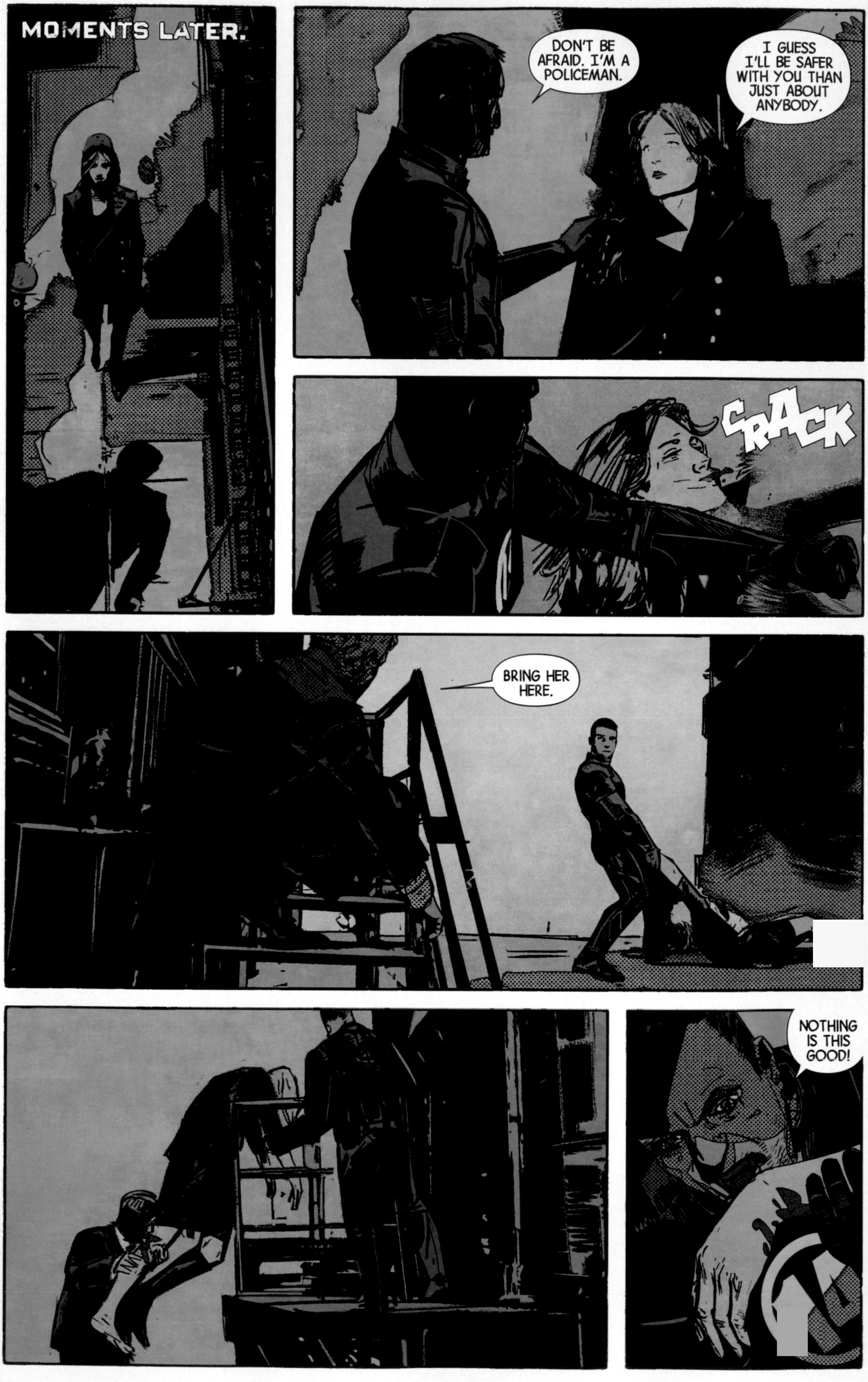
MOMENTS LATER.
DON'T BE AFRAID. I'M A POLICEMAN.
I GUESS I'LL BE SAFER WITH YOU THAN JUST ABOUT ANYBODY.
CRACK
BRING HER HERE.
NOTHING IS THIS GOOD!

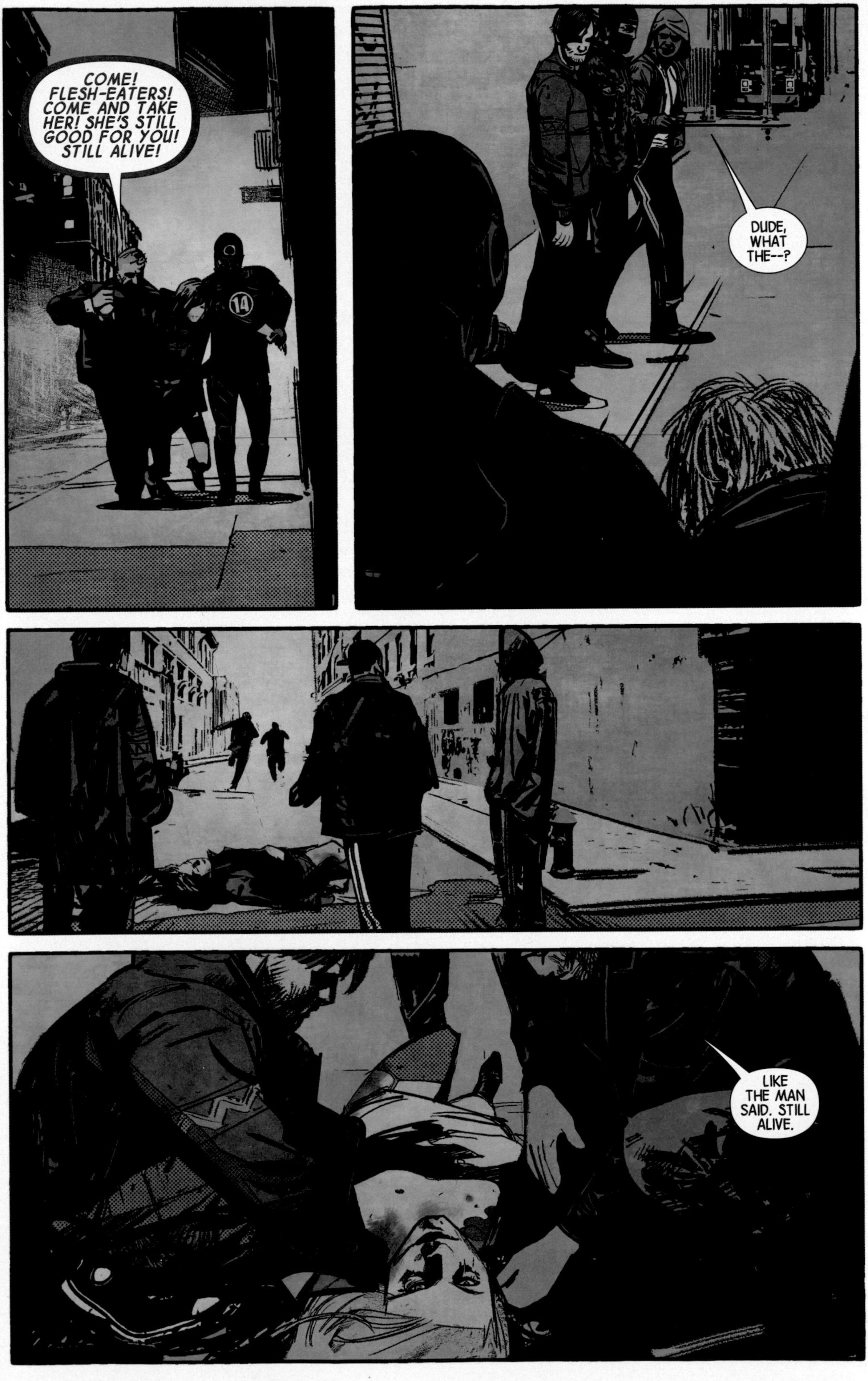
COME! FLESH-EATERS! COME AND TAKE HER! SHE'S STILL GOOD FOR YOU! STILL ALIVE!
DUDE, WHAT THE--?
LIKE THE MAN SAID. STILL ALIVE.

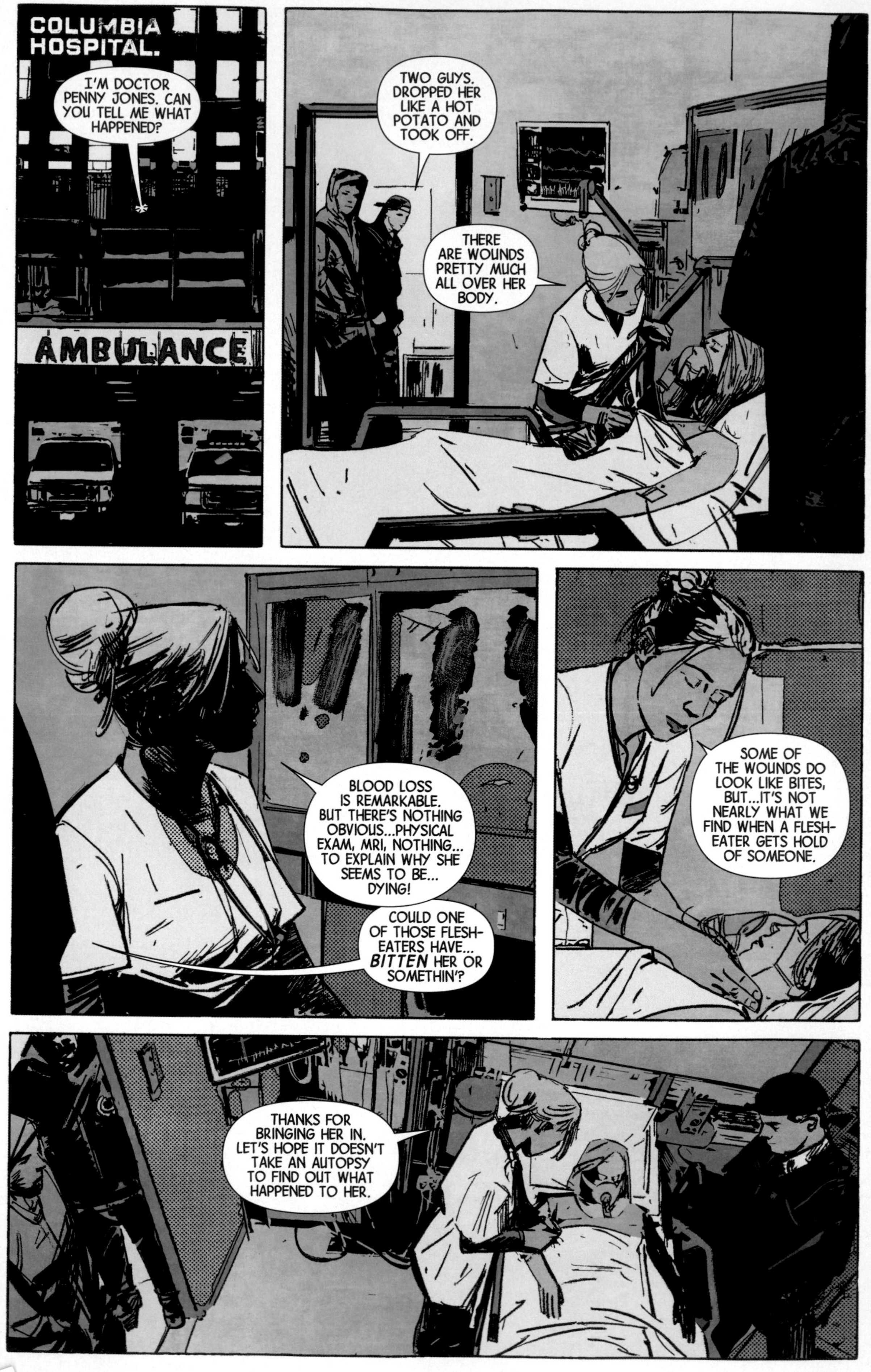
COLUMBIA HOSPITAL.
I'M DOCTOR PENNY JONES. CAN YOU TELL ME WHAT HAPPENED?
AMBULANCE
TWO GUYS. DROPPED HER LIKE A HOT POTATO AND TOOK OFF.
THERE ARE WOUNDS PRETTY MUCH ALL OVER HER BODY.
BLOOD LOSS IS REMARKABLE. BUT THERE'S NOTHING OBVIOUS...PHYSICAL EXAM, MRI, NOTHING... TO EXPLAIN WHY SHE SEEMS TO BE... DYING!
COULD ONE OF THOSE FLESH-EATERS HAVE... BITTEN HER OR SOMETHIN'?
SOME OF THE WOUNDS DO LOOK LIKE BITES, BUT...IT'S NOT NEARLY WHAT WE FIND WHEN A FLESH-EATER GETS HOLD OF SOMEONE.
THANKS FOR BRINGING HER IN. LET'S HOPE IT DOESN'T TAKE AN AUTOPSY TO FIND OUT WHAT HAPPENED TO HER.

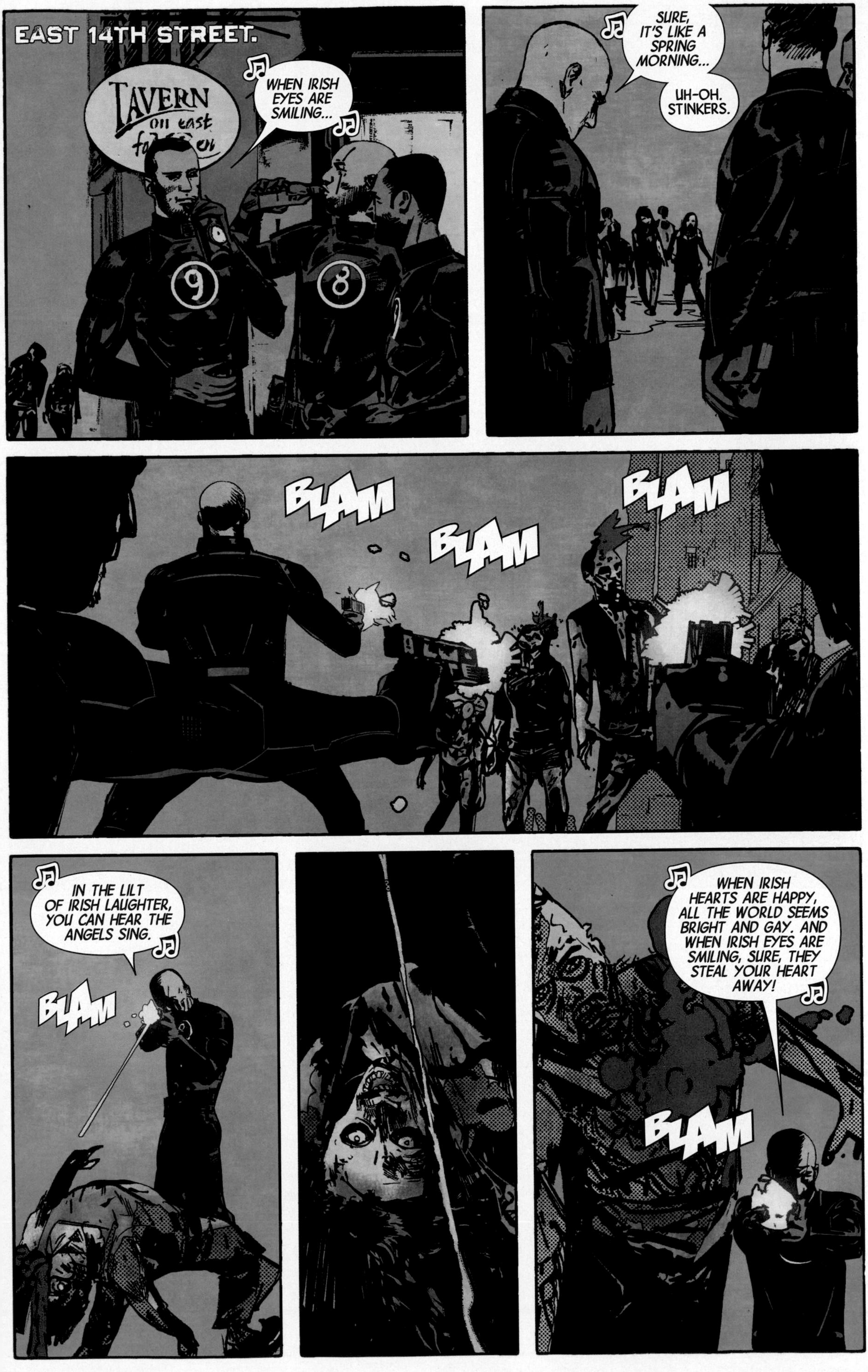
EAST 14TH STREET.
TAVERN on east fo...
WHEN IRISH EYES ARE SMILING...
SURE, IT'S LIKE A SPRING MORNING...
UH-OH. STINKERS.
BLAM
BLAM
BLAM
IN THE LILT OF IRISH LAUGHTER, YOU CAN HEAR THE ANGELS SING.
BLAM
WHEN IRISH HEARTS ARE HAPPY, ALL THE WORLD SEEMS BRIGHT AND GAY. AND WHEN IRISH EYES ARE SMILING, SURE, THEY STEAL YOUR HEART AWAY!
BLAM

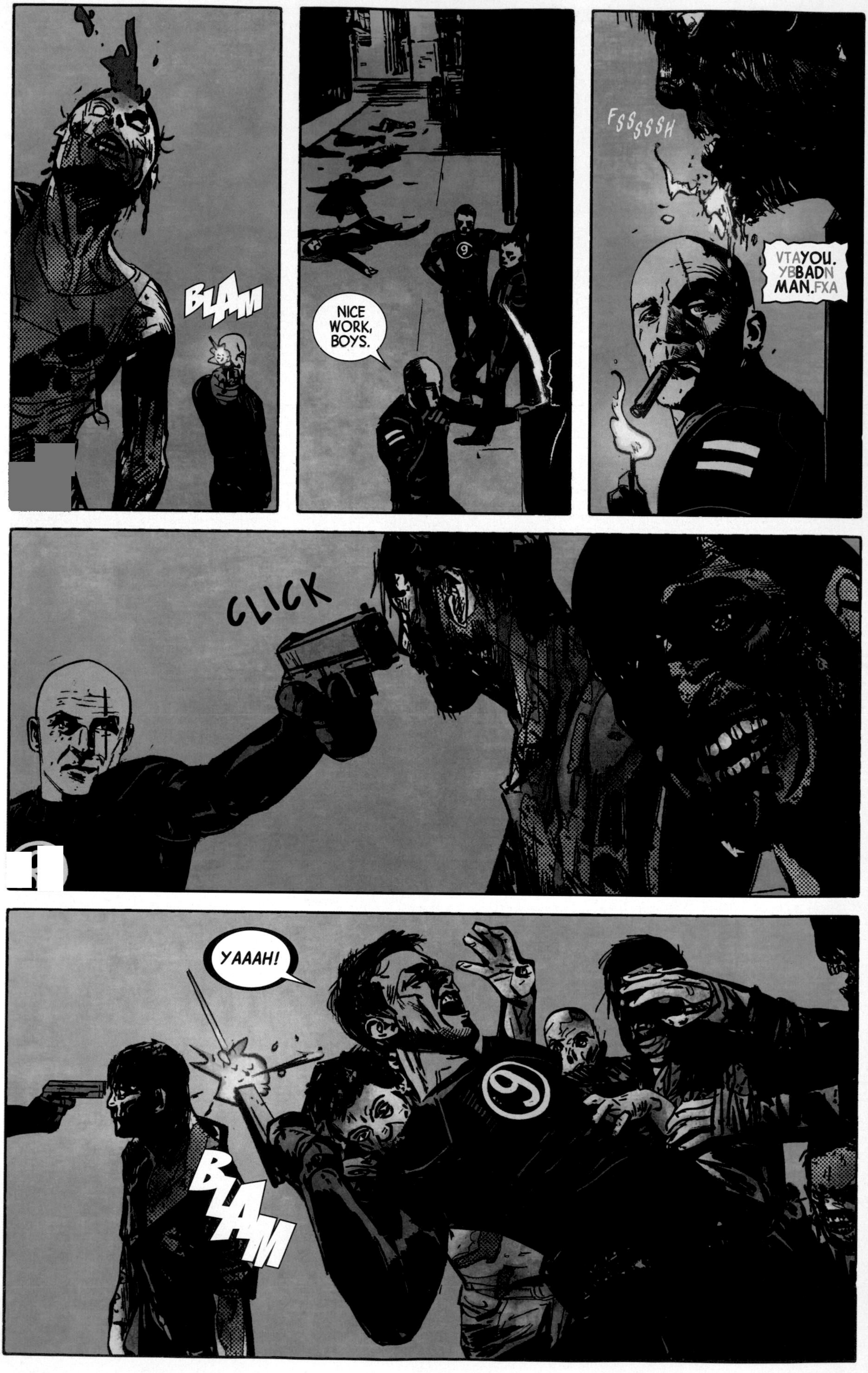
BLAM
NICE WORK, BOYS.
FSSSSSH
VTAYOU. YBBADN MAN.FXA
CLICK
YAAAH!
BLAM

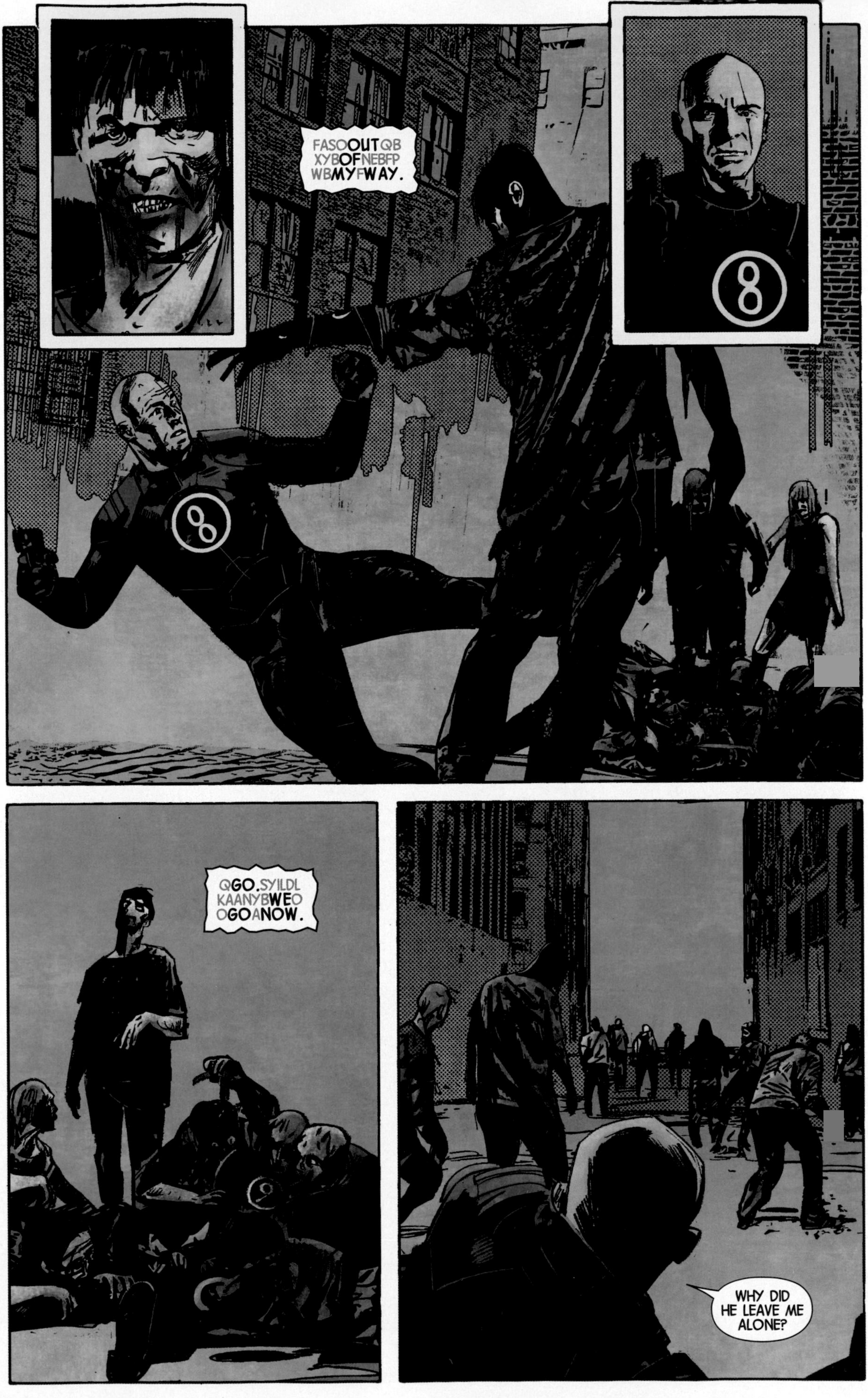
FASOOUTQB XYBOFNEBFP WBMYFWAY.
QGO.SYILDL KAANYBWEO OGOANOW.
WHY DID HE LEAVE ME ALONE?

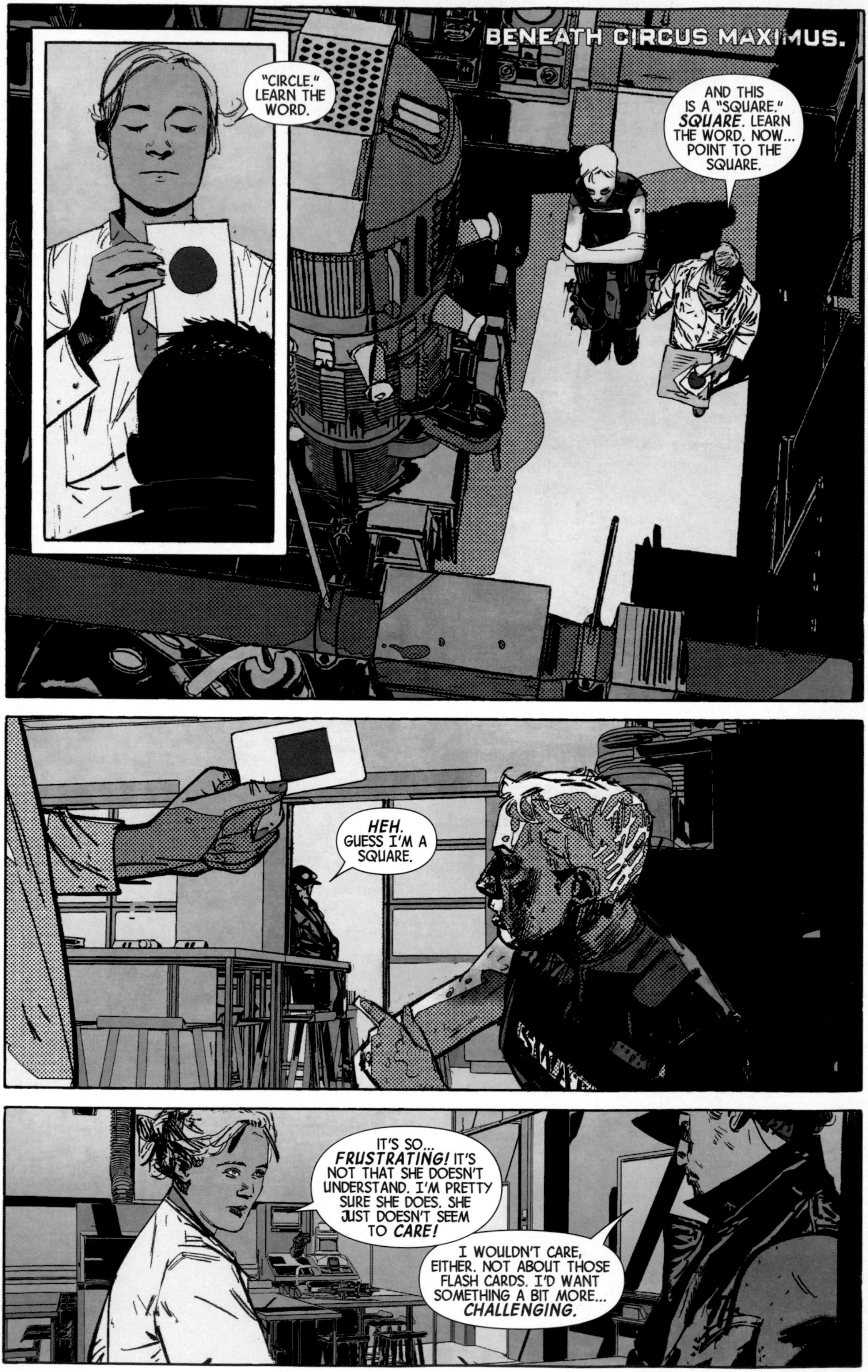
BENEATH CIRCUS MAXIMUS.
"CIRCLE." LEARN THE WORD.
AND THIS IS A "SQUARE." SQUARE. LEARN THE WORD. NOW... POINT TO THE SQUARE.
HEH. GUESS I'M A SQUARE.
IT'S SO... FRUSTRATING! IT'S NOT THAT SHE DOESN'T UNDERSTAND. I'M PRETTY SURE SHE DOES. SHE JUST DOESN'T SEEM TO CARE!
I WOULDN'T CARE, EITHER. NOT ABOUT THOSE FLASH CARDS. I'D WANT SOMETHING A BIT MORE... CHALLENGING.

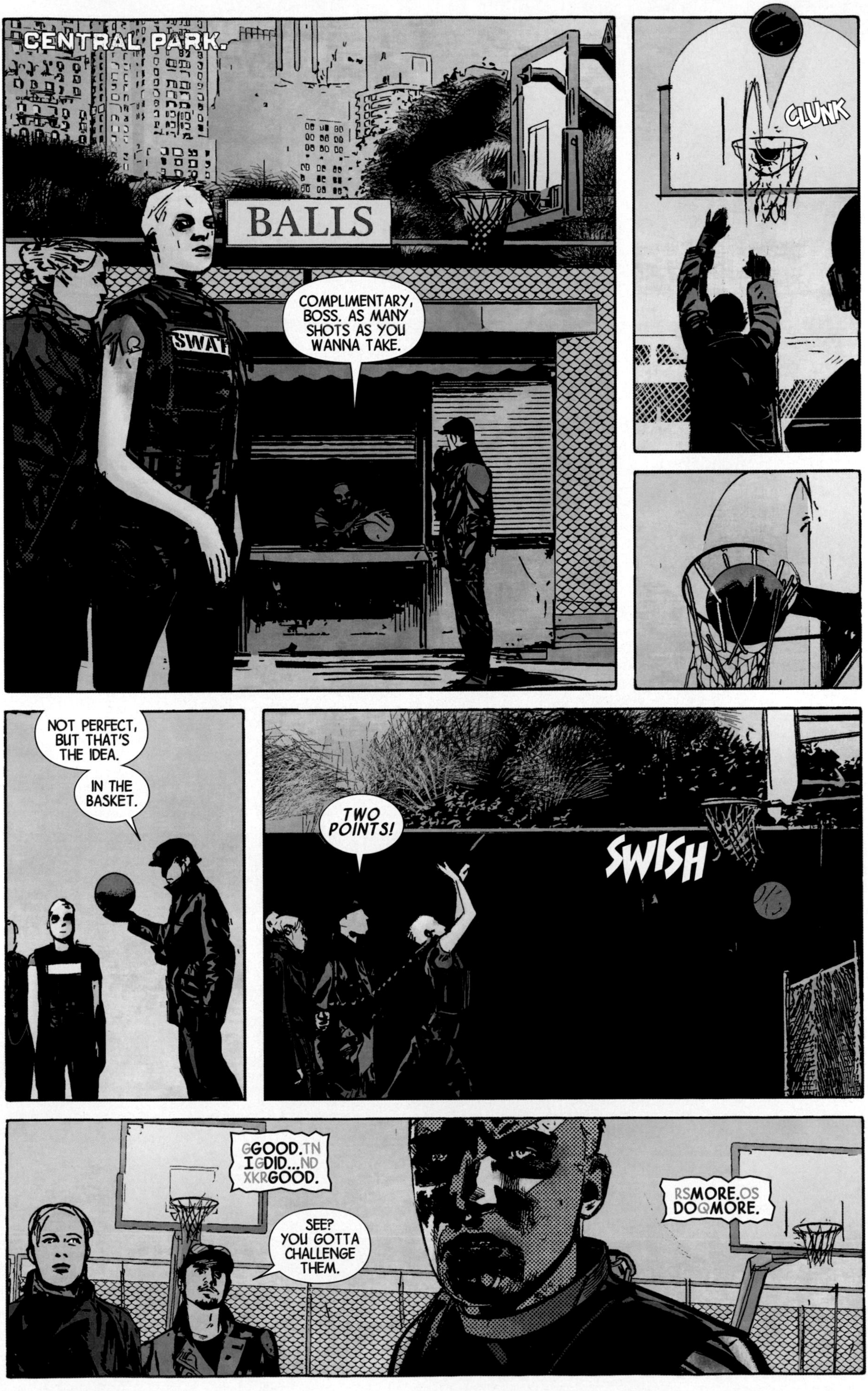
CENTRAL PARK.
BALLS
SWAT
COMPLIMENTARY, BOSS. AS MANY SHOTS AS YOU WANNA TAKE.
CLUNK
NOT PERFECT, BUT THAT'S THE IDEA.
IN THE BASKET.
TWO POINTS!
SWISH
GGOOD.TN IGDID...ND XKRGOOD.
SEE? YOU GOTTA CHALLENGE THEM.
RSMORE.OS DOQMORE.

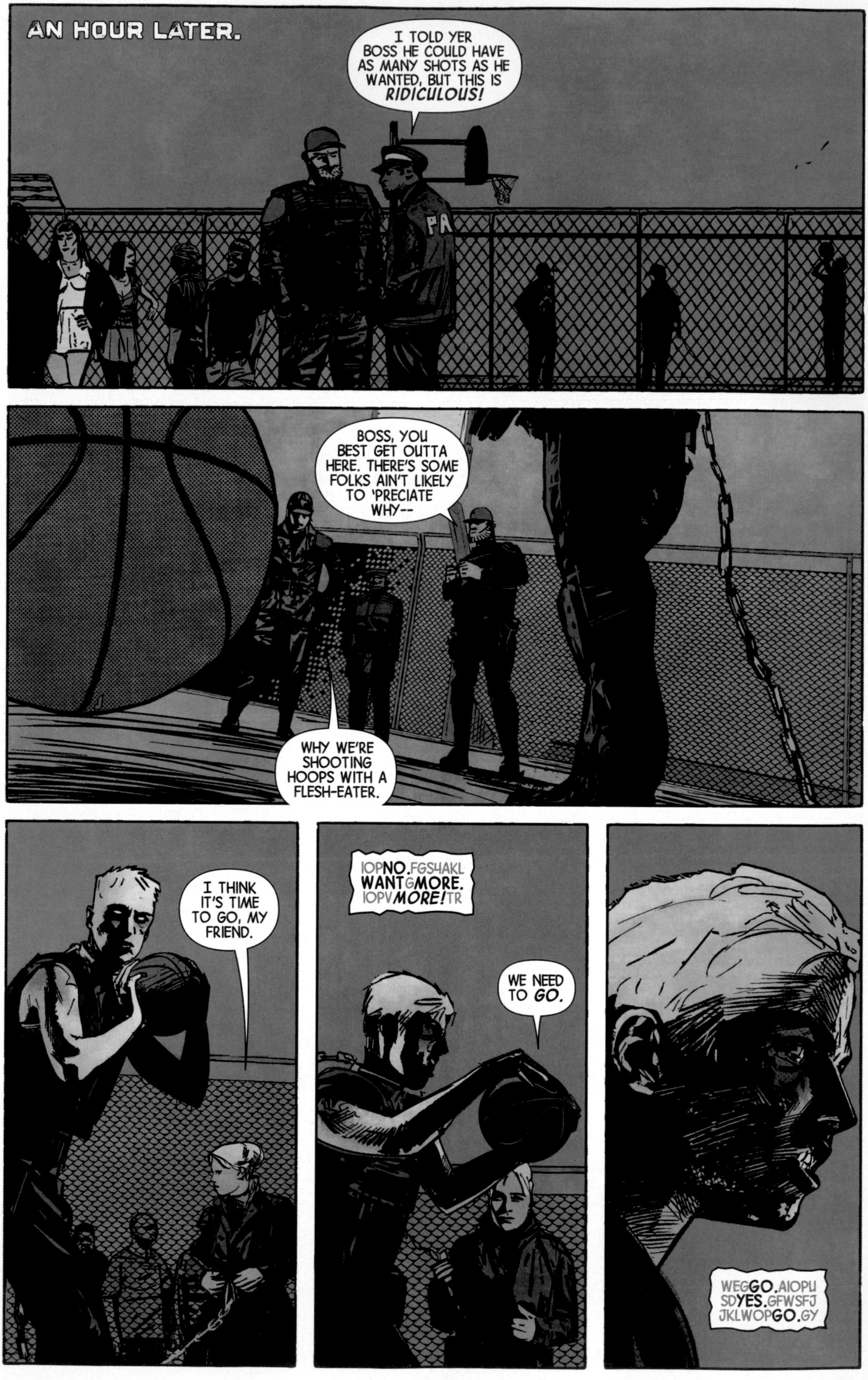
AN HOUR LATER.
I TOLD YER BOSS HE COULD HAVE AS MANY SHOTS AS HE WANTED, BUT THIS IS *RIDICULOUS!*
BOSS, YOU BEST GET OUTTA HERE. THERE'S SOME FOLKS AIN'T LIKELY TO 'PRECIATE WHY--
WHY WE'RE SHOOTING HOOPS WITH A FLESH-EATER.
I THINK IT'S TIME TO GO, MY FRIEND.
IOPNO.FGS4AKL WANTGMORE. IOPV*MORE!*TR
WE NEED TO *GO*.
WEGGO.AIOPU SDYES.GFWSFJ JKLWOPGO.GY

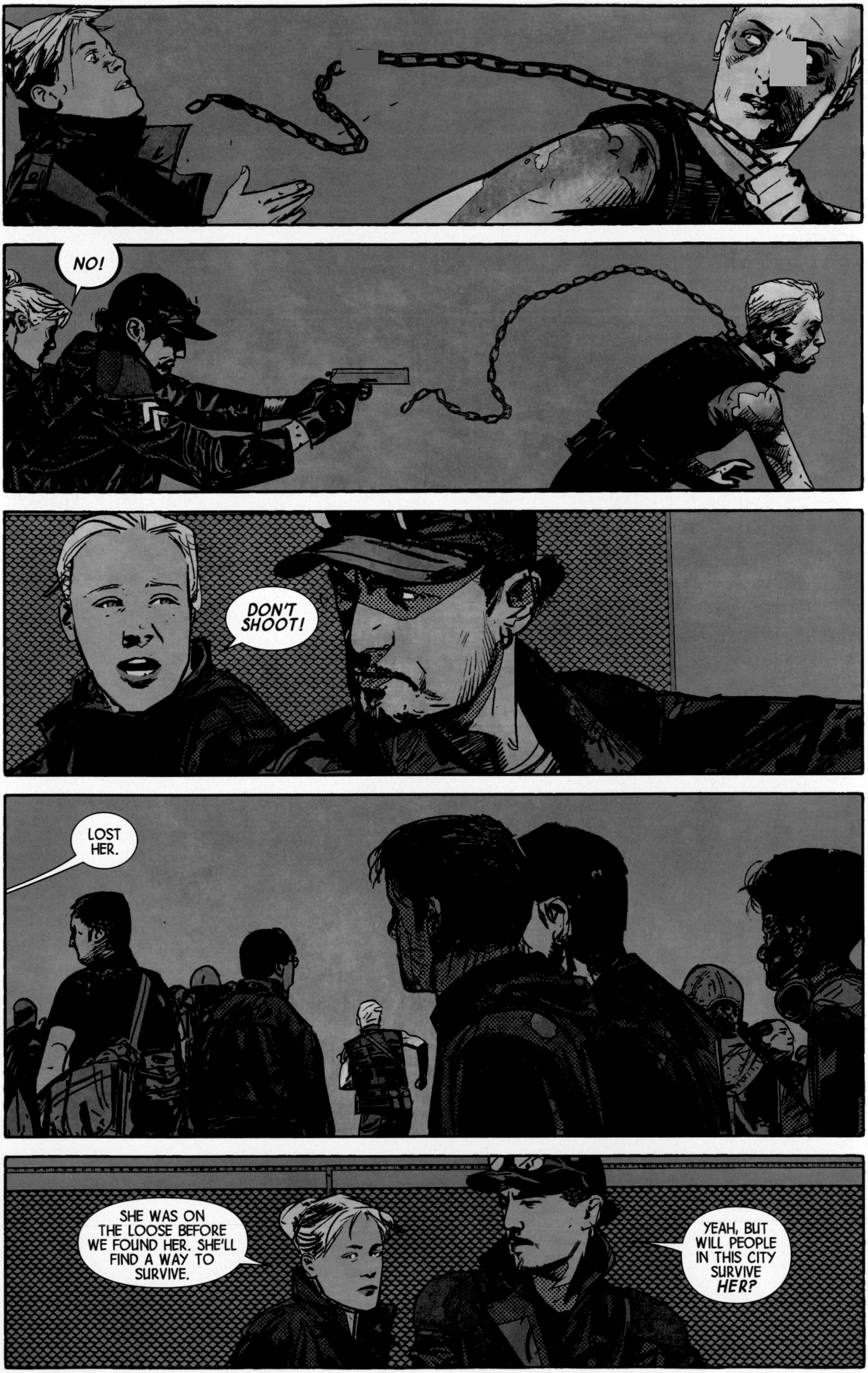
NO!
DON'T SHOOT!
LOST HER.
SHE WAS ON THE LOOSE BEFORE WE FOUND HER. SHE'LL FIND A WAY TO SURVIVE.
YEAH, BUT WILL PEOPLE IN THIS CITY SURVIVE *HER?*

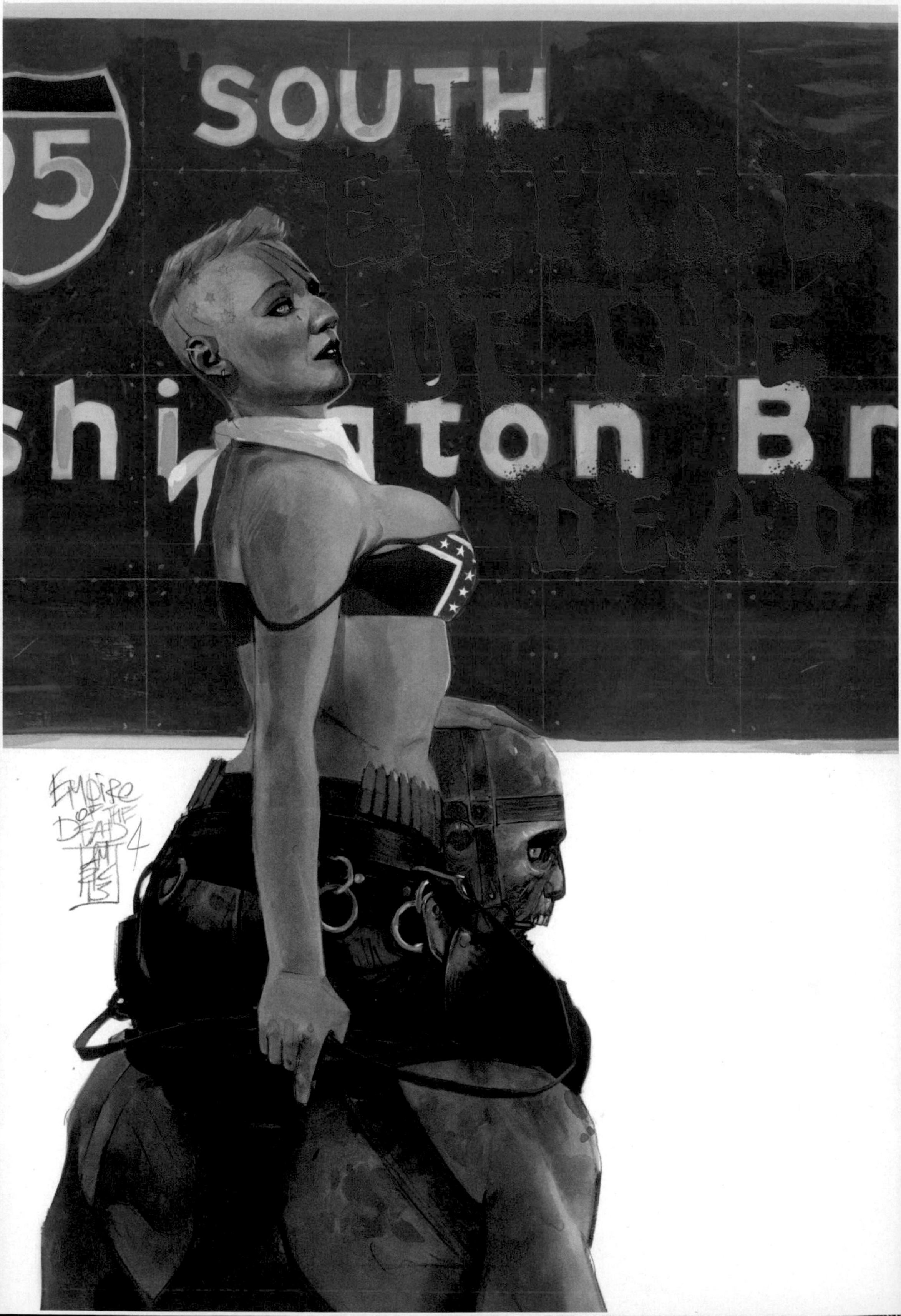
95
SOUTH
Empire of the Dead 4

FOUR

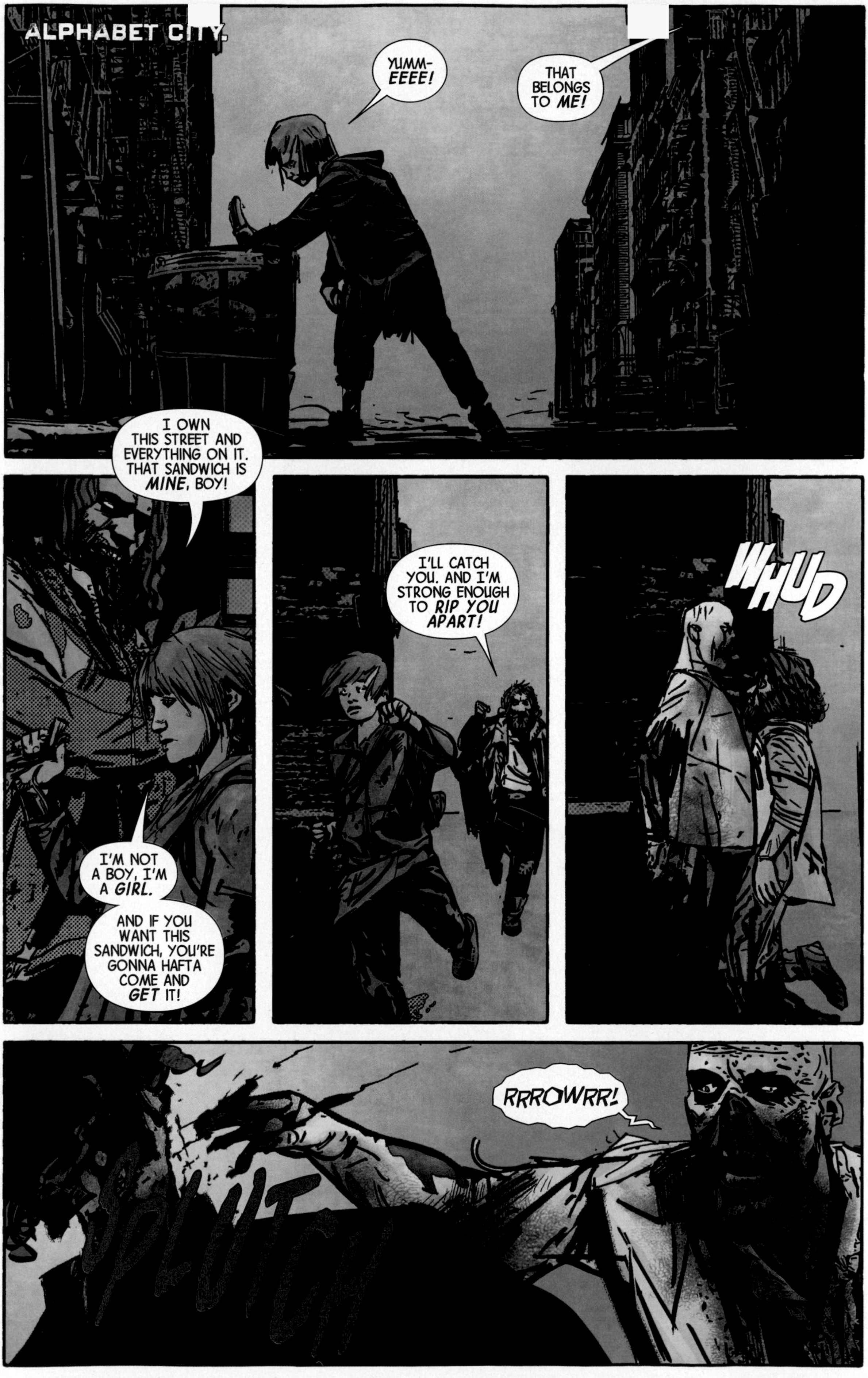
ALPHABET CITY.
YUMM-EEEE!
THAT BELONGS TO ME!
I OWN THIS STREET AND EVERYTHING ON IT. THAT SANDWICH IS MINE, BOY!
I'M NOT A BOY, I'M A GIRL.
AND IF YOU WANT THIS SANDWICH, YOU'RE GONNA HAFTA COME AND GET IT!
I'LL CATCH YOU. AND I'M STRONG ENOUGH TO RIP YOU APART!
WHUD
RRROWRR!

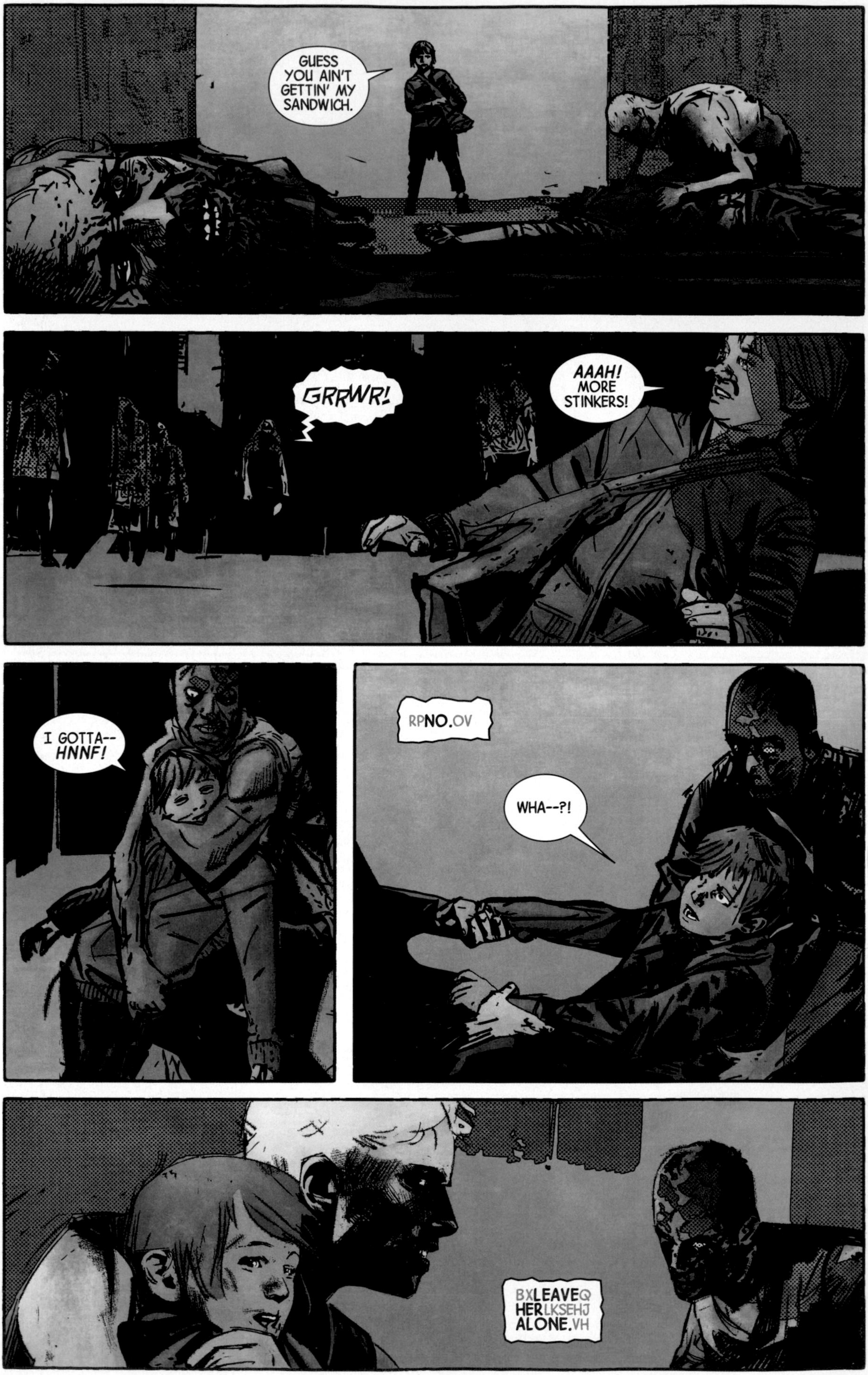
GUESS YOU AIN'T GETTIN' MY SANDWICH.
GRRWR!
AAAH! MORE STINKERS!
I GOTTA-- HNNF!
RPNO.OV
WHA--?!
BXLEAVEQ
HERLKSEHJ
ALONE.VH

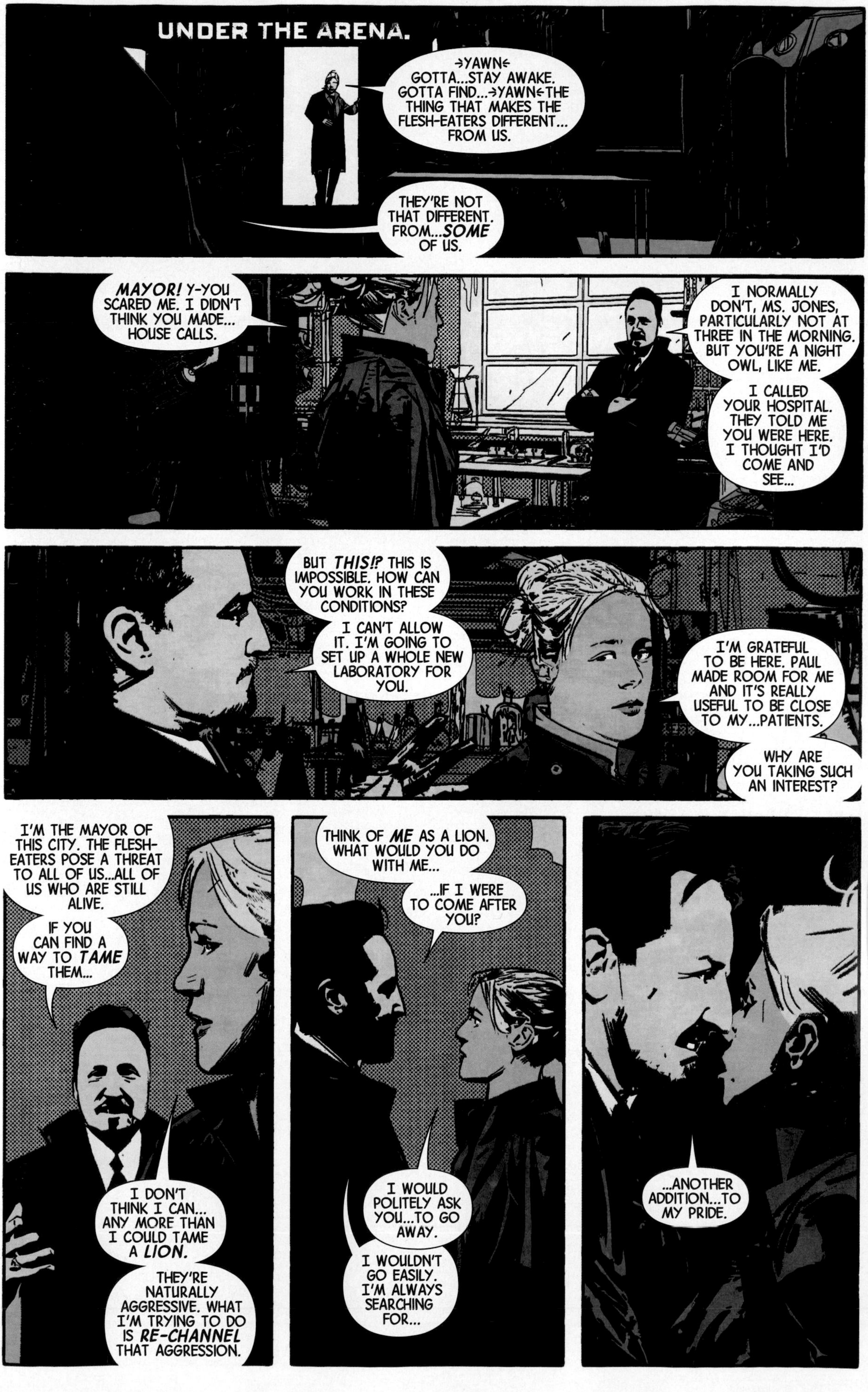
UNDER THE ARENA.
→YAWN← GOTTA...STAY AWAKE. GOTTA FIND...→YAWN← THE THING THAT MAKES THE FLESH-EATERS DIFFERENT... FROM US.
THEY'RE NOT THAT DIFFERENT. FROM...SOME OF US.
MAYOR! Y-YOU SCARED ME. I DIDN'T THINK YOU MADE... HOUSE CALLS.
I NORMALLY DON'T, MS. JONES, PARTICULARLY NOT AT THREE IN THE MORNING. BUT YOU'RE A NIGHT OWL, LIKE ME.
I CALLED YOUR HOSPITAL. THEY TOLD ME YOU WERE HERE. I THOUGHT I'D COME AND SEE...
BUT THIS!? THIS IS IMPOSSIBLE. HOW CAN YOU WORK IN THESE CONDITIONS?
I CAN'T ALLOW IT. I'M GOING TO SET UP A WHOLE NEW LABORATORY FOR YOU.
I'M GRATEFUL TO BE HERE. PAUL MADE ROOM FOR ME AND IT'S REALLY USEFUL TO BE CLOSE TO MY...PATIENTS.
WHY ARE YOU TAKING SUCH AN INTEREST?
I'M THE MAYOR OF THIS CITY. THE FLESH-EATERS POSE A THREAT TO ALL OF US...ALL OF US WHO ARE STILL ALIVE.
IF YOU CAN FIND A WAY TO TAME THEM...
I DON'T THINK I CAN... ANY MORE THAN I COULD TAME A LION.
THEY'RE NATURALLY AGGRESSIVE. WHAT I'M TRYING TO DO IS RE-CHANNEL THAT AGGRESSION.
THINK OF ME AS A LION. WHAT WOULD YOU DO WITH ME...
...IF I WERE TO COME AFTER YOU?
I WOULD POLITELY ASK YOU...TO GO AWAY.
I WOULDN'T GO EASILY. I'M ALWAYS SEARCHING FOR...
...ANOTHER ADDITION...TO MY PRIDE.

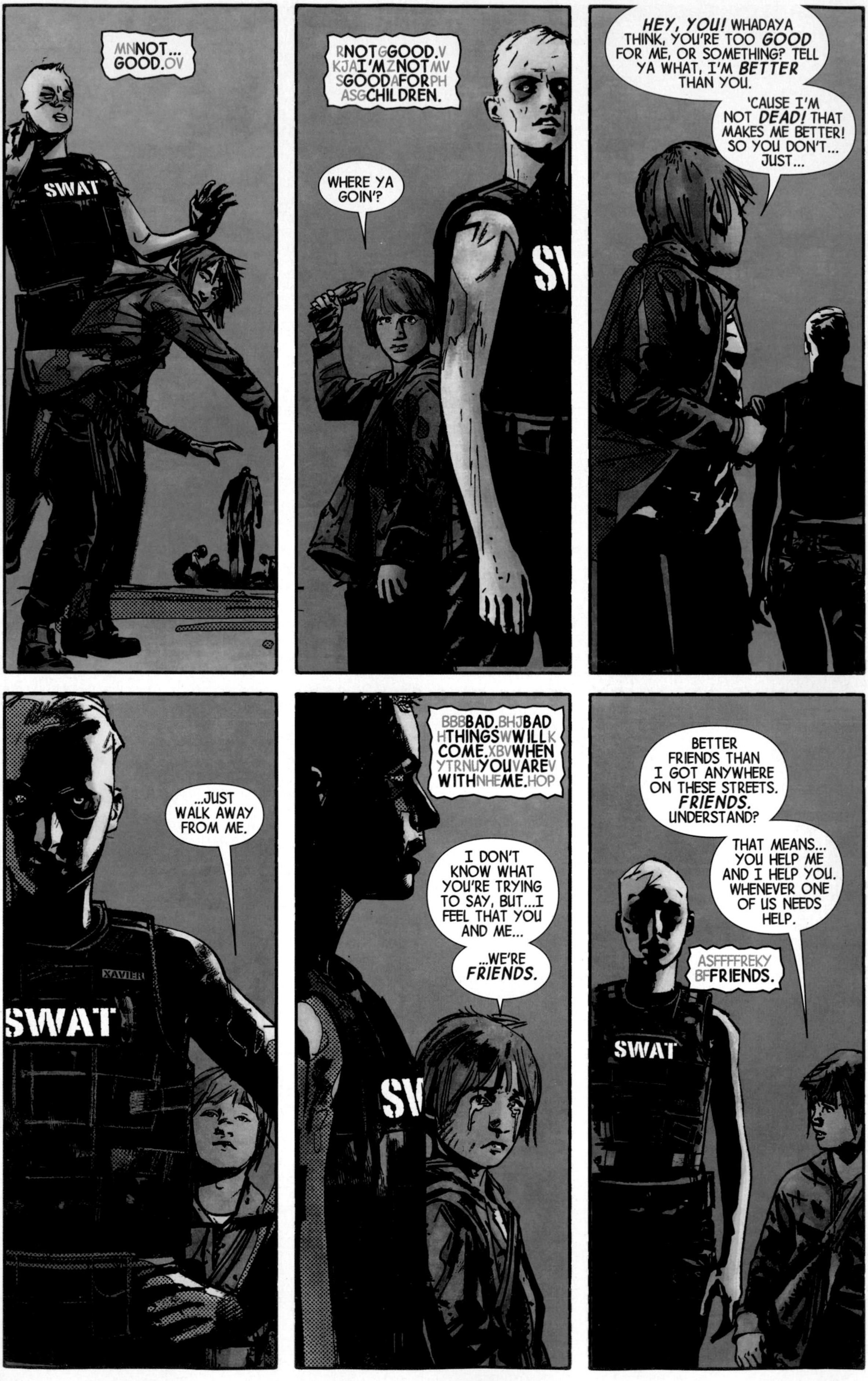
MNNOT... GOOD.OV
RNOTGGOOD.V KJAI'MZNOTMV SGOODAFORPH ASGCHILDREN.
WHERE YA GOIN'?
SWAT
HEY, YOU! WHADAYA THINK, YOU'RE TOO GOOD FOR ME, OR SOMETHING? TELL YA WHAT, I'M BETTER THAN YOU.
'CAUSE I'M NOT DEAD! THAT MAKES ME BETTER! SO YOU DON'T... JUST...
...JUST WALK AWAY FROM ME.
XAVIER
SWAT
BBBBAD.BHJBAD HTHINGSWWILLK COME.XBVWHEN YTRNUYOUVAREV WITHNHEME.HOP
I DON'T KNOW WHAT YOU'RE TRYING TO SAY, BUT...I FEEL THAT YOU AND ME...
...WE'RE FRIENDS.
BETTER FRIENDS THAN I GOT ANYWHERE ON THESE STREETS. FRIENDS. UNDERSTAND?
THAT MEANS... YOU HELP ME AND I HELP YOU. WHENEVER ONE OF US NEEDS HELP.
ASFFFFREKY BFFRIENDS.
SWAT

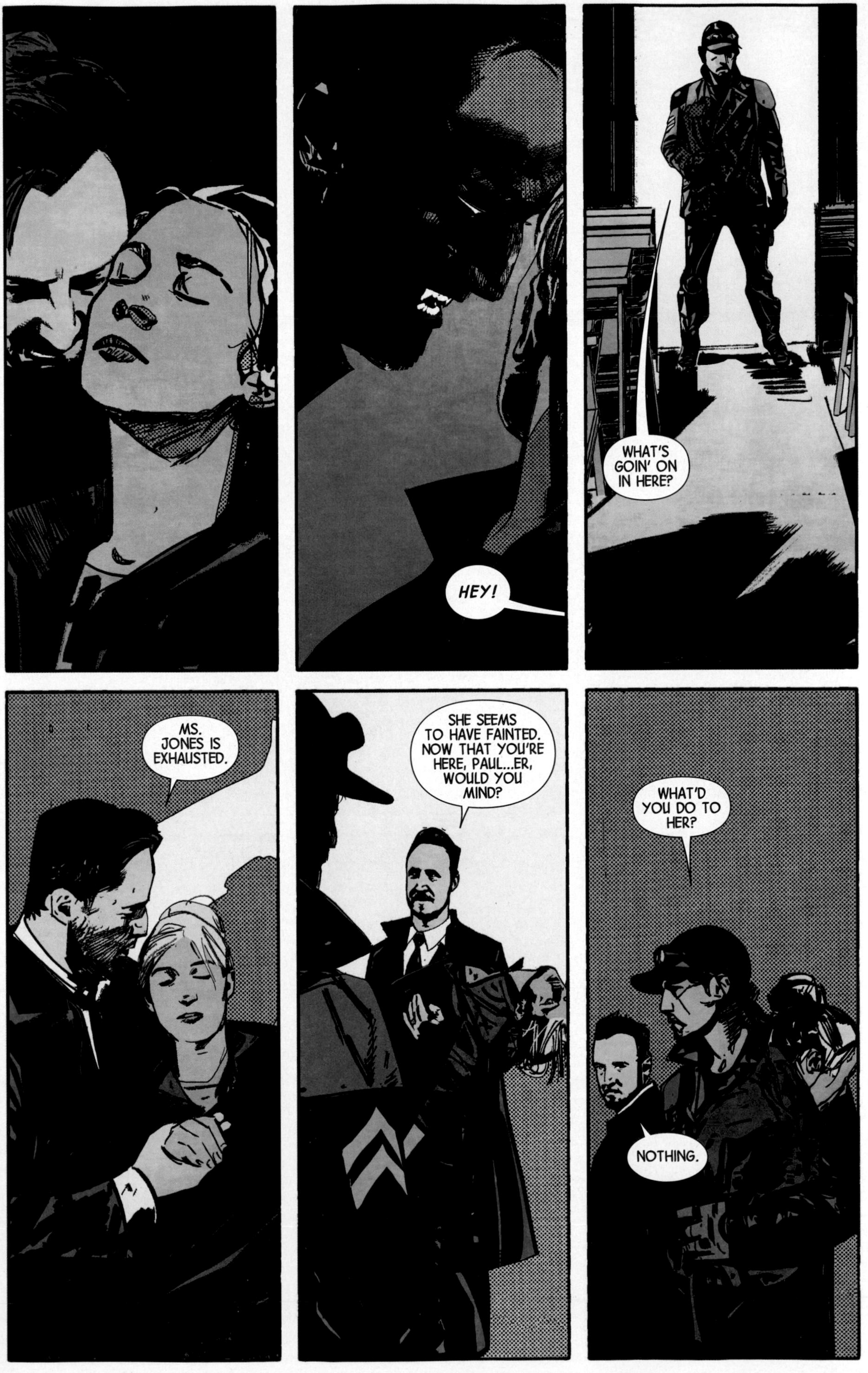
HEY!
WHAT'S GOIN' ON IN HERE?
MS. JONES IS EXHAUSTED.
SHE SEEMS TO HAVE FAINTED. NOW THAT YOU'RE HERE, PAUL...ER, WOULD YOU MIND?
WHAT'D YOU DO TO HER?
NOTHING.

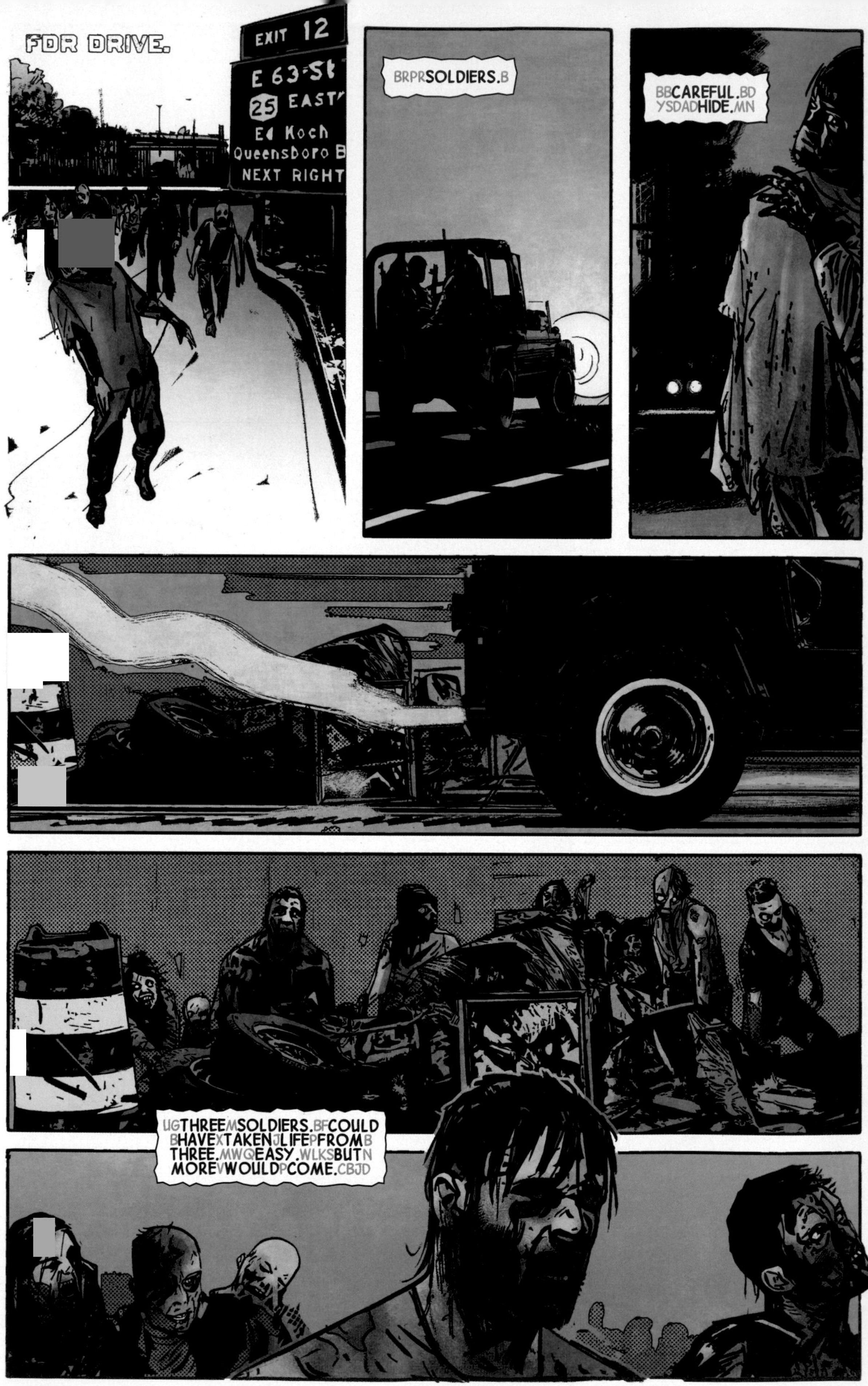
FDR DRIVE.
EXIT 12
E 63 St
25 EAST
Ed Koch
Queensboro B
NEXT RIGHT
SOLDIERS.
CAREFUL.
HIDE.
THREE SOLDIERS. COULD HAVE TAKEN LIFE FROM THREE. EASY. BUT MORE WOULD COME.

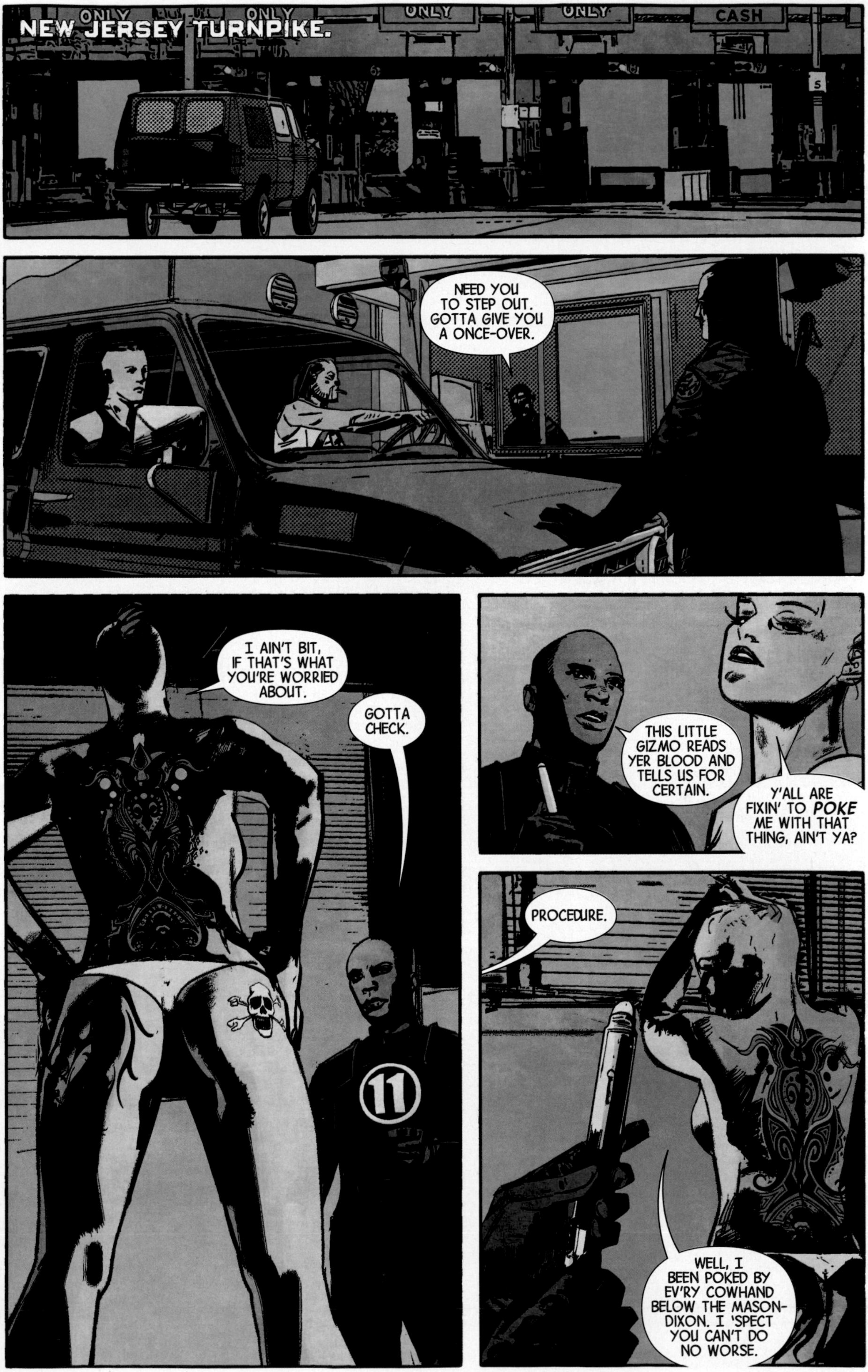

NEW JERSEY TURNPIKE.
NEED YOU TO STEP OUT. GOTTA GIVE YOU A ONCE-OVER.
I AIN'T BIT, IF THAT'S WHAT YOU'RE WORRIED ABOUT.
GOTTA CHECK.
THIS LITTLE GIZMO READS YER BLOOD AND TELLS US FOR CERTAIN.
Y'ALL ARE FIXIN' TO POKE ME WITH THAT THING, AIN'T YA?
PROCEDURE.
WELL, I BEEN POKED BY EV'RY COWHAND BELOW THE MASON-DIXON. I 'SPECT YOU CAN'T DO NO WORSE.

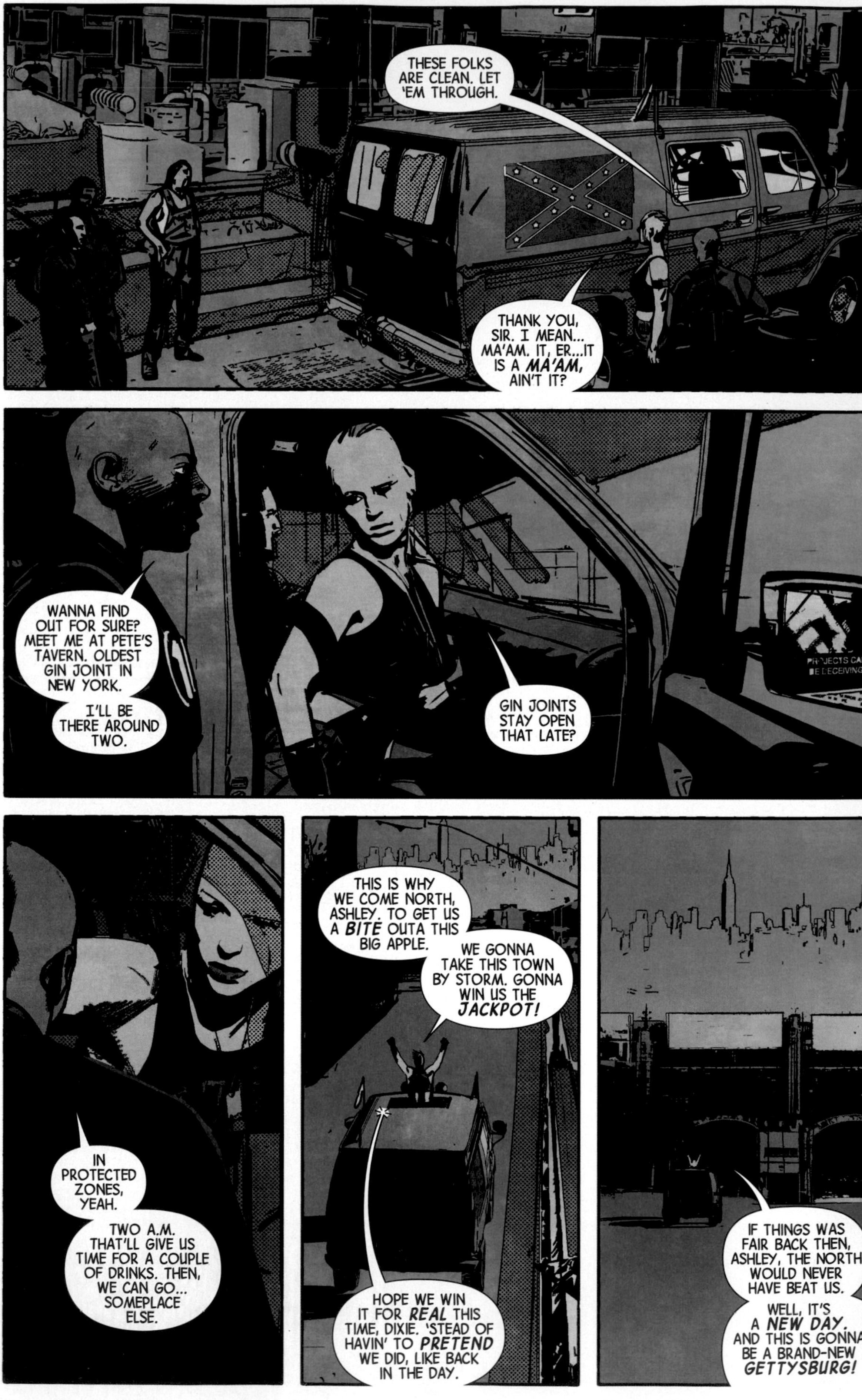

THESE FOLKS ARE CLEAN. LET 'EM THROUGH.
THANK YOU, SIR. I MEAN... MA'AM. IT, ER...IT IS A *MA'AM,* AIN'T IT?
WANNA FIND OUT FOR SURE? MEET ME AT PETE'S TAVERN. OLDEST GIN JOINT IN NEW YORK.
I'LL BE THERE AROUND TWO.
GIN JOINTS STAY OPEN THAT LATE?
IN PROTECTED ZONES, YEAH.
TWO A.M. THAT'LL GIVE US TIME FOR A COUPLE OF DRINKS. THEN, WE CAN GO... SOMEPLACE ELSE.
THIS IS WHY WE COME NORTH, ASHLEY. TO GET US A *BITE* OUTA THIS BIG APPLE.
WE GONNA TAKE THIS TOWN BY STORM. GONNA WIN US THE *JACKPOT!*
HOPE WE WIN IT FOR *REAL* THIS TIME, DIXIE. 'STEAD OF HAVIN' TO *PRETEND* WE DID, LIKE BACK IN THE DAY.
IF THINGS WAS FAIR BACK THEN, ASHLEY, THE NORTH WOULD NEVER HAVE BEAT US.
WELL, IT'S A *NEW DAY.* AND THIS IS GONNA BE A BRAND-NEW *GETTYSBURG!*

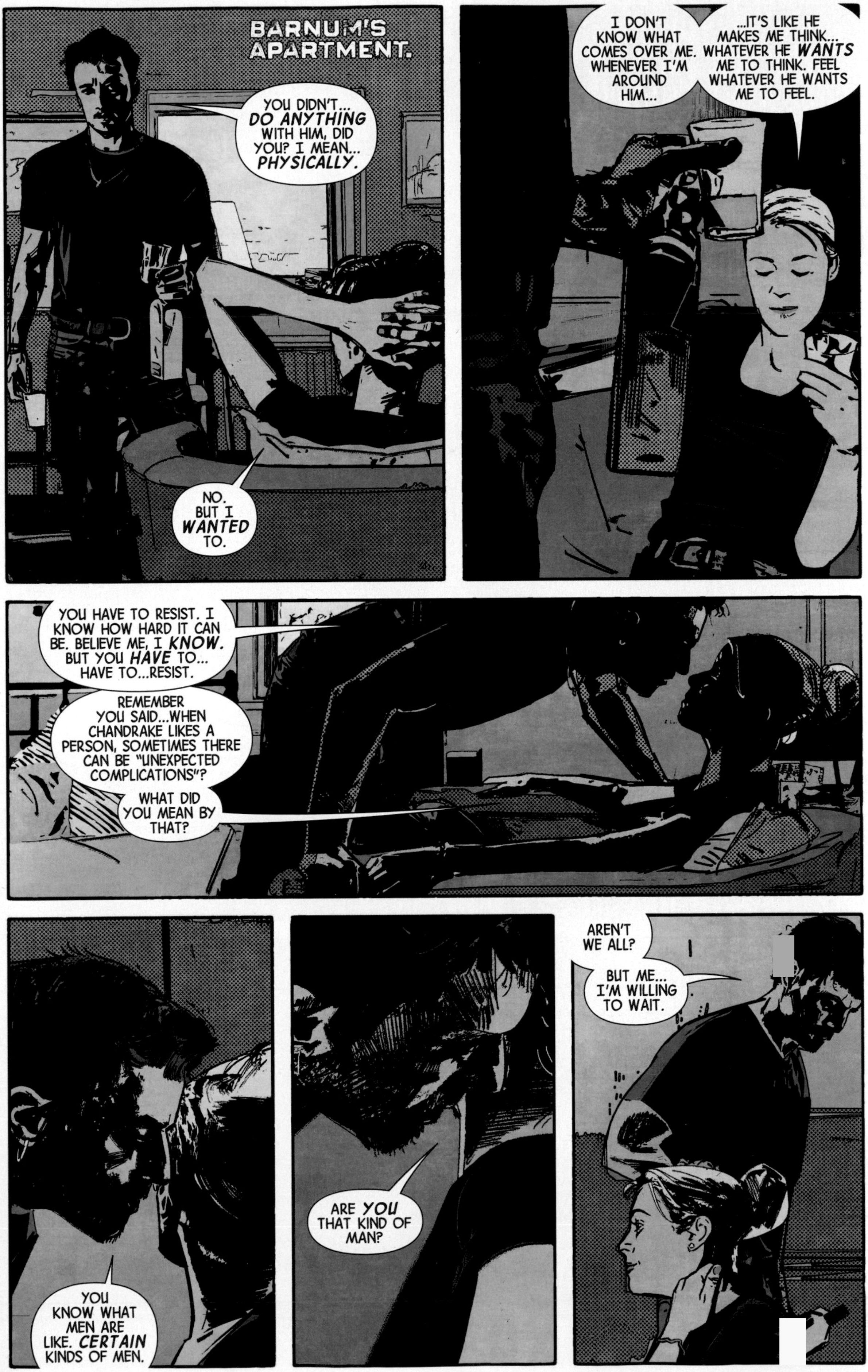
BARNUM'S APARTMENT.
YOU DIDN'T... DO ANYTHING WITH HIM, DID YOU? I MEAN... PHYSICALLY.
NO. BUT I WANTED TO.
I DON'T KNOW WHAT COMES OVER ME. WHENEVER I'M AROUND HIM...
...IT'S LIKE HE MAKES ME THINK... WHATEVER HE WANTS ME TO THINK. FEEL WHATEVER HE WANTS ME TO FEEL.
YOU HAVE TO RESIST. I KNOW HOW HARD IT CAN BE. BELIEVE ME, I KNOW. BUT YOU HAVE TO... HAVE TO...RESIST.
REMEMBER YOU SAID...WHEN CHANDRAKE LIKES A PERSON, SOMETIMES THERE CAN BE "UNEXPECTED COMPLICATIONS"?
WHAT DID YOU MEAN BY THAT?
YOU KNOW WHAT MEN ARE LIKE. CERTAIN KINDS OF MEN.
ARE YOU THAT KIND OF MAN?
AREN'T WE ALL?
BUT ME... I'M WILLING TO WAIT.

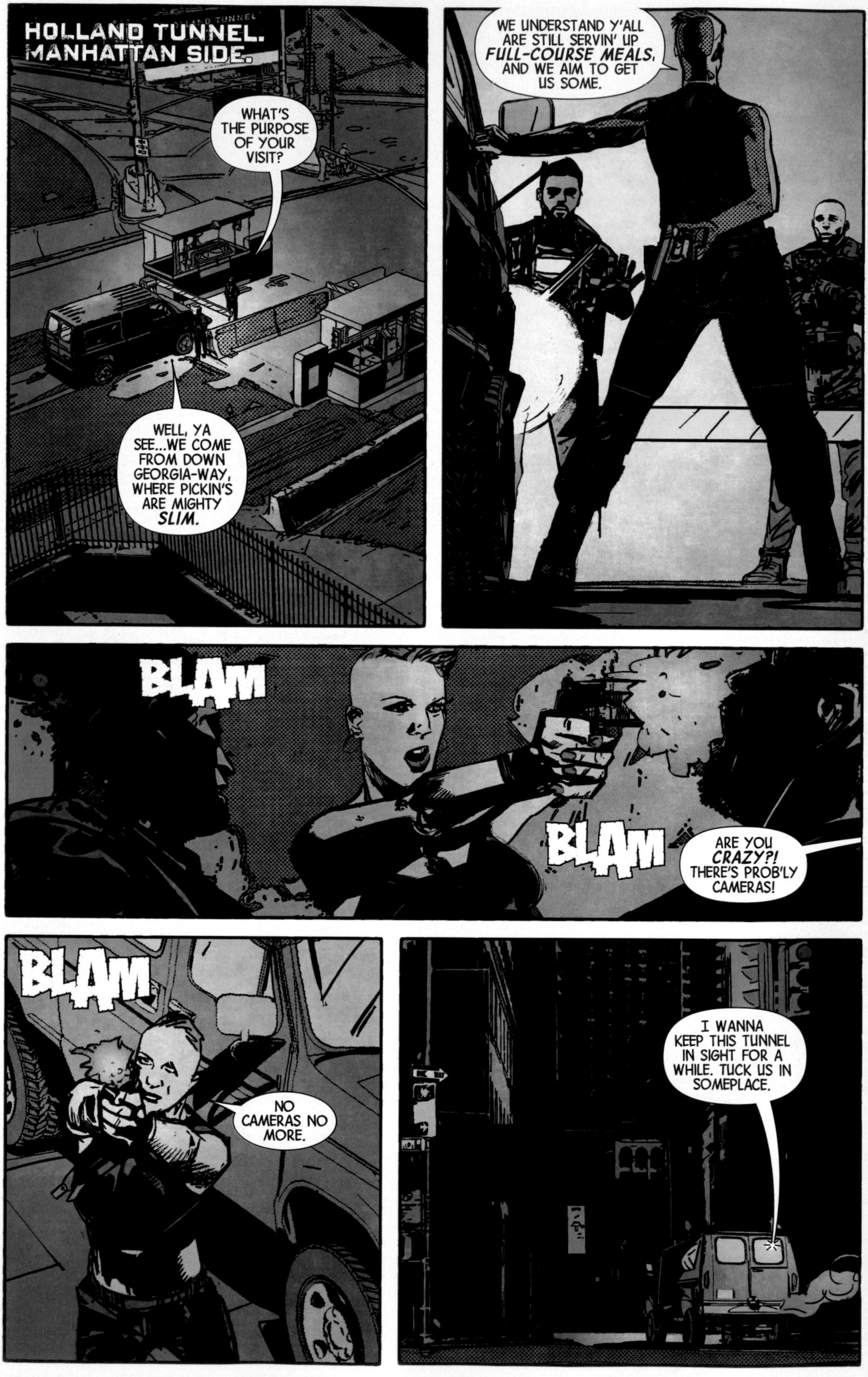
HOLLAND TUNNEL. MANHATTAN SIDE.
WHAT'S THE PURPOSE OF YOUR VISIT?
WELL, YA SEE...WE COME FROM DOWN GEORGIA-WAY, WHERE PICKIN'S ARE MIGHTY SLIM.
WE UNDERSTAND Y'ALL ARE STILL SERVIN' UP FULL-COURSE MEALS, AND WE AIM TO GET US SOME.
BLAM
BLAM
ARE YOU CRAZY?! THERE'S PROB'LY CAMERAS!
BLAM
NO CAMERAS NO MORE.
I WANNA KEEP THIS TUNNEL IN SIGHT FOR A WHILE. TUCK US IN SOMEPLACE.

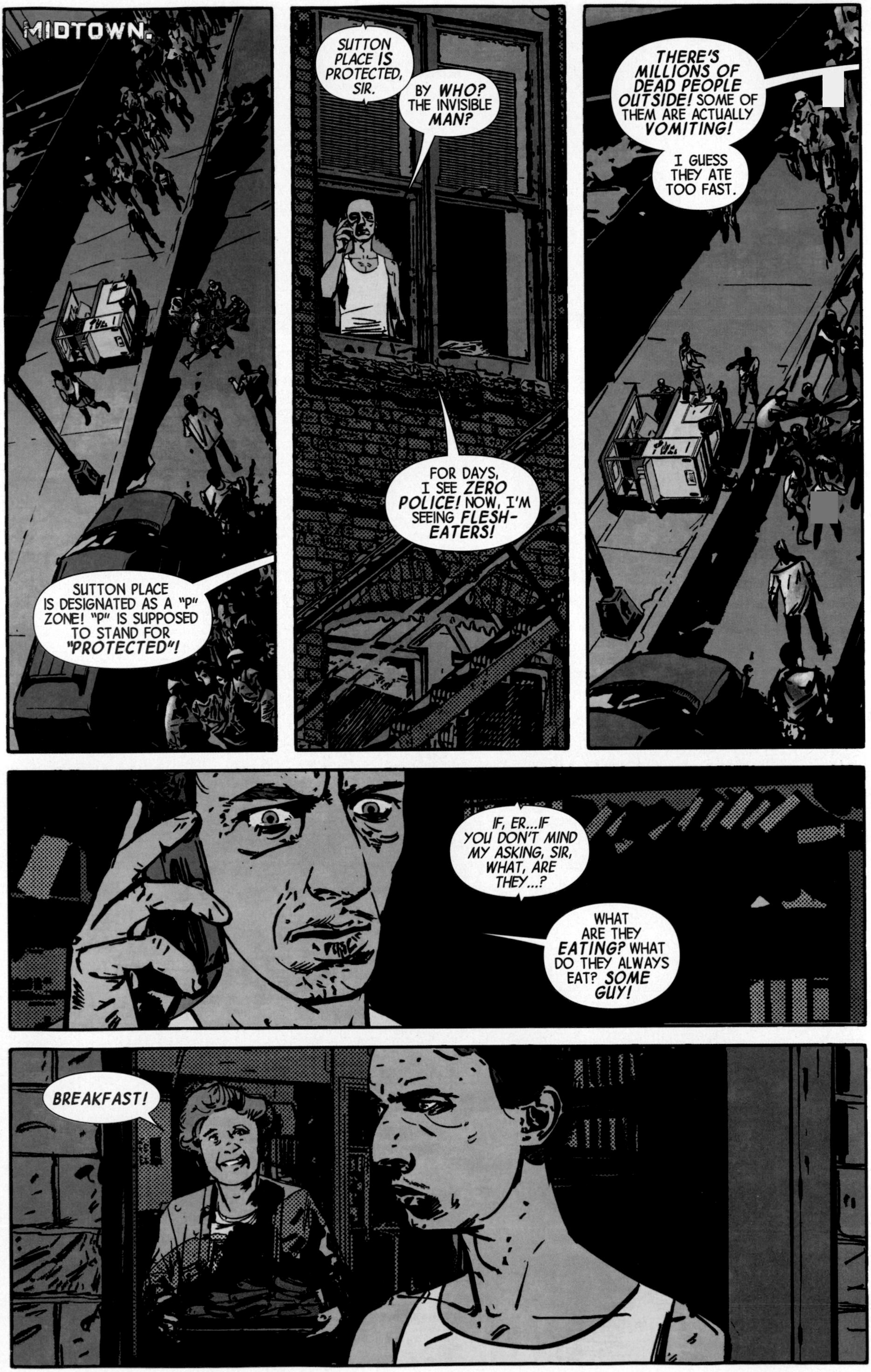
MIDTOWN.
SUTTON PLACE IS DESIGNATED AS A "P" ZONE! "P" IS SUPPOSED TO STAND FOR "PROTECTED"!
SUTTON PLACE IS PROTECTED, SIR.
BY WHO? THE INVISIBLE MAN?
FOR DAYS, I SEE ZERO POLICE! NOW, I'M SEEING FLESH-EATERS!
THERE'S MILLIONS OF DEAD PEOPLE OUTSIDE! SOME OF THEM ARE ACTUALLY VOMITING!
I GUESS THEY ATE TOO FAST.
IF, ER...IF YOU DON'T MIND MY ASKING, SIR, WHAT, ARE THEY...?
WHAT ARE THEY EATING? WHAT DO THEY ALWAYS EAT? SOME GUY!
BREAKFAST!

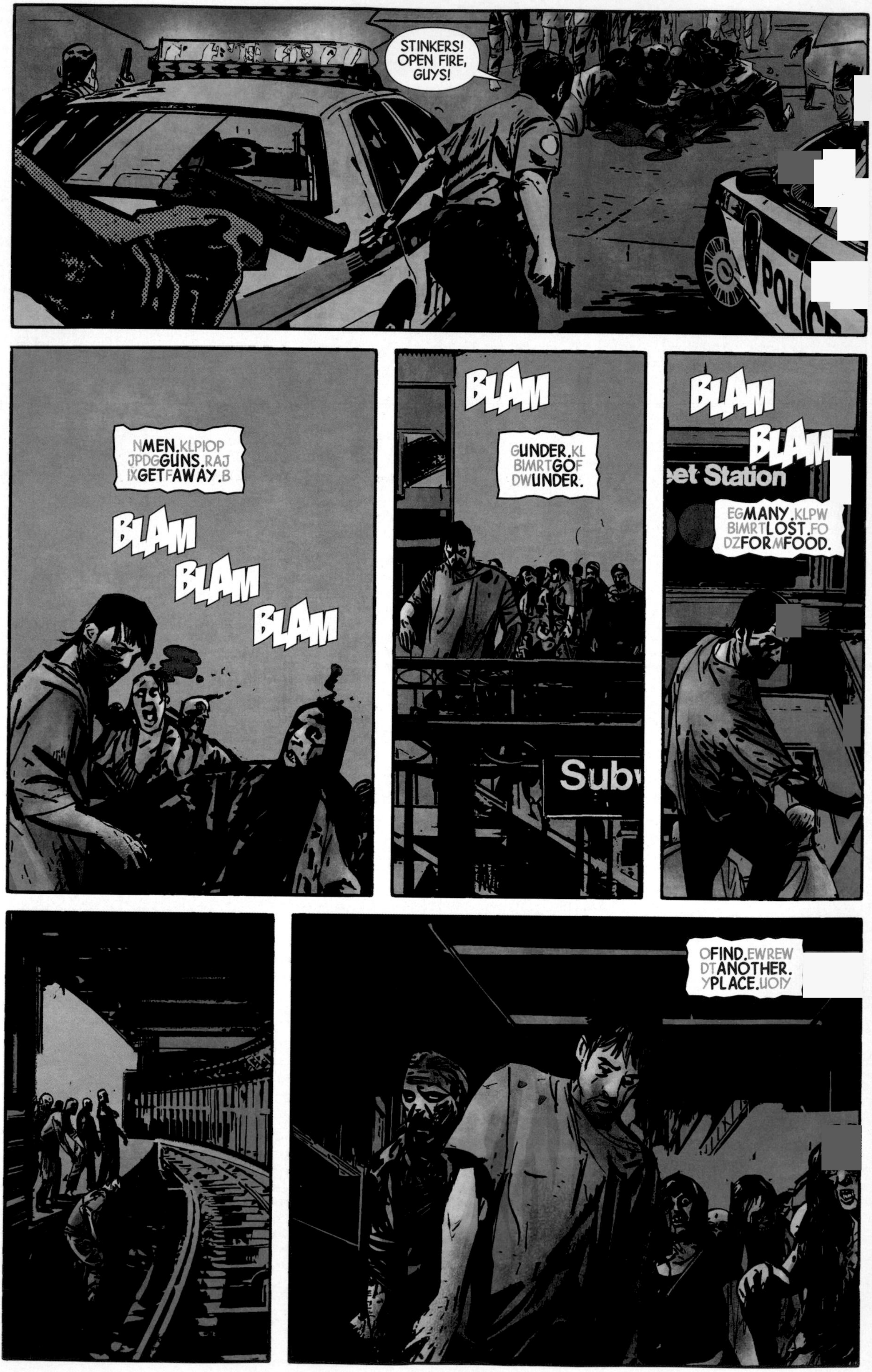

STINKERS! OPEN FIRE, GUYS!
NMEN.KLPIOP JPDGGUNS.RAJ IXGETFAWAY.B
BLAM
BLAM
BLAM
BLAM
GUNDER.KL BIMRTGOF DWUNDER.
Subw
BLAM
BLAM
eet Station
EGMANY.KLPW BIMRTLOST.FO DZFORMFOOD.
OFIND.EWREW DTANOTHER. YPLACE.UOIY

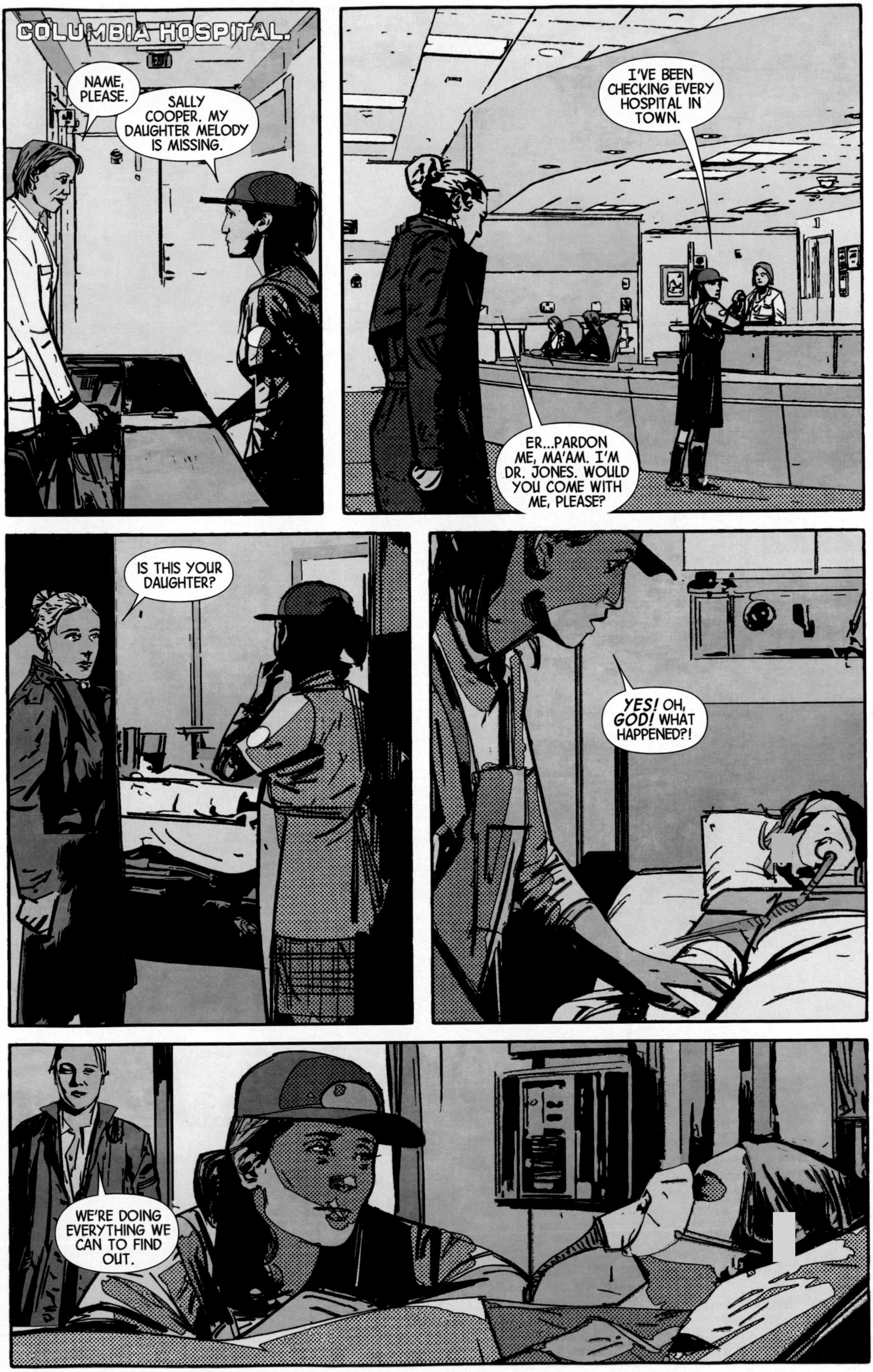
COLUMBIA HOSPITAL.
NAME, PLEASE.
SALLY COOPER. MY DAUGHTER MELODY IS MISSING.
I'VE BEEN CHECKING EVERY HOSPITAL IN TOWN.
ER...PARDON ME, MA'AM. I'M DR. JONES. WOULD YOU COME WITH ME, PLEASE?
IS THIS YOUR DAUGHTER?
YES! OH, GOD! WHAT HAPPENED?!
WE'RE DOING EVERYTHING WE CAN TO FIND OUT.

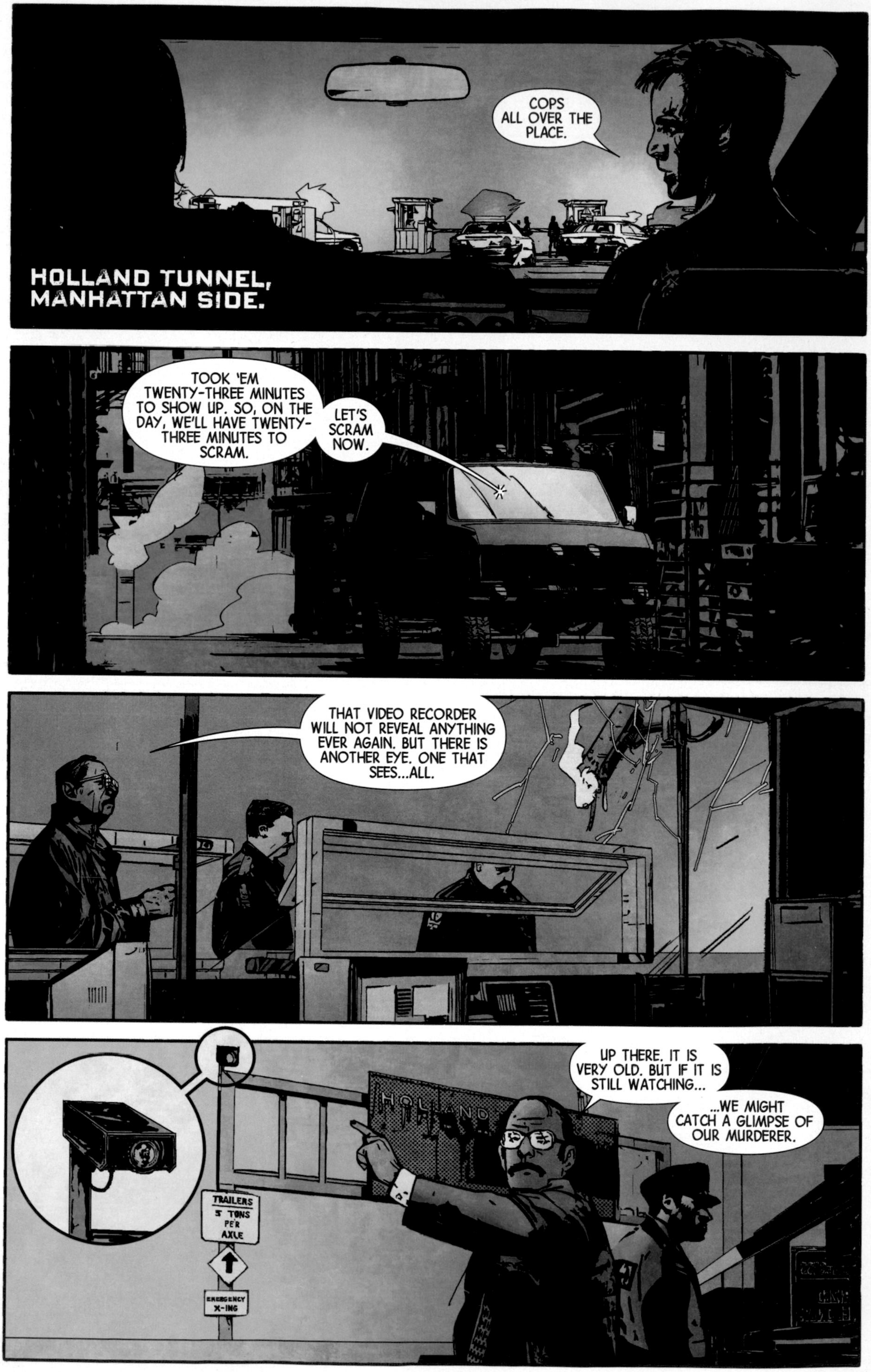
COPS ALL OVER THE PLACE.
HOLLAND TUNNEL, MANHATTAN SIDE.
TOOK 'EM TWENTY-THREE MINUTES TO SHOW UP. SO, ON THE DAY, WE'LL HAVE TWENTY-THREE MINUTES TO SCRAM.
LET'S SCRAM NOW.
THAT VIDEO RECORDER WILL NOT REVEAL ANYTHING EVER AGAIN. BUT THERE IS ANOTHER EYE. ONE THAT SEES...ALL.
UP THERE. IT IS VERY OLD. BUT IF IT IS STILL WATCHING...
...WE MIGHT CATCH A GLIMPSE OF OUR MURDERER.
HOLLAND
TRAILERS
5 TONS PER AXLE
EMERGENCY X-ING

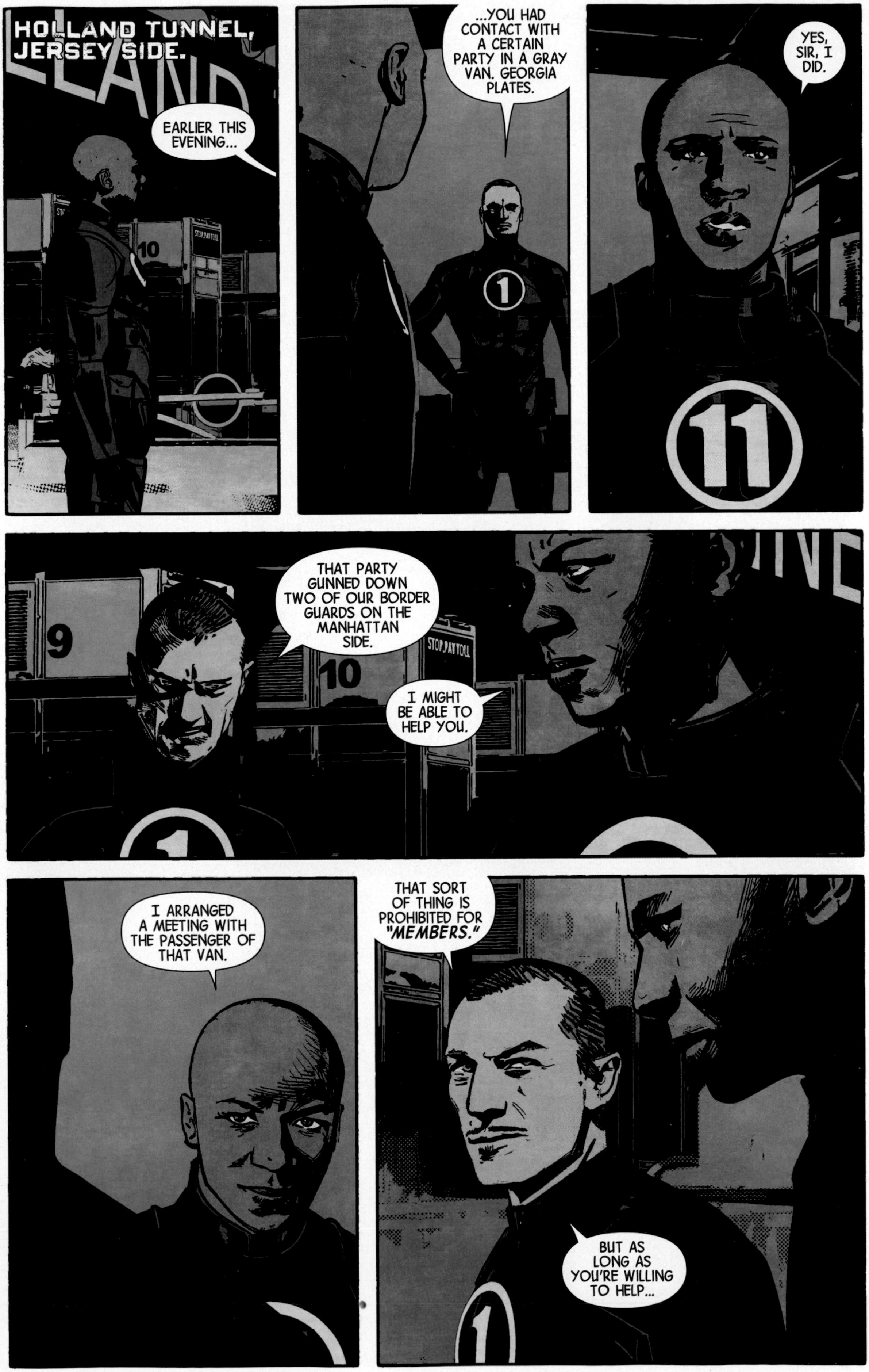
HOLLAND TUNNEL, JERSEY SIDE.
EARLIER THIS EVENING...
...YOU HAD CONTACT WITH A CERTAIN PARTY IN A GRAY VAN. GEORGIA PLATES.
YES, SIR, I DID.
THAT PARTY GUNNED DOWN TWO OF OUR BORDER GUARDS ON THE MANHATTAN SIDE.
I MIGHT BE ABLE TO HELP YOU.
I ARRANGED A MEETING WITH THE PASSENGER OF THAT VAN.
THAT SORT OF THING IS PROHIBITED FOR "MEMBERS."
BUT AS LONG AS YOU'RE WILLING TO HELP...

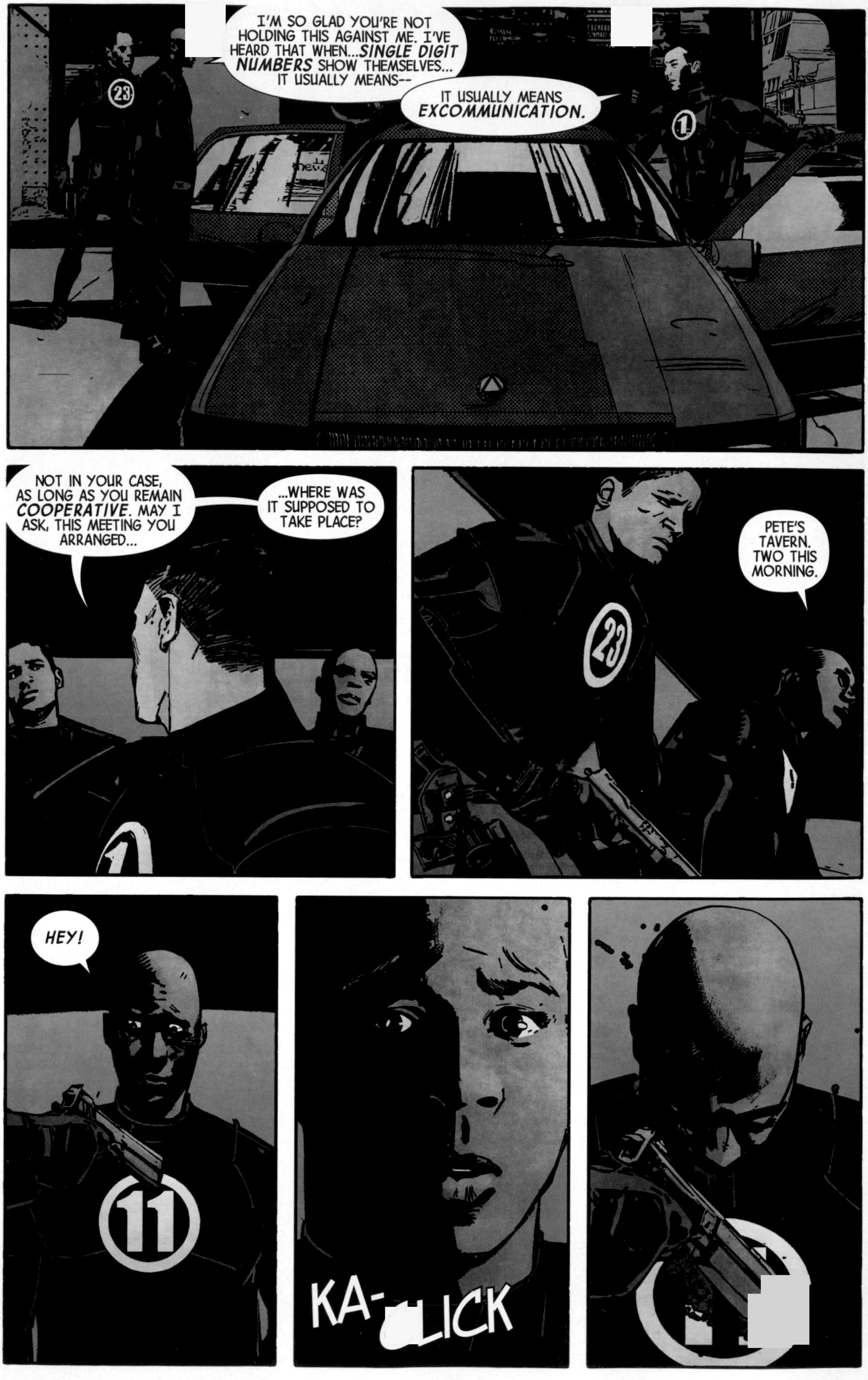
I'M SO GLAD YOU'RE NOT HOLDING THIS AGAINST ME. I'VE HEARD THAT WHEN...SINGLE DIGIT NUMBERS SHOW THEMSELVES... IT USUALLY MEANS--
IT USUALLY MEANS EXCOMMUNICATION.
NOT IN YOUR CASE, AS LONG AS YOU REMAIN COOPERATIVE. MAY I ASK, THIS MEETING YOU ARRANGED...
...WHERE WAS IT SUPPOSED TO TAKE PLACE?
PETE'S TAVERN. TWO THIS MORNING.
HEY!
KA-LICK

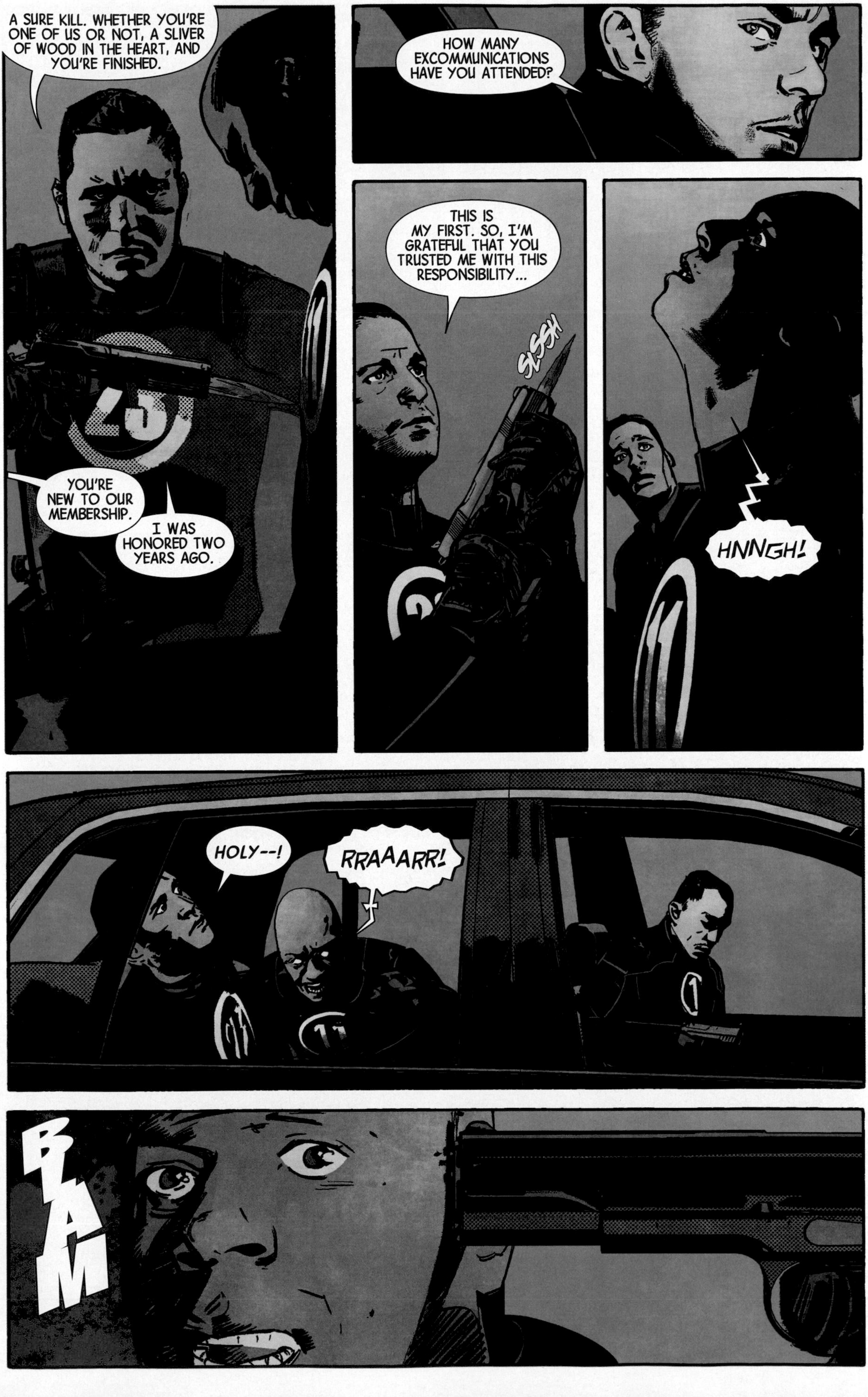
A SURE KILL. WHETHER YOU'RE ONE OF US OR NOT, A SLIVER OF WOOD IN THE HEART, AND YOU'RE FINISHED.
YOU'RE NEW TO OUR MEMBERSHIP.
I WAS HONORED TWO YEARS AGO.
HOW MANY EXCOMMUNICATIONS HAVE YOU ATTENDED?
THIS IS MY FIRST. SO, I'M GRATEFUL THAT YOU TRUSTED ME WITH THIS RESPONSIBILITY...
SLSSH
HNNGH!
HOLY--!
RRAAARR!
BLAM

OUR MEMBERS HAVE ALWAYS HAD A HARD TIME UNDERSTANDING THAT ANYONE--

--ANYONE--

--WHO DIES THESE DAYS, BECOMES A FLESH-EATER.

BUT YOU AND I, SIR--

--AND THIS ONE--

--WE ALL DIED.

ONCE. AND WHEN WE DID, SOME STRANGE *FORCE* CAME OVER US. WHATEVER THAT FORCE IS, WHATEVER IT IS THAT *INFECTS* US, THAT SAME MAGICAL, MYSTERIOUS GERM *PRESERVES* US SOMEHOW.

IT'S A BLESSING... AND A CURSE.

CURSE?

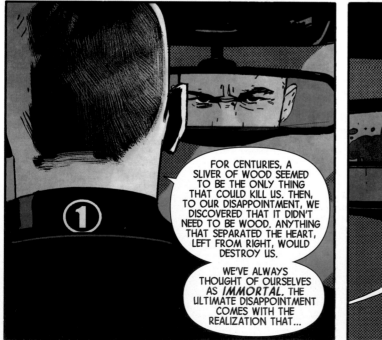

FOR CENTURIES, A SLIVER OF WOOD SEEMED TO BE THE ONLY THING THAT COULD KILL US. THEN, TO OUR DISAPPOINTMENT, WE DISCOVERED THAT IT DIDN'T NEED TO BE WOOD. ANYTHING THAT SEPARATED THE HEART, LEFT FROM RIGHT, WOULD DESTROY US.

WE'VE ALWAYS THOUGHT OF OURSELVES AS *IMMORTAL.* THE ULTIMATE DISAPPOINTMENT COMES WITH THE REALIZATION THAT...

...WE STILL HAVE TO FACE DEATH.

IN THAT WAY, WE MIGHT AS WELL BE *HUMAN.*

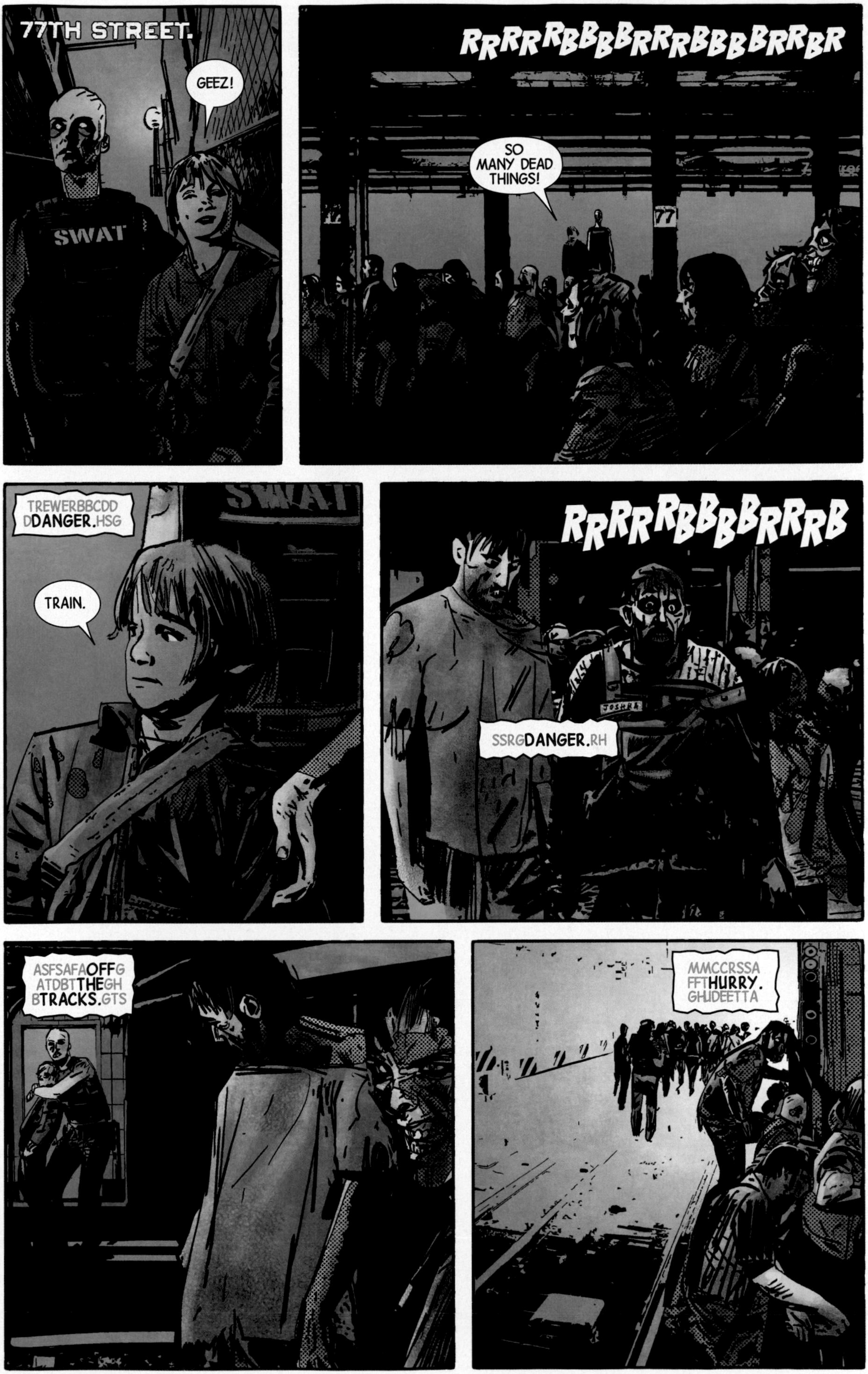
77TH STREET.
GEEZ!
RRRRRBBBRRRRBBBBRRRBR
SO MANY DEAD THINGS!
TREWERBBCDD DDANGER.HSG
TRAIN.
RRRRRBBBRRRRB
SSRGDANGER.RH
ASFSAFAOFFG ATDBTTHEGH BTRACKS.GTS
MMCCRSSA FFTHURRY. GHJDEETTA

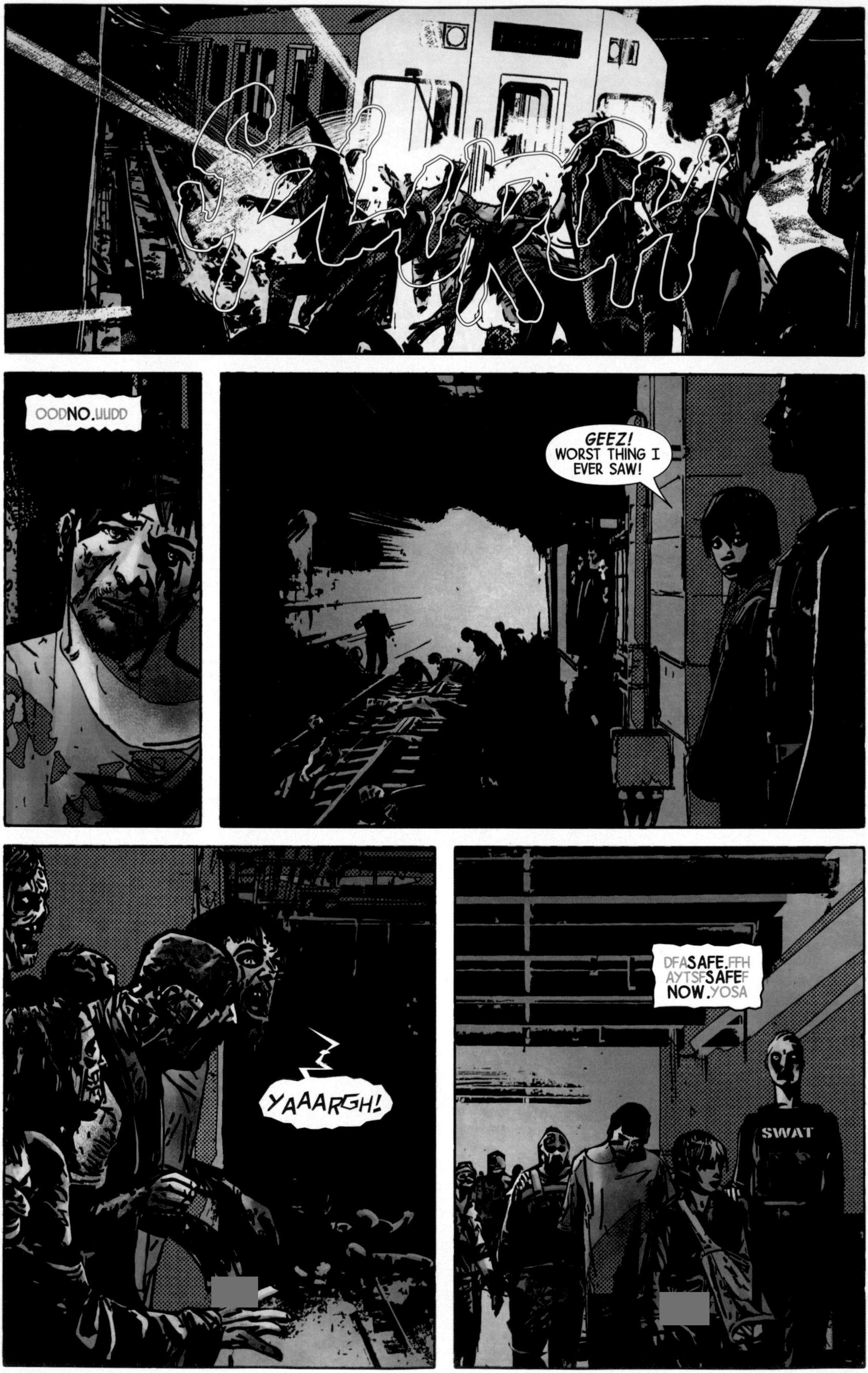
OODNO.UUDD
GEEZ! WORST THING I EVER SAW!
YAAARGH!
DFASAFE.FFH
AYTSFSAFEF
NOW.YOSA
SWAT

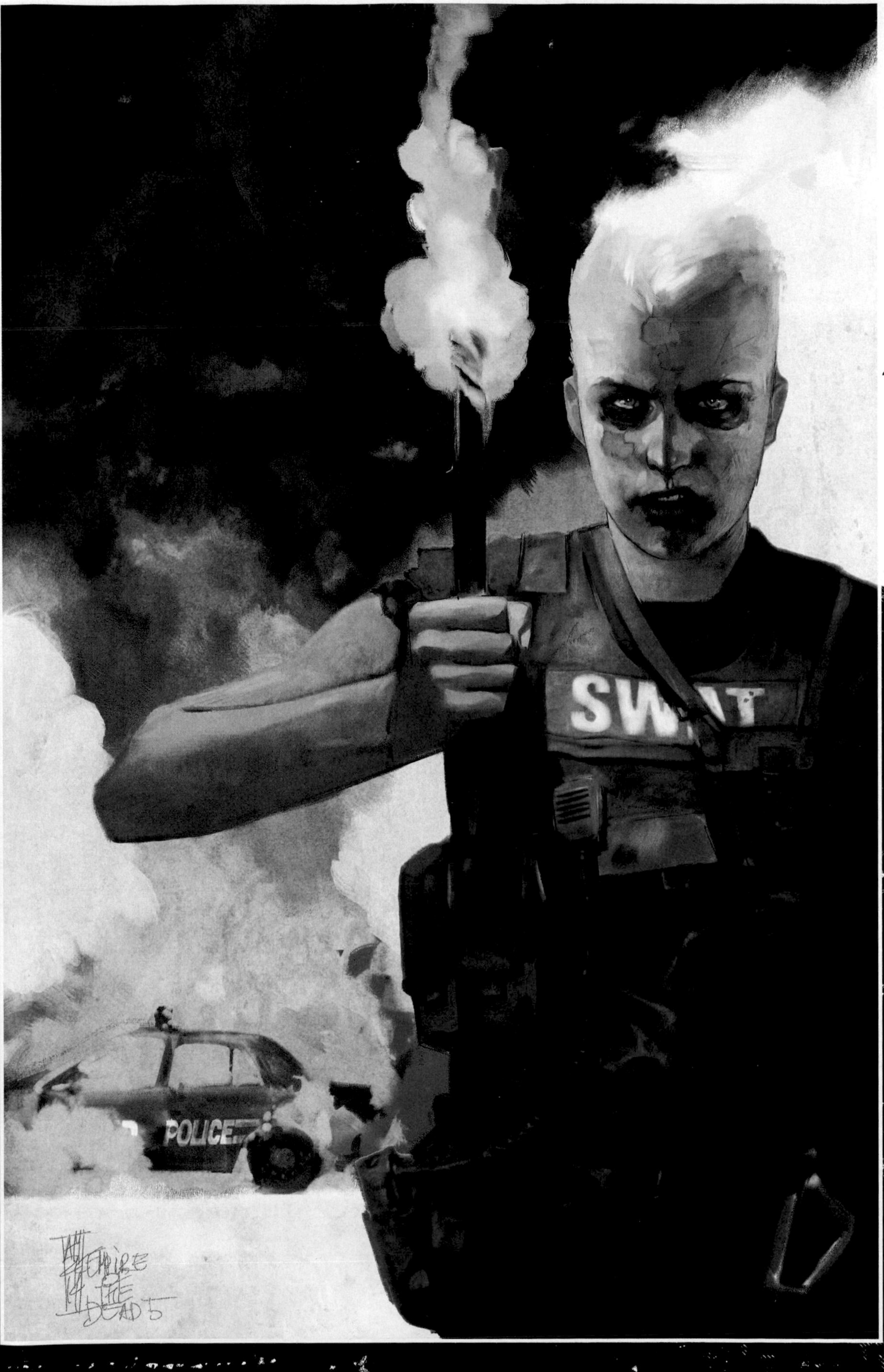
SWAT
POLICE
EMPIRE OF THE DEAD 5

FIVE

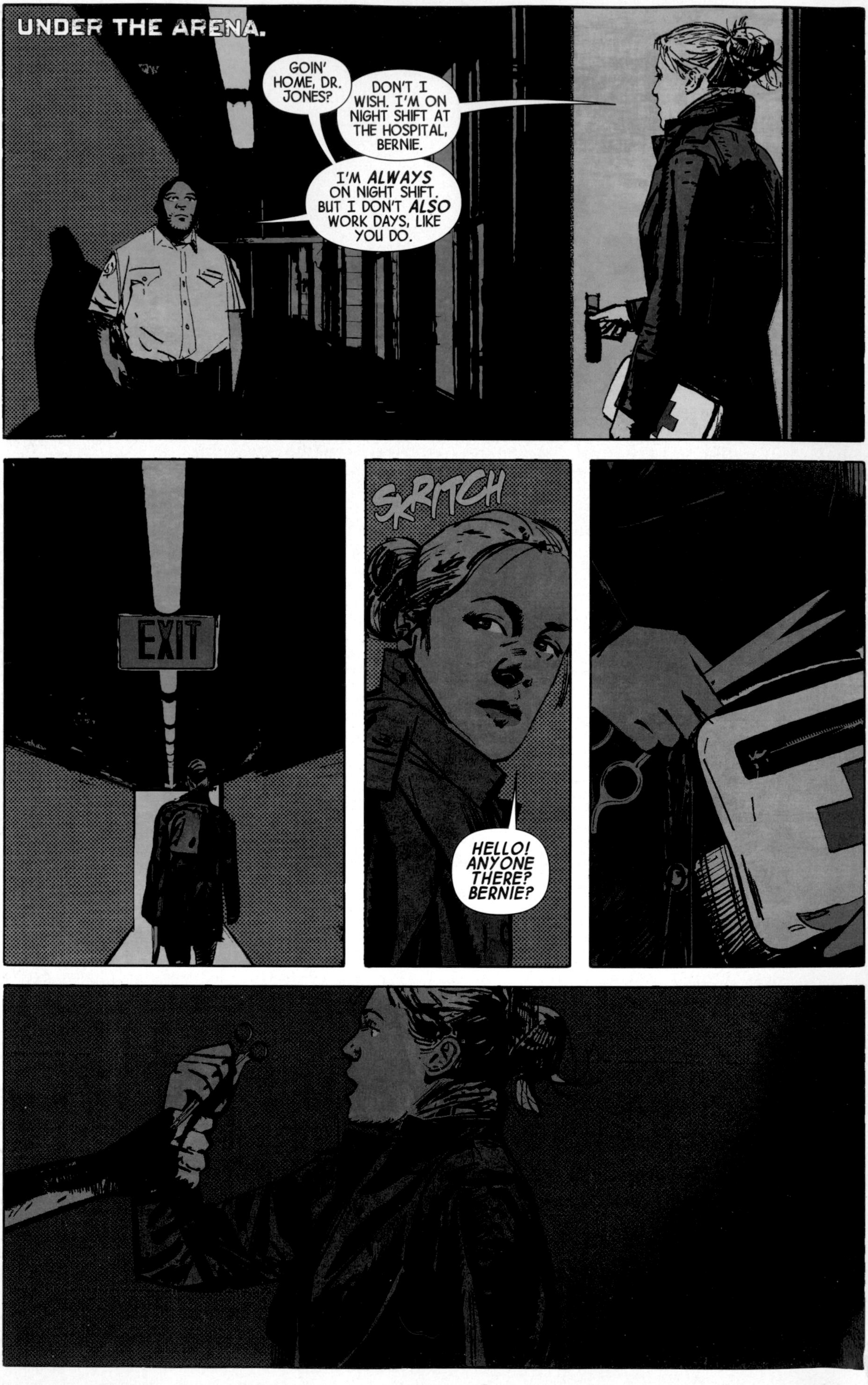
UNDER THE ARENA.
GOIN' HOME, DR. JONES?
DON'T I WISH. I'M ON NIGHT SHIFT AT THE HOSPITAL, BERNIE.
I'M *ALWAYS* ON NIGHT SHIFT. BUT I DON'T *ALSO* WORK DAYS, LIKE YOU DO.
EXIT
SKRITCH
HELLO! ANYONE THERE? BERNIE?

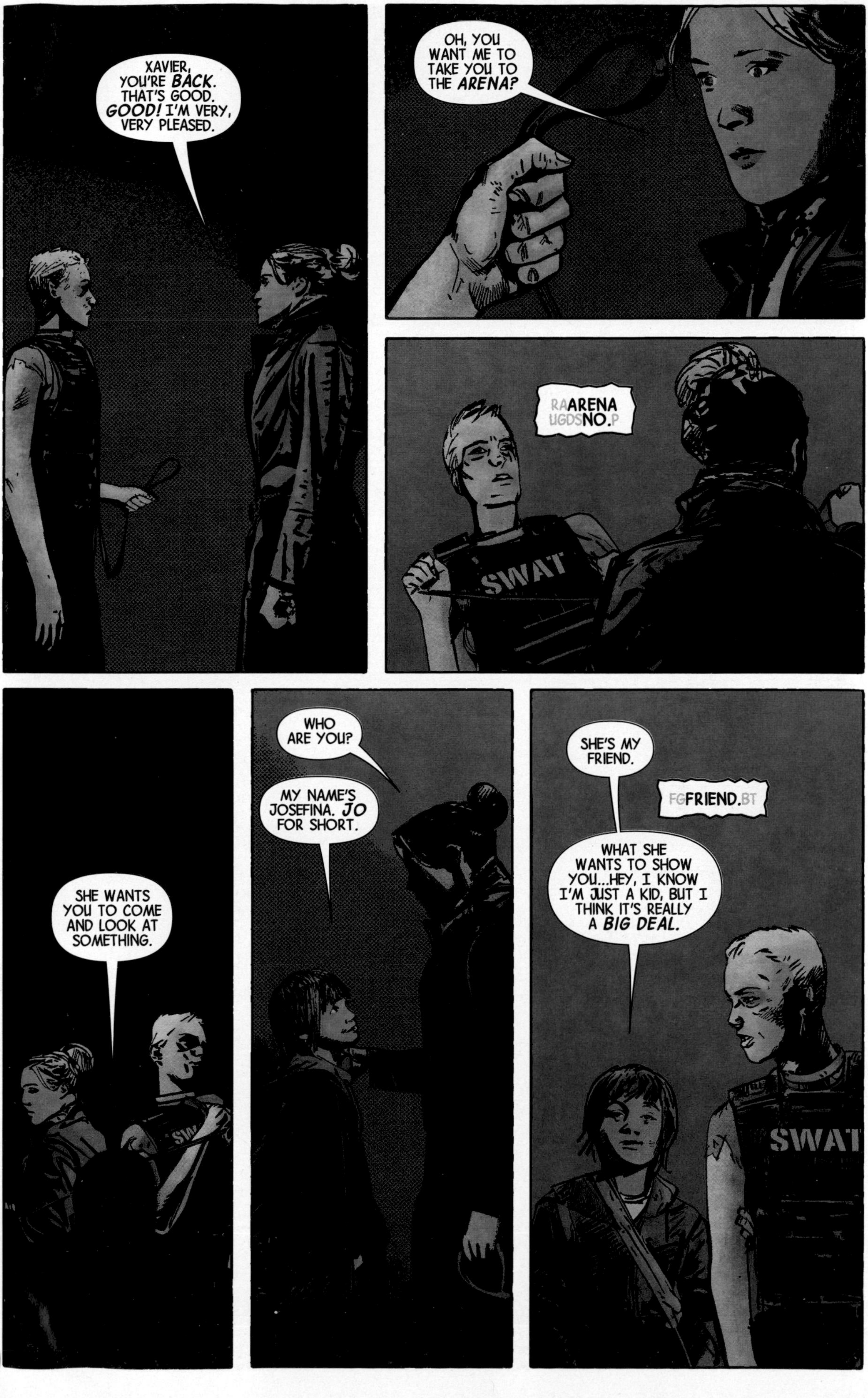
XAVIER, YOU'RE BACK. THAT'S GOOD. GOOD! I'M VERY, VERY PLEASED.
OH, YOU WANT ME TO TAKE YOU TO THE ARENA?
RAARENA UGDSNO.P
SHE WANTS YOU TO COME AND LOOK AT SOMETHING.
WHO ARE YOU?
MY NAME'S JOSEFINA. JO FOR SHORT.
SHE'S MY FRIEND.
FGFRIEND.BT
WHAT SHE WANTS TO SHOW YOU...HEY, I KNOW I'M JUST A KID, BUT I THINK IT'S REALLY A BIG DEAL.

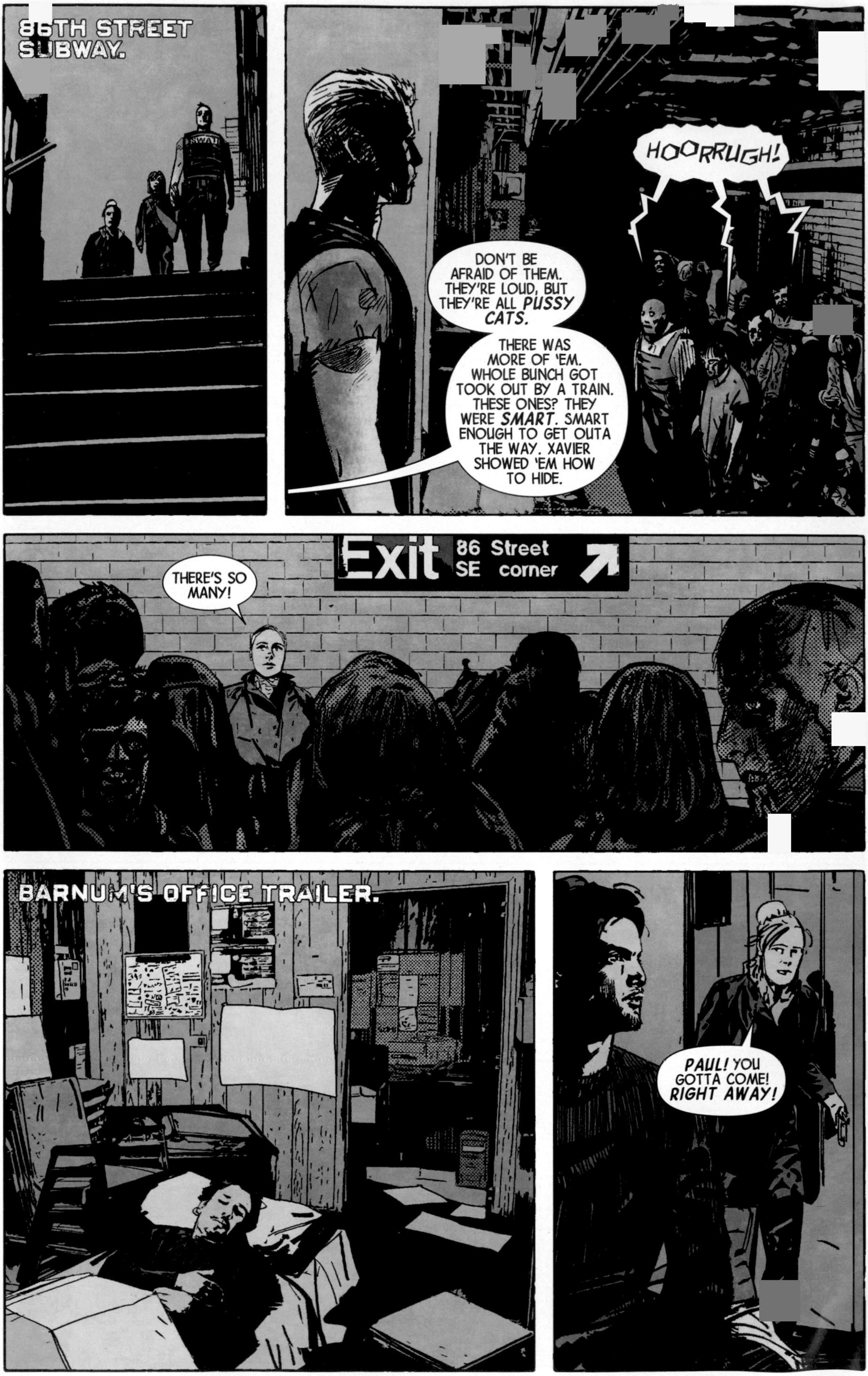
86TH STREET SUBWAY.
HOORRUGH!
DON'T BE AFRAID OF THEM. THEY'RE LOUD, BUT THEY'RE ALL PUSSY CATS.
THERE WAS MORE OF 'EM. WHOLE BUNCH GOT TOOK OUT BY A TRAIN. THESE ONES? THEY WERE SMART. SMART ENOUGH TO GET OUTA THE WAY. XAVIER SHOWED 'EM HOW TO HIDE.
Exit 86 Street SE corner
THERE'S SO MANY!
BARNUM'S OFFICE TRAILER.
PAUL! YOU GOTTA COME! RIGHT AWAY!

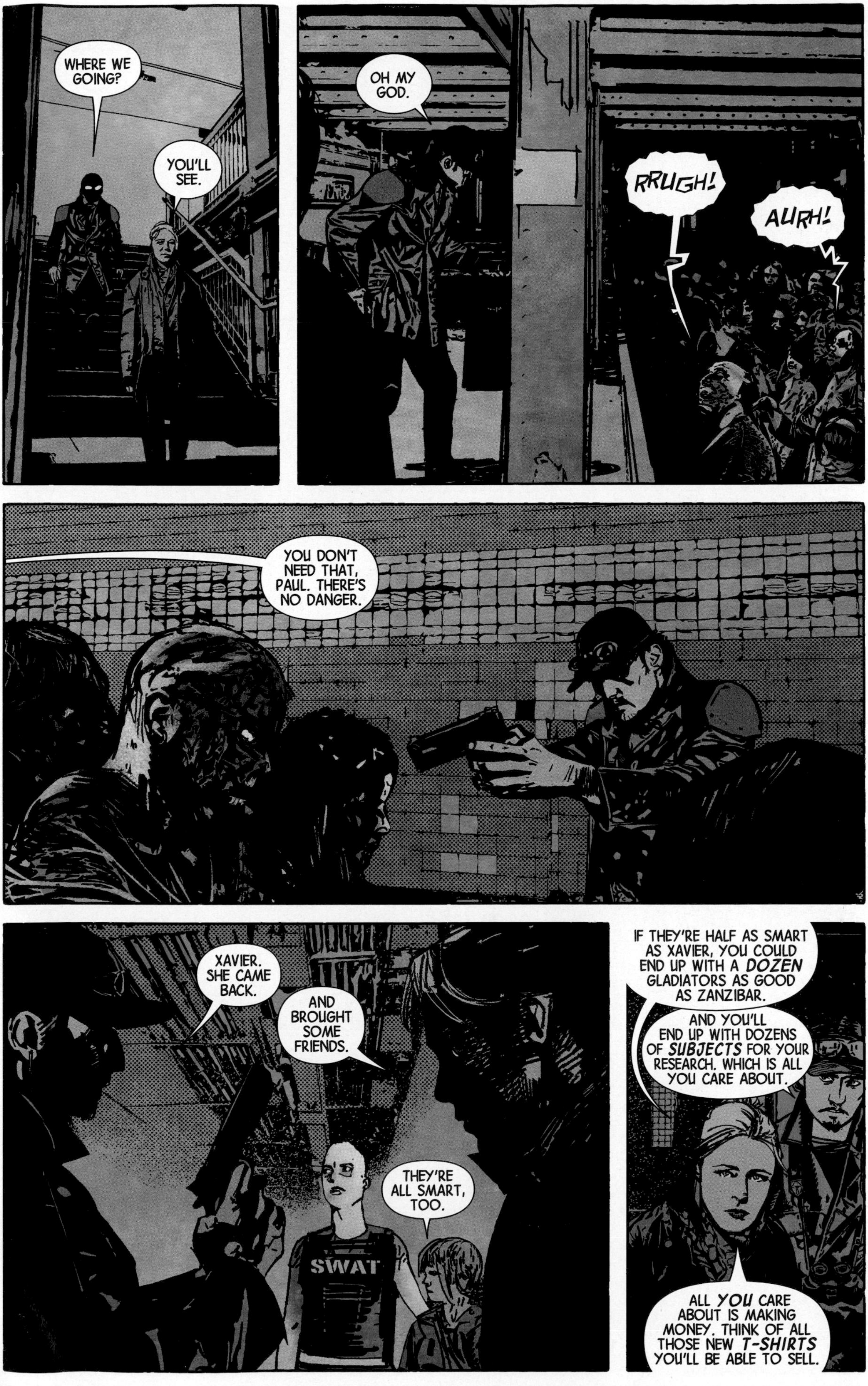
WHERE WE GOING?
YOU'LL SEE.
OH MY GOD.
RRUGH!
AURH!
YOU DON'T NEED THAT, PAUL. THERE'S NO DANGER.
XAVIER. SHE CAME BACK.
AND BROUGHT SOME FRIENDS.
THEY'RE ALL SMART, TOO.
SWAT
IF THEY'RE HALF AS SMART AS XAVIER, YOU COULD END UP WITH A DOZEN GLADIATORS AS GOOD AS ZANZIBAR.
AND YOU'LL END UP WITH DOZENS OF SUBJECTS FOR YOUR RESEARCH. WHICH IS ALL YOU CARE ABOUT.
ALL YOU CARE ABOUT IS MAKING MONEY. THINK OF ALL THOSE NEW T-SHIRTS YOU'LL BE ABLE TO SELL.

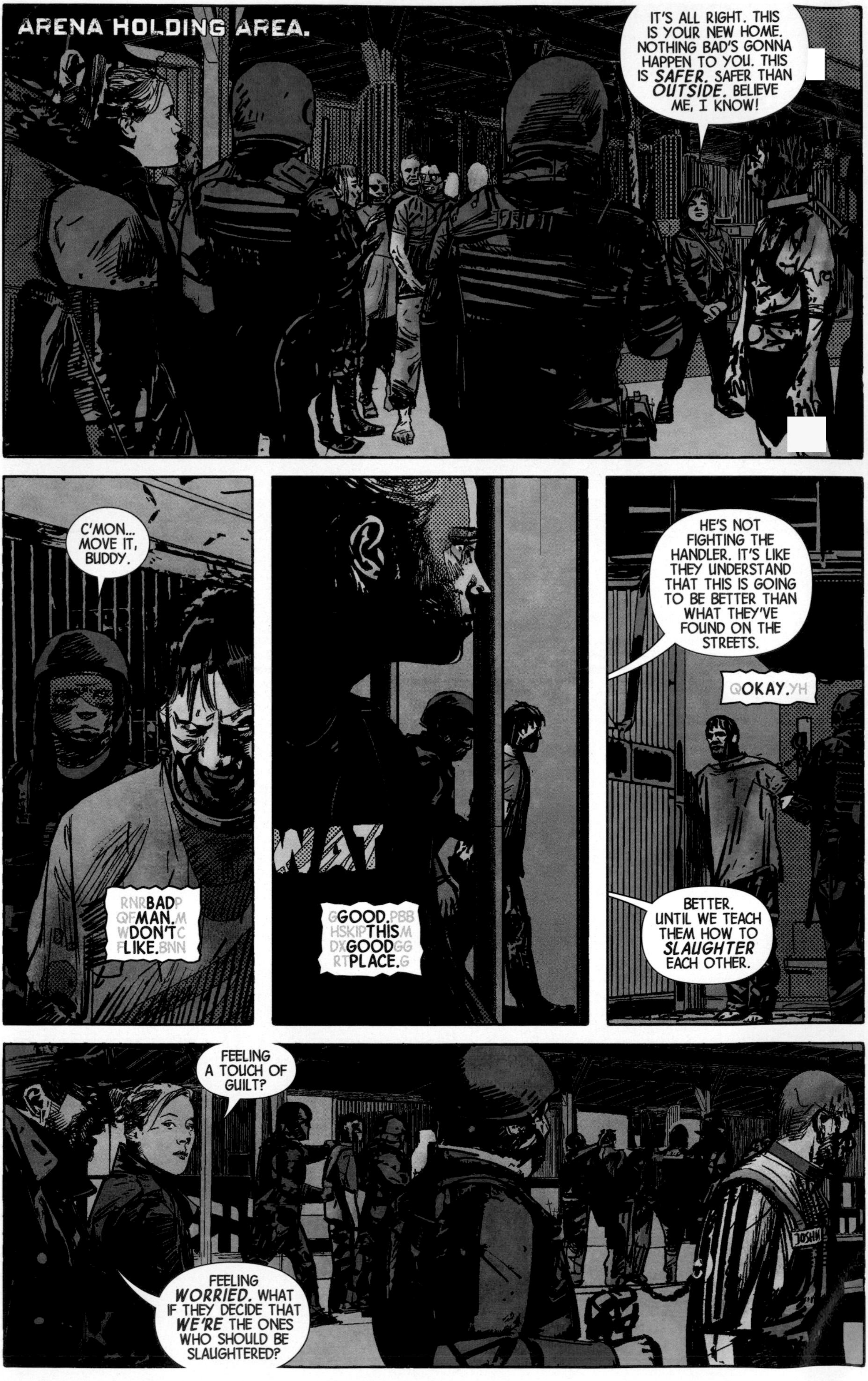
ARENA HOLDING AREA.
IT'S ALL RIGHT. THIS IS YOUR NEW HOME. NOTHING BAD'S GONNA HAPPEN TO YOU. THIS IS SAFER. SAFER THAN OUTSIDE. BELIEVE ME, I KNOW!
C'MON... MOVE IT, BUDDY.
RNRBADP QFMAN.M WDON'TC FLIKE.BNN
GGOOD.PBB HSKIPTHISM DXGOODGG RTPLACE.G
HE'S NOT FIGHTING THE HANDLER. IT'S LIKE THEY UNDERSTAND THAT THIS IS GOING TO BE BETTER THAN WHAT THEY'VE FOUND ON THE STREETS.
QOKAY.YH
BETTER. UNTIL WE TEACH THEM HOW TO SLAUGHTER EACH OTHER.
FEELING A TOUCH OF GUILT?
FEELING WORRIED. WHAT IF THEY DECIDE THAT WE'RE THE ONES WHO SHOULD BE SLAUGHTERED?

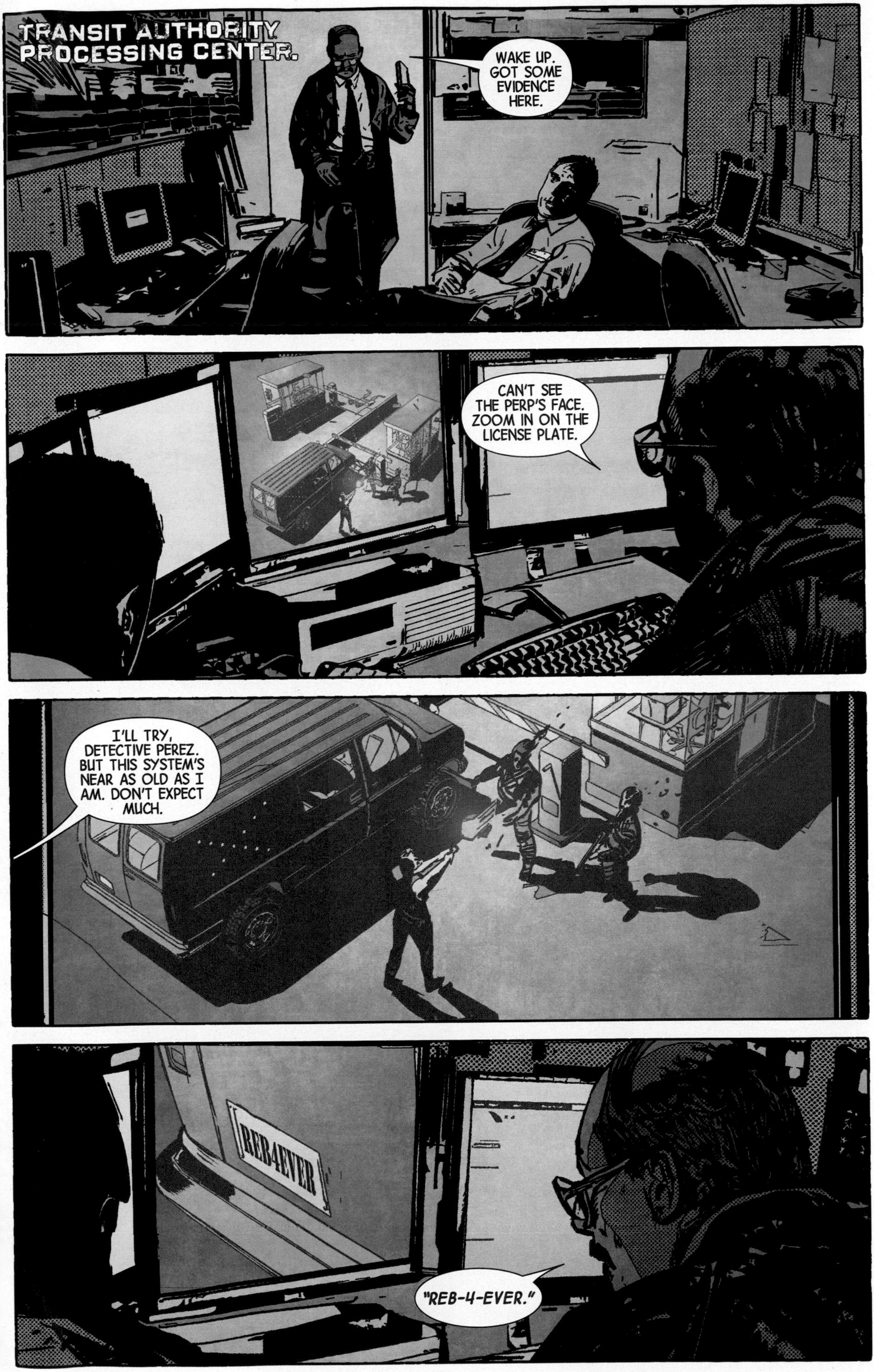
TRANSIT AUTHORITY PROCESSING CENTER.
WAKE UP. GOT SOME EVIDENCE HERE.
CAN'T SEE THE PERP'S FACE. ZOOM IN ON THE LICENSE PLATE.
I'LL TRY, DETECTIVE PEREZ. BUT THIS SYSTEM'S NEAR AS OLD AS I AM. DON'T EXPECT MUCH.
REB4EVER
"REB-4-EVER."

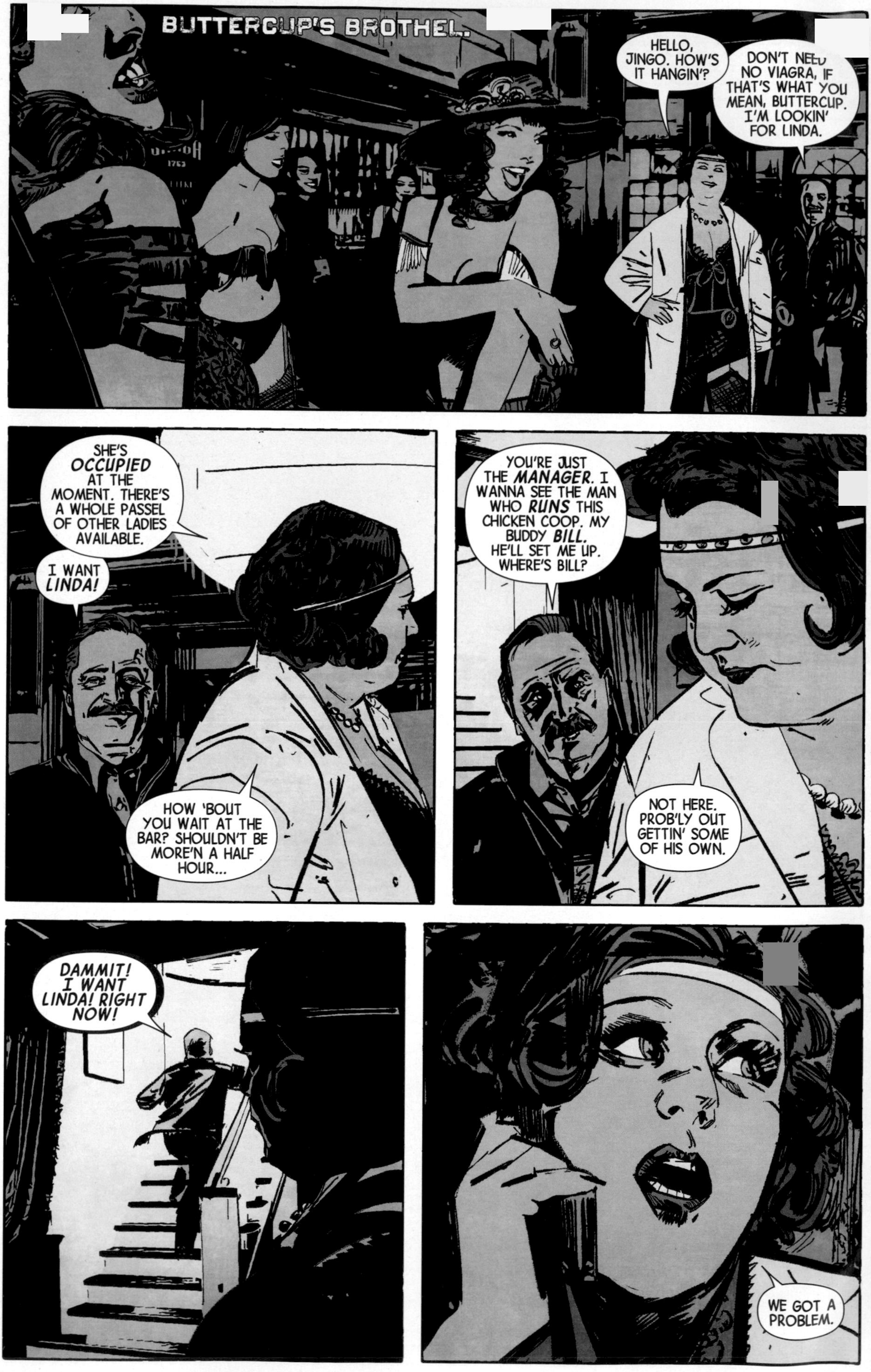

BUTTERCUP'S BROTHEL.
HELLO, JINGO. HOW'S IT HANGIN'?
DON'T NEED NO VIAGRA, IF THAT'S WHAT YOU MEAN, BUTTERCUP. I'M LOOKIN' FOR LINDA.
SHE'S OCCUPIED AT THE MOMENT. THERE'S A WHOLE PASSEL OF OTHER LADIES AVAILABLE.
I WANT LINDA!
HOW 'BOUT YOU WAIT AT THE BAR? SHOULDN'T BE MORE'N A HALF HOUR...
YOU'RE JUST THE MANAGER. I WANNA SEE THE MAN WHO RUNS THIS CHICKEN COOP. MY BUDDY BILL. HE'LL SET ME UP. WHERE'S BILL?
NOT HERE. PROB'LY OUT GETTIN' SOME OF HIS OWN.
DAMMIT! I WANT LINDA! RIGHT NOW!
WE GOT A PROBLEM.

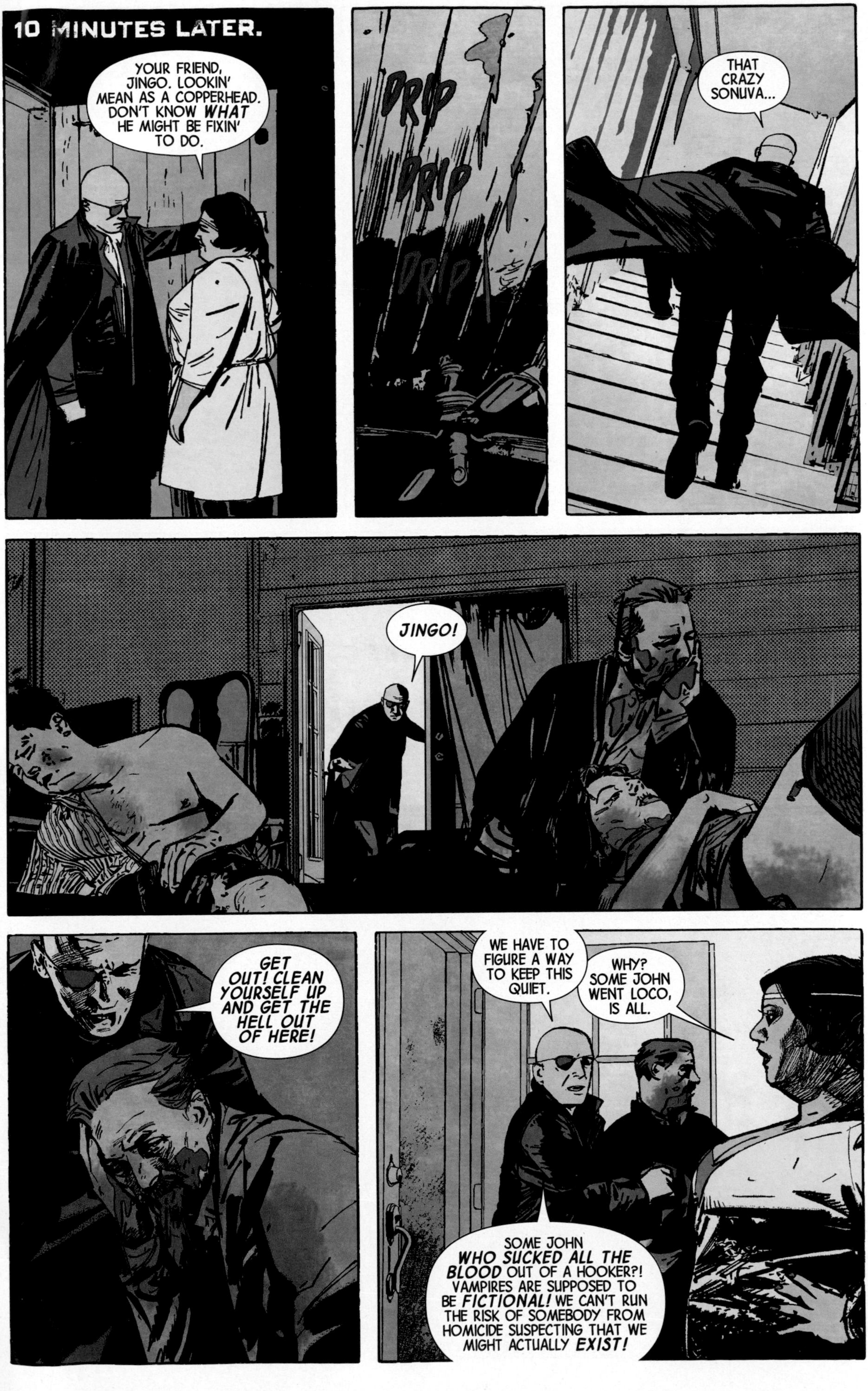
10 MINUTES LATER.
YOUR FRIEND, JINGO. LOOKIN' MEAN AS A COPPERHEAD. DON'T KNOW WHAT HE MIGHT BE FIXIN' TO DO.
DRIP
DRIP
DRIP
THAT CRAZY SONUVA...
JINGO!
GET OUT! CLEAN YOURSELF UP AND GET THE HELL OUT OF HERE!
WE HAVE TO FIGURE A WAY TO KEEP THIS QUIET.
WHY? SOME JOHN WENT LOCO, IS ALL.
SOME JOHN WHO SUCKED ALL THE BLOOD OUT OF A HOOKER?! VAMPIRES ARE SUPPOSED TO BE FICTIONAL! WE CAN'T RUN THE RISK OF SOMEBODY FROM HOMICIDE SUSPECTING THAT WE MIGHT ACTUALLY EXIST!

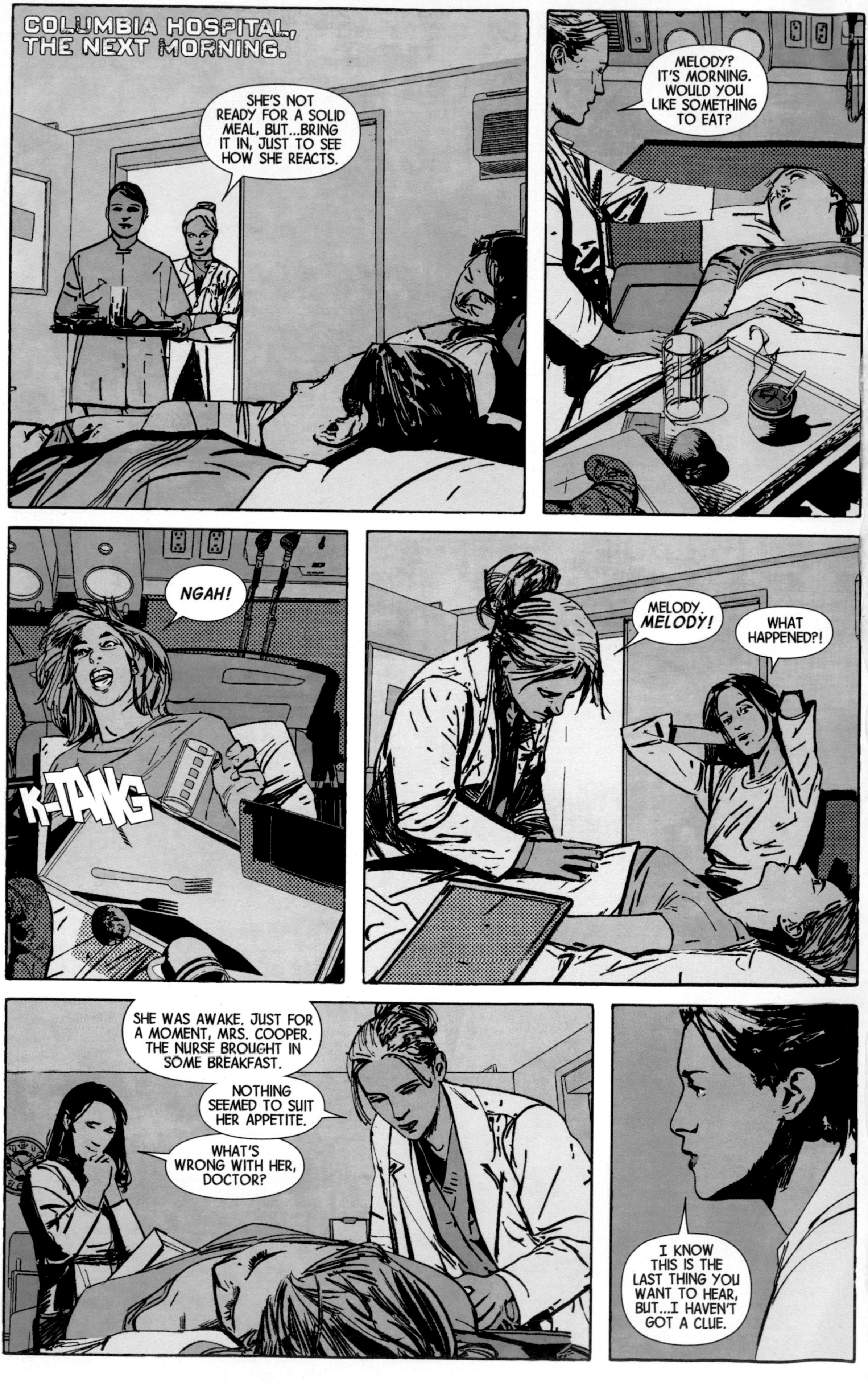
COLUMBIA HOSPITAL, THE NEXT MORNING.
SHE'S NOT READY FOR A SOLID MEAL, BUT...BRING IT IN, JUST TO SEE HOW SHE REACTS.
MELODY? IT'S MORNING. WOULD YOU LIKE SOMETHING TO EAT?
NGAH!
K-TANG
MELODY. MELODY!
WHAT HAPPENED?!
SHE WAS AWAKE. JUST FOR A MOMENT, MRS. COOPER. THE NURSE BROUGHT IN SOME BREAKFAST.
NOTHING SEEMED TO SUIT HER APPETITE.
WHAT'S WRONG WITH HER, DOCTOR?
I KNOW THIS IS THE LAST THING YOU WANT TO HEAR, BUT...I HAVEN'T GOT A CLUE.

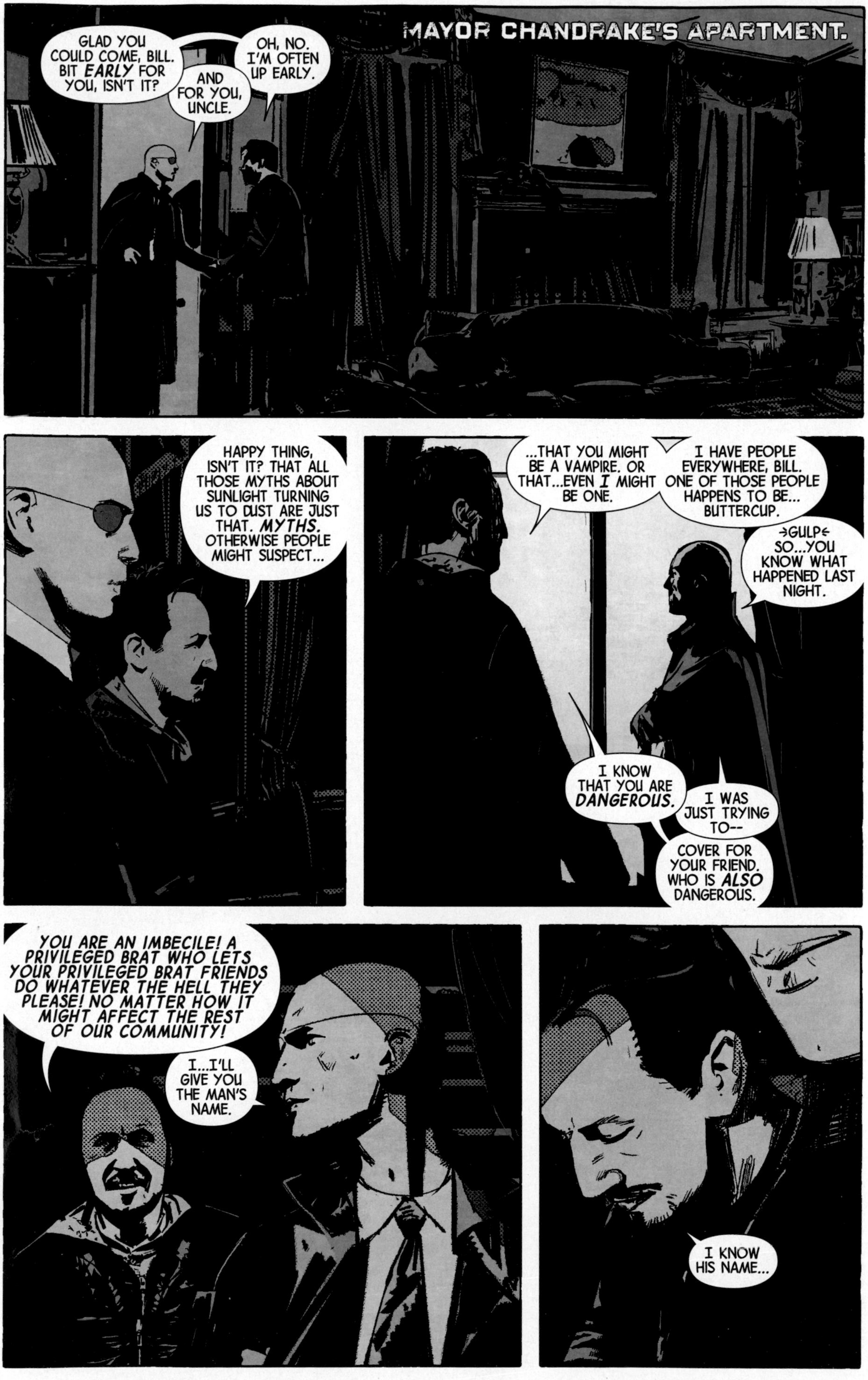
MAYOR CHANDRAKE'S APARTMENT.
GLAD YOU COULD COME, BILL. BIT EARLY FOR YOU, ISN'T IT?
OH, NO. I'M OFTEN UP EARLY.
AND FOR YOU, UNCLE.
HAPPY THING, ISN'T IT? THAT ALL THOSE MYTHS ABOUT SUNLIGHT TURNING US TO DUST ARE JUST THAT. MYTHS. OTHERWISE PEOPLE MIGHT SUSPECT...
...THAT YOU MIGHT BE A VAMPIRE. OR THAT...EVEN I MIGHT BE ONE.
I HAVE PEOPLE EVERYWHERE, BILL. ONE OF THOSE PEOPLE HAPPENS TO BE... BUTTERCUP.
→GULP← SO...YOU KNOW WHAT HAPPENED LAST NIGHT.
I KNOW THAT YOU ARE DANGEROUS.
I WAS JUST TRYING TO--
COVER FOR YOUR FRIEND. WHO IS ALSO DANGEROUS.
YOU ARE AN IMBECILE! A PRIVILEGED BRAT WHO LETS YOUR PRIVILEGED BRAT FRIENDS DO WHATEVER THE HELL THEY PLEASE! NO MATTER HOW IT MIGHT AFFECT THE REST OF OUR COMMUNITY!
I...I'LL GIVE YOU THE MAN'S NAME.
I KNOW HIS NAME...

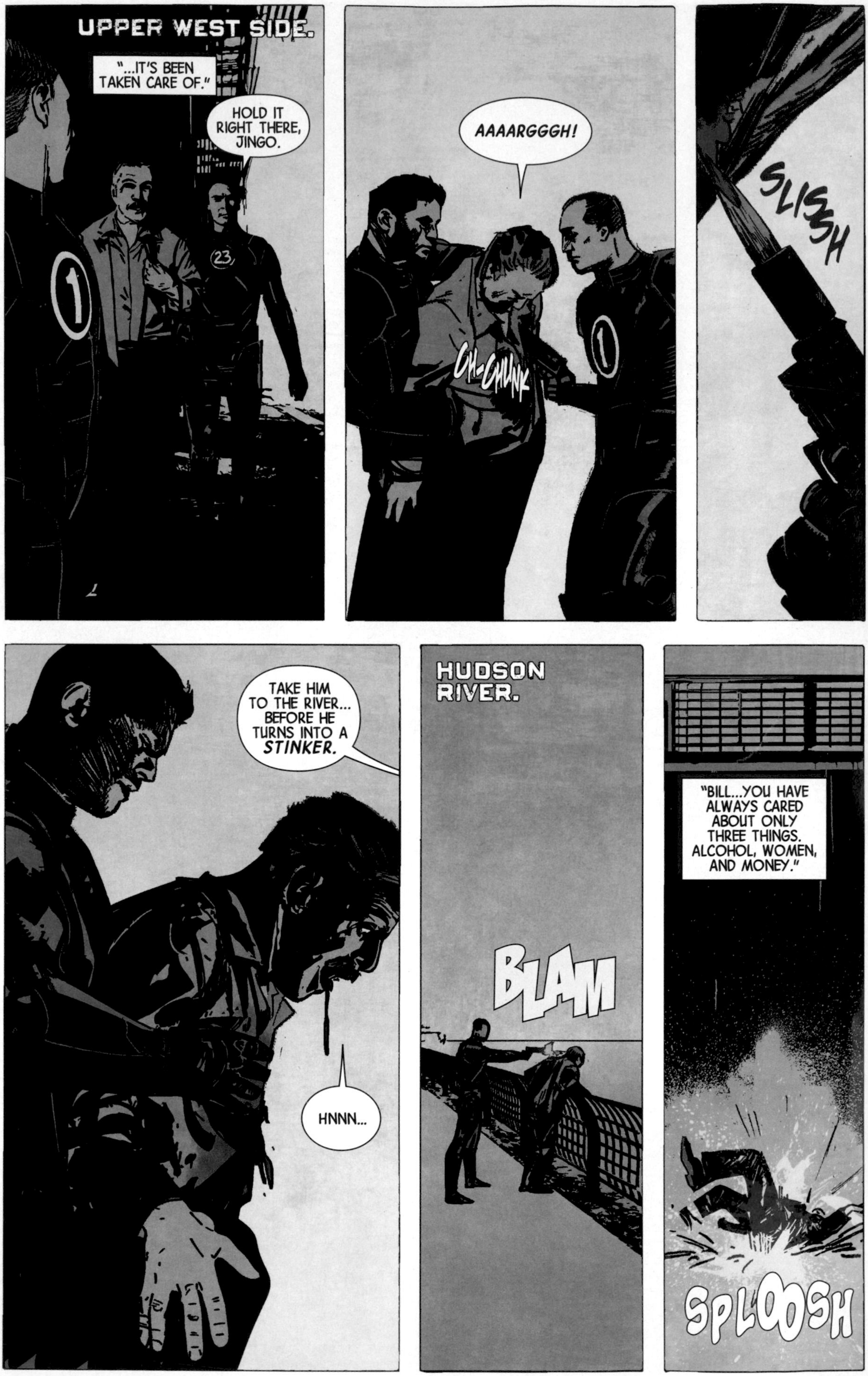
UPPER WEST SIDE.
"...IT'S BEEN TAKEN CARE OF."
HOLD IT RIGHT THERE, JINGO.
AAAARGGGH!
CH-CHUNK
SLISSH
TAKE HIM TO THE RIVER... BEFORE HE TURNS INTO A STINKER.
HNNN...
HUDSON RIVER.
BLAM
"BILL...YOU HAVE ALWAYS CARED ABOUT ONLY THREE THINGS. ALCOHOL, WOMEN, AND MONEY."
SPLOOSH

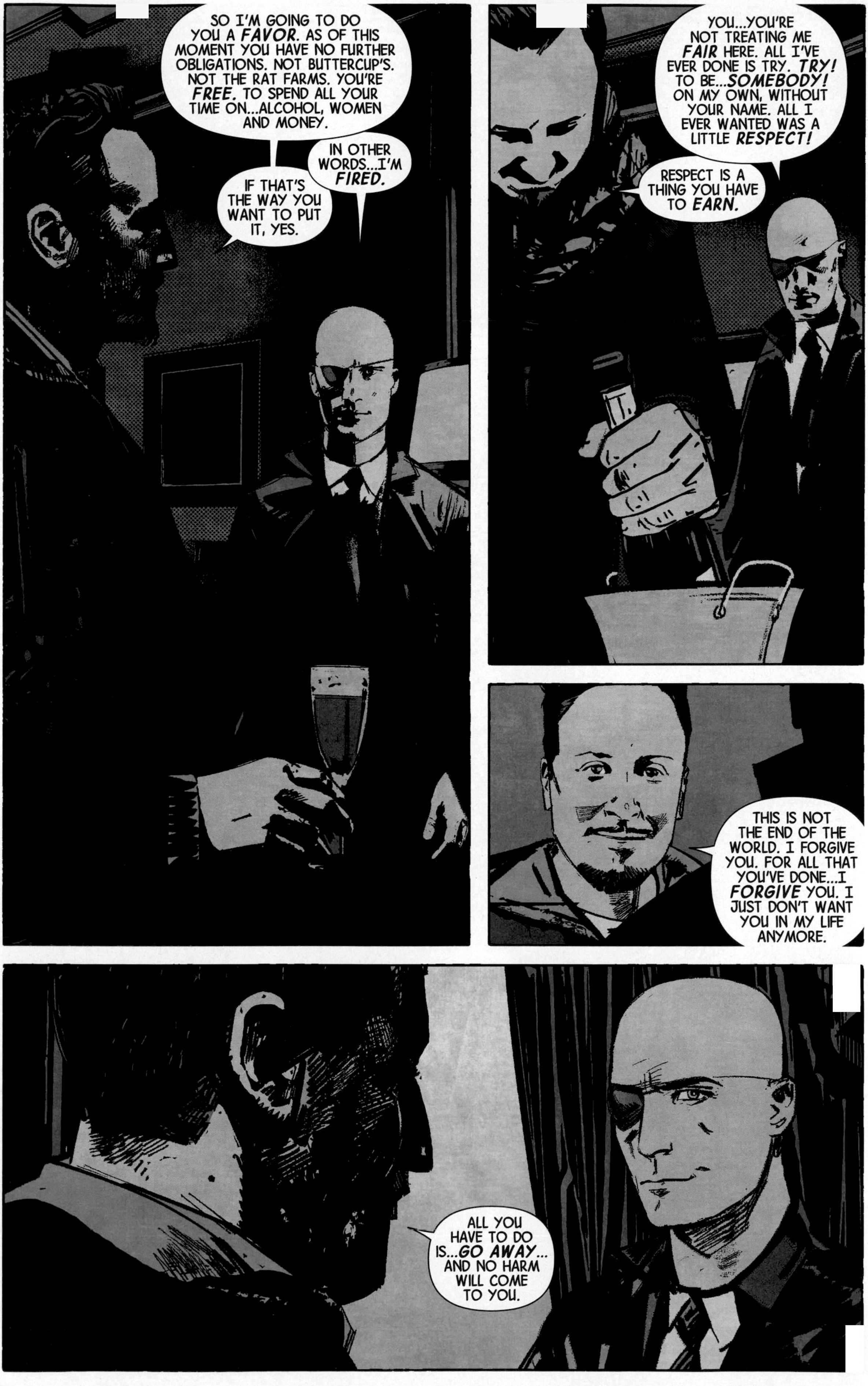
SO I'M GOING TO DO YOU A FAVOR. AS OF THIS MOMENT YOU HAVE NO FURTHER OBLIGATIONS. NOT BUTTERCUP'S. NOT THE RAT FARMS. YOU'RE FREE. TO SPEND ALL YOUR TIME ON...ALCOHOL, WOMEN AND MONEY.
IN OTHER WORDS...I'M FIRED.
IF THAT'S THE WAY YOU WANT TO PUT IT, YES.
YOU...YOU'RE NOT TREATING ME FAIR HERE. ALL I'VE EVER DONE IS TRY. TRY! TO BE...SOMEBODY! ON MY OWN, WITHOUT YOUR NAME. ALL I EVER WANTED WAS A LITTLE RESPECT!
RESPECT IS A THING YOU HAVE TO EARN.
THIS IS NOT THE END OF THE WORLD. I FORGIVE YOU. FOR ALL THAT YOU'VE DONE...I FORGIVE YOU. I JUST DON'T WANT YOU IN MY LIFE ANYMORE.
ALL YOU HAVE TO DO IS...GO AWAY... AND NO HARM WILL COME TO YOU.

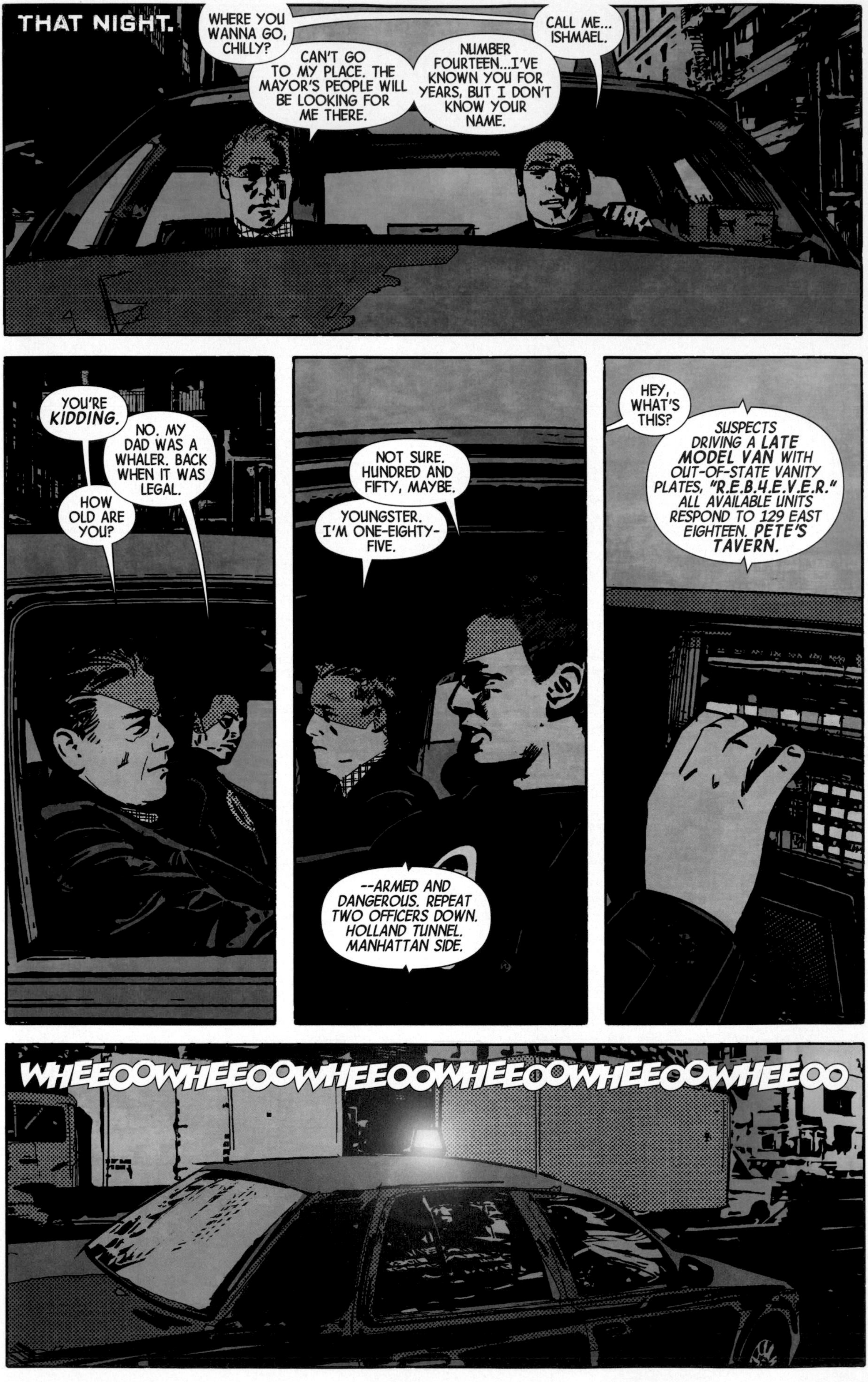
THAT NIGHT.
WHERE YOU WANNA GO, CHILLY?
CAN'T GO TO MY PLACE. THE MAYOR'S PEOPLE WILL BE LOOKING FOR ME THERE.
NUMBER FOURTEEN...I'VE KNOWN YOU FOR YEARS, BUT I DON'T KNOW YOUR NAME.
CALL ME... ISHMAEL.
YOU'RE KIDDING.
NO. MY DAD WAS A WHALER. BACK WHEN IT WAS LEGAL.
HOW OLD ARE YOU?
NOT SURE. HUNDRED AND FIFTY, MAYBE.
YOUNGSTER. I'M ONE-EIGHTY-FIVE.
--ARMED AND DANGEROUS. REPEAT TWO OFFICERS DOWN. HOLLAND TUNNEL. MANHATTAN SIDE.
HEY, WHAT'S THIS?
SUSPECTS DRIVING A LATE MODEL VAN WITH OUT-OF-STATE VANITY PLATES, "R.E.B.4.E.V.E.R." ALL AVAILABLE UNITS RESPOND TO 129 EAST EIGHTEEN. PETE'S TAVERN.
WHEEOOWHEEOOWHEEOOWHEEOOWHEEOOWHEEOO

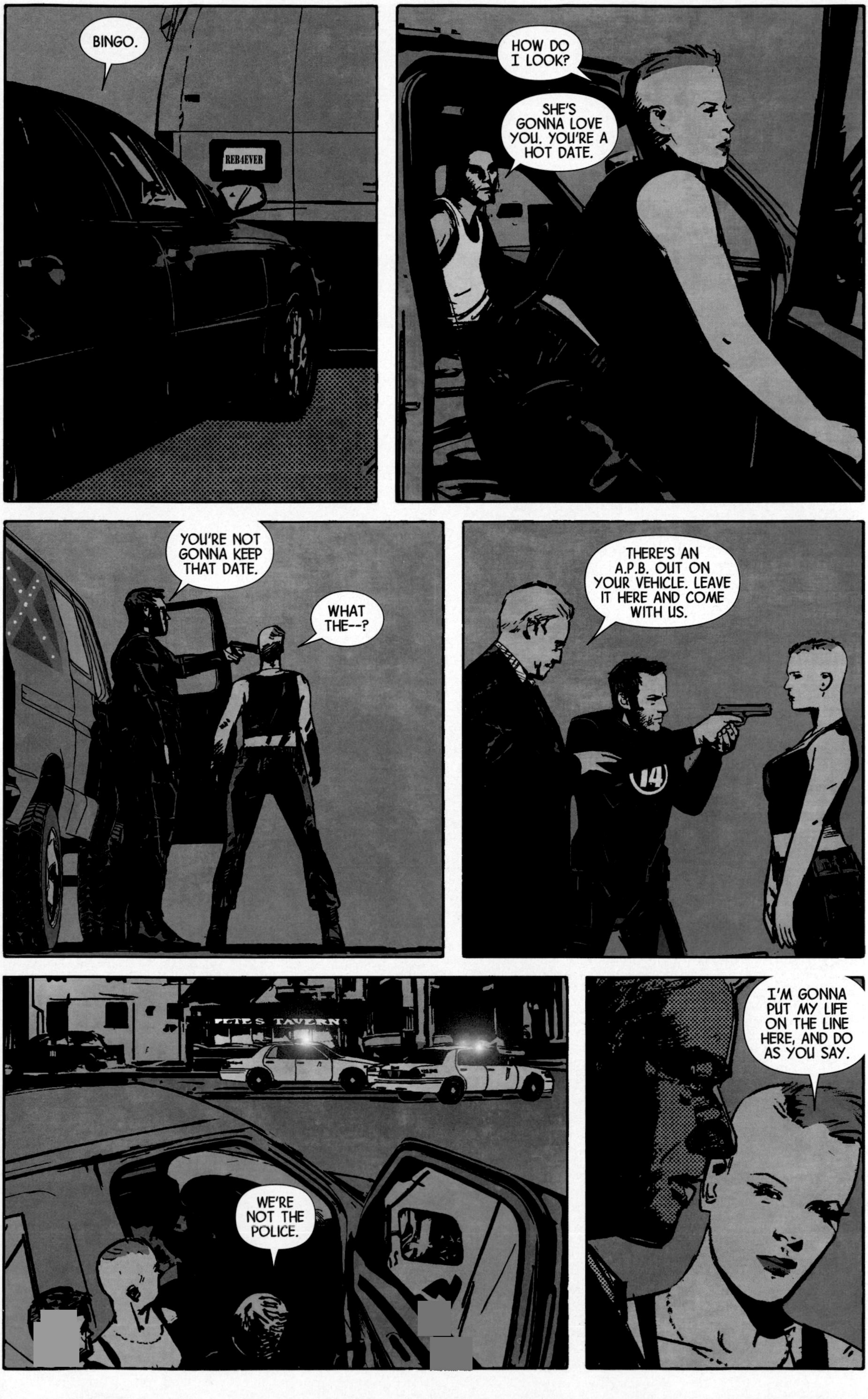
BINGO.
REB4EVER
HOW DO I LOOK?
SHE'S GONNA LOVE YOU. YOU'RE A HOT DATE.
YOU'RE NOT GONNA KEEP THAT DATE.
WHAT THE--?
THERE'S AN A.P.B. OUT ON YOUR VEHICLE. LEAVE IT HERE AND COME WITH US.
PETE'S TAVERN
WE'RE NOT THE POLICE.
I'M GONNA PUT MY LIFE ON THE LINE HERE, AND DO AS YOU SAY.

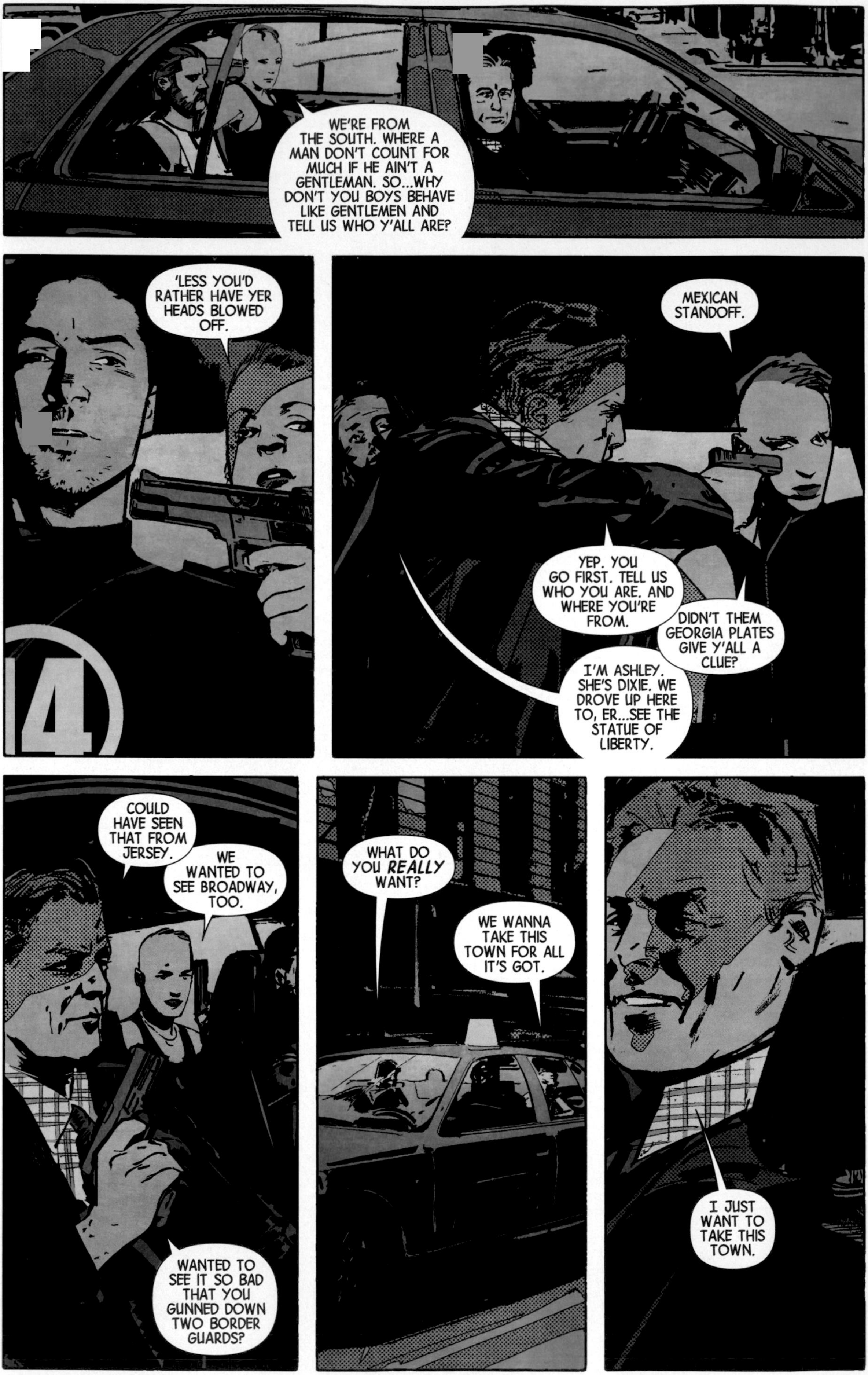
WE'RE FROM THE SOUTH. WHERE A MAN DON'T COUNT FOR MUCH IF HE AIN'T A GENTLEMAN. SO...WHY DON'T YOU BOYS BEHAVE LIKE GENTLEMEN AND TELL US WHO Y'ALL ARE?
'LESS YOU'D RATHER HAVE YER HEADS BLOWED OFF.
MEXICAN STANDOFF.
YEP. YOU GO FIRST. TELL US WHO YOU ARE. AND WHERE YOU'RE FROM.
DIDN'T THEM GEORGIA PLATES GIVE Y'ALL A CLUE?
I'M ASHLEY. SHE'S DIXIE. WE DROVE UP HERE TO, ER...SEE THE STATUE OF LIBERTY.
COULD HAVE SEEN THAT FROM JERSEY.
WE WANTED TO SEE BROADWAY, TOO.
WANTED TO SEE IT SO BAD THAT YOU GUNNED DOWN TWO BORDER GUARDS?
WHAT DO YOU REALLY WANT?
WE WANNA TAKE THIS TOWN FOR ALL IT'S GOT.
I JUST WANT TO TAKE THIS TOWN.

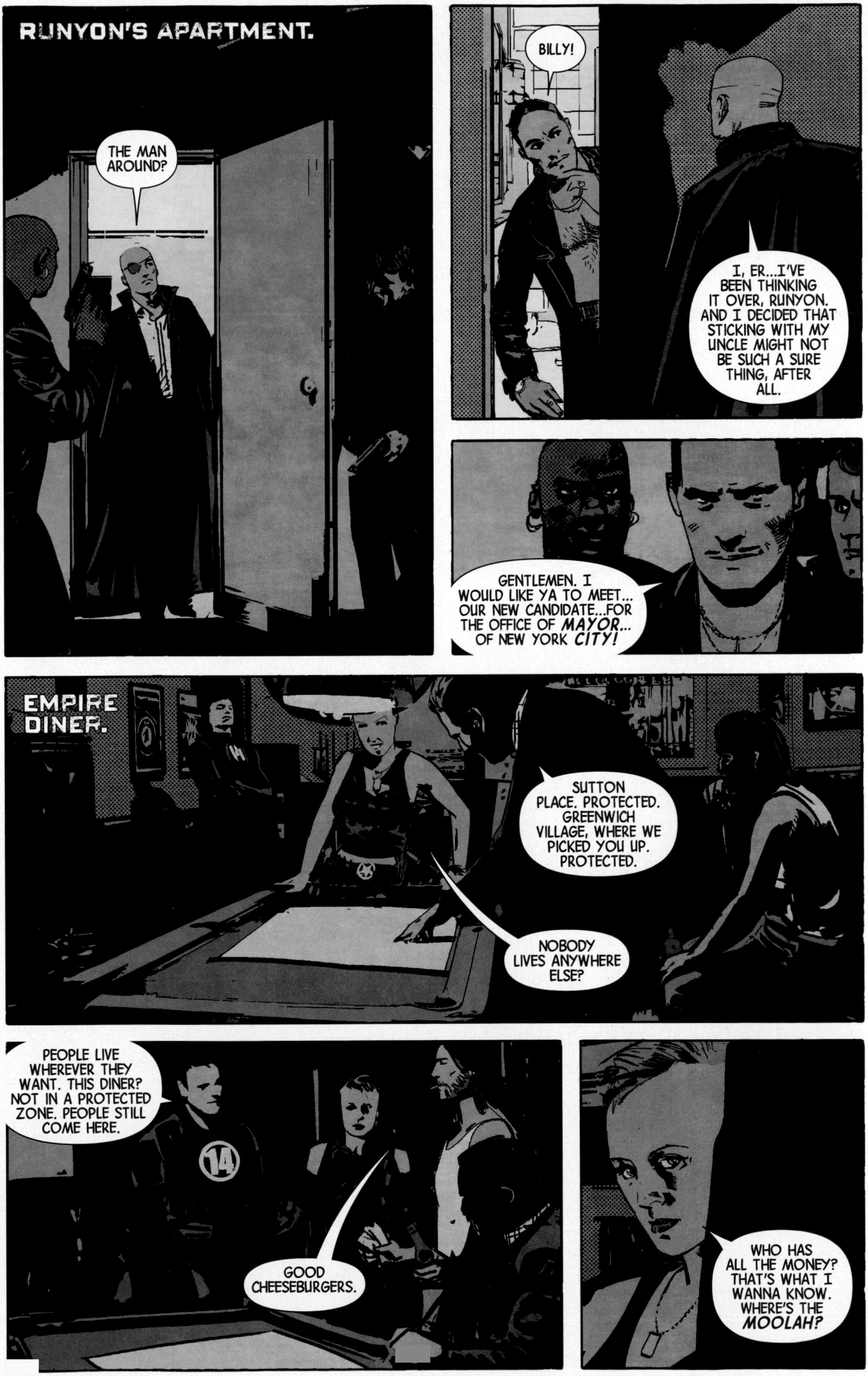
RUNYON'S APARTMENT.
THE MAN AROUND?
BILLY!
I, ER...I'VE BEEN THINKING IT OVER, RUNYON. AND I DECIDED THAT STICKING WITH MY UNCLE MIGHT NOT BE SUCH A SURE THING, AFTER ALL.
GENTLEMEN. I WOULD LIKE YA TO MEET... OUR NEW CANDIDATE...FOR THE OFFICE OF MAYOR... OF NEW YORK CITY!
EMPIRE DINER.
SUTTON PLACE. PROTECTED. GREENWICH VILLAGE, WHERE WE PICKED YOU UP. PROTECTED.
NOBODY LIVES ANYWHERE ELSE?
PEOPLE LIVE WHEREVER THEY WANT. THIS DINER? NOT IN A PROTECTED ZONE. PEOPLE STILL COME HERE.
GOOD CHEESEBURGERS.
WHO HAS ALL THE MONEY? THAT'S WHAT I WANNA KNOW. WHERE'S THE MOOLAH?

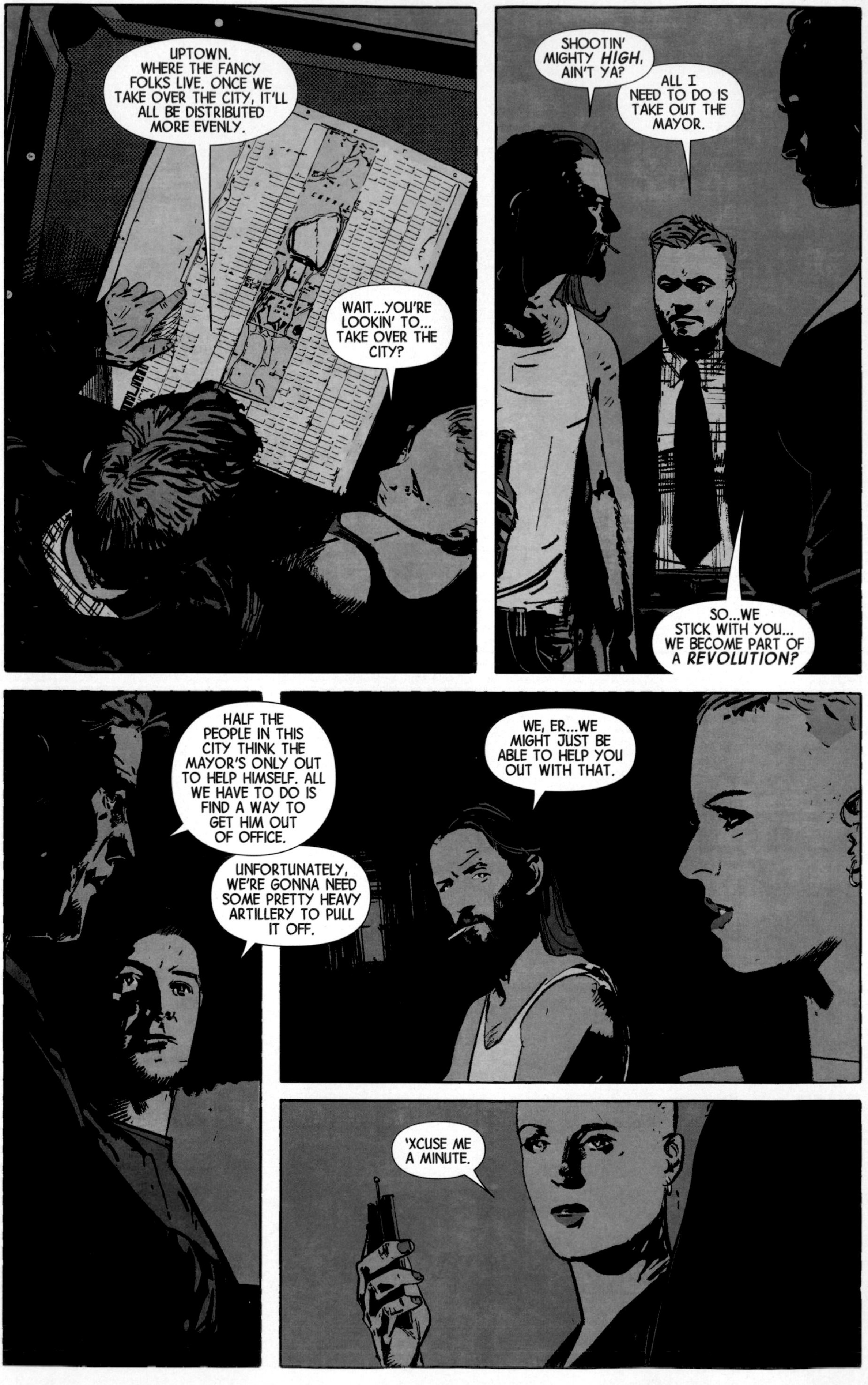
UPTOWN. WHERE THE FANCY FOLKS LIVE. ONCE WE TAKE OVER THE CITY, IT'LL ALL BE DISTRIBUTED MORE EVENLY.
WAIT...YOU'RE LOOKIN' TO... TAKE OVER THE CITY?
SHOOTIN' MIGHTY HIGH, AIN'T YA?
ALL I NEED TO DO IS TAKE OUT THE MAYOR.
SO...WE STICK WITH YOU... WE BECOME PART OF A REVOLUTION?
HALF THE PEOPLE IN THIS CITY THINK THE MAYOR'S ONLY OUT TO HELP HIMSELF. ALL WE HAVE TO DO IS FIND A WAY TO GET HIM OUT OF OFFICE.
UNFORTUNATELY, WE'RE GONNA NEED SOME PRETTY HEAVY ARTILLERY TO PULL IT OFF.
WE, ER...WE MIGHT JUST BE ABLE TO HELP YOU OUT WITH THAT.
'XCUSE ME A MINUTE.

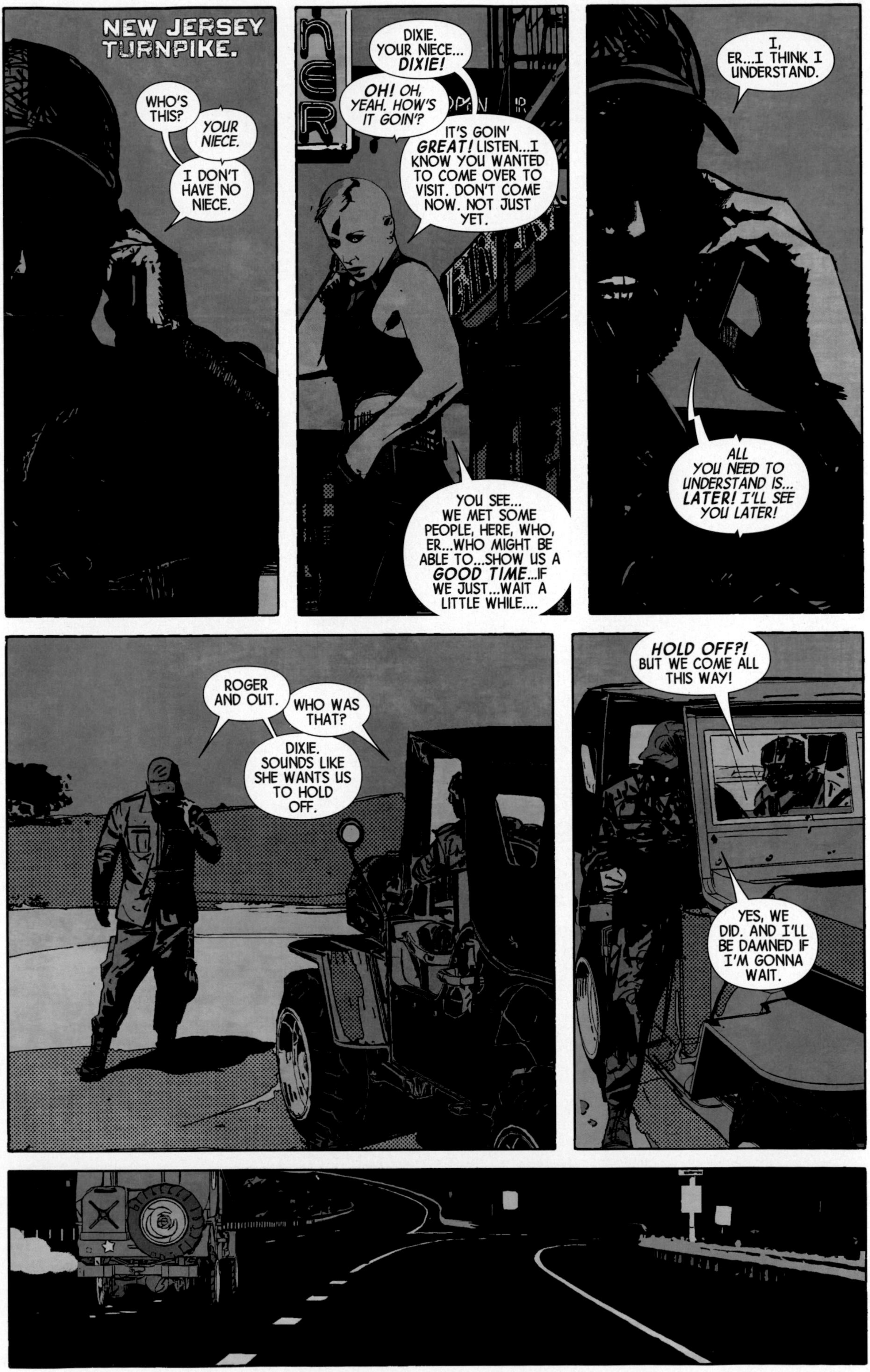
NEW JERSEY TURNPIKE.
WHO'S THIS?
YOUR NIECE.
I DON'T HAVE NO NIECE.
DIXIE. YOUR NIECE... DIXIE!
OH! OH, YEAH. HOW'S IT GOIN'?
IT'S GOIN' GREAT! LISTEN...I KNOW YOU WANTED TO COME OVER TO VISIT. DON'T COME NOW. NOT JUST YET.
YOU SEE... WE MET SOME PEOPLE, HERE, WHO, ER...WHO MIGHT BE ABLE TO...SHOW US A GOOD TIME...IF WE JUST...WAIT A LITTLE WHILE....
I, ER...I THINK I UNDERSTAND.
ALL YOU NEED TO UNDERSTAND IS... LATER! I'LL SEE YOU LATER!
ROGER AND OUT.
WHO WAS THAT?
DIXIE. SOUNDS LIKE SHE WANTS US TO HOLD OFF.
HOLD OFF?! BUT WE COME ALL THIS WAY!
YES, WE DID. AND I'LL BE DAMNED IF I'M GONNA WAIT.

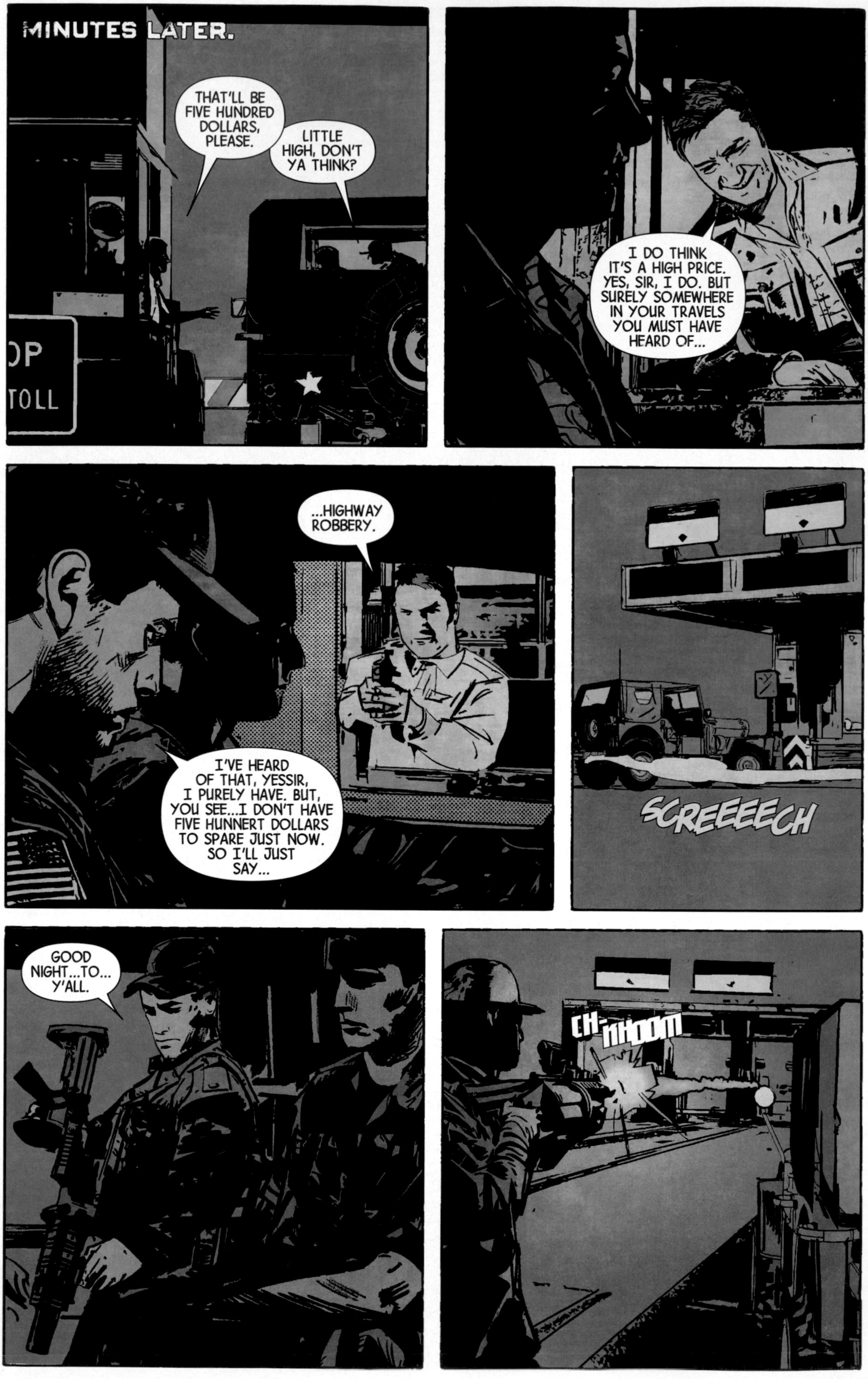
MINUTES LATER.
THAT'LL BE FIVE HUNDRED DOLLARS, PLEASE.
LITTLE HIGH, DON'T YA THINK?
OP
TOLL
I DO THINK IT'S A HIGH PRICE. YES, SIR, I DO. BUT SURELY SOMEWHERE IN YOUR TRAVELS YOU MUST HAVE HEARD OF...
...HIGHWAY ROBBERY.
I'VE HEARD OF THAT, YESSIR, I PURELY HAVE. BUT, YOU SEE...I DON'T HAVE FIVE HUNNERT DOLLARS TO SPARE JUST NOW. SO I'LL JUST SAY...
SCREEEECH
GOOD NIGHT...TO... Y'ALL.
CH-KHOOM

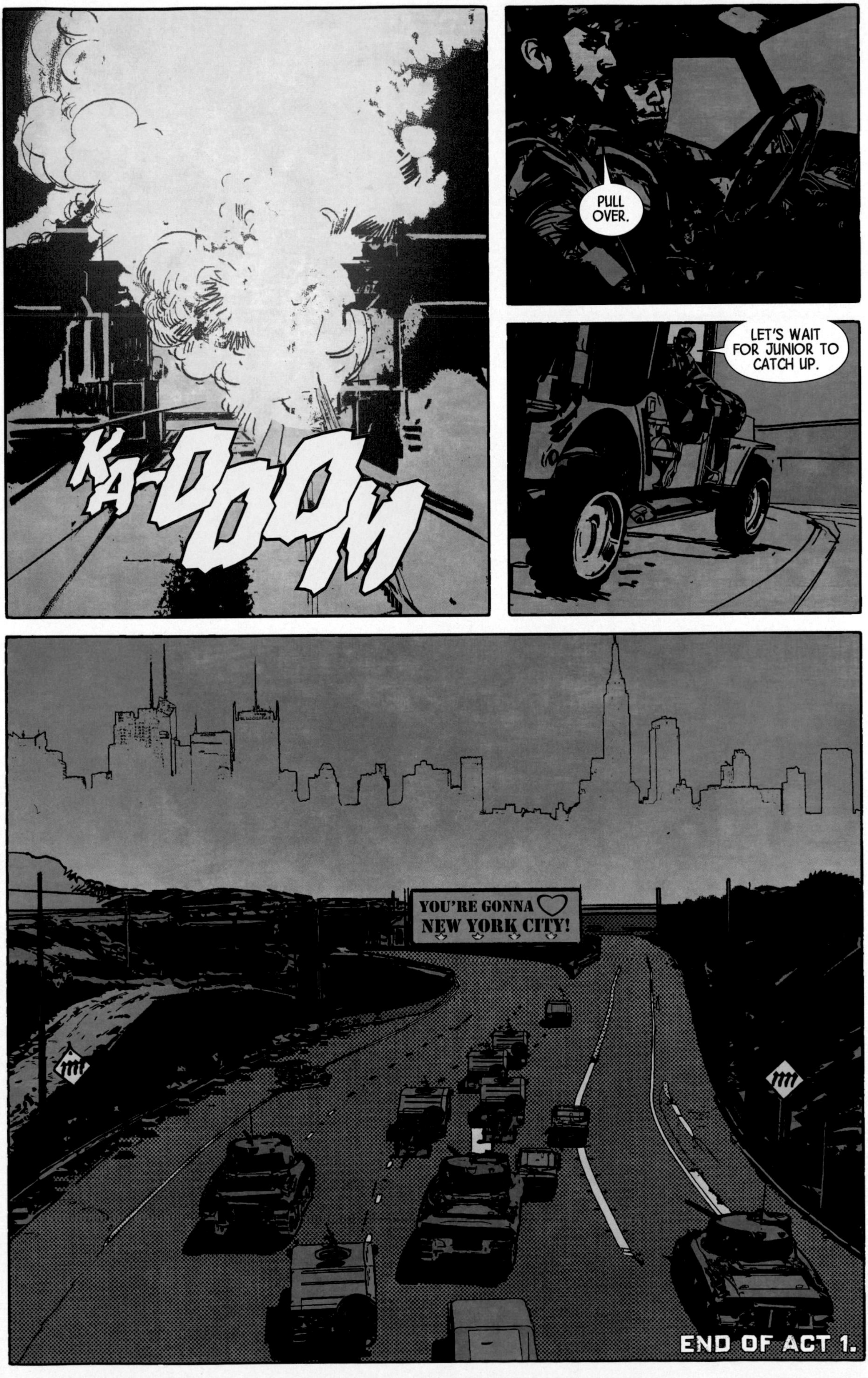
KA-DOOOM
PULL OVER.
LET'S WAIT FOR JUNIOR TO CATCH UP.
YOU'RE GONNA ♡ NEW YORK CITY!
END OF ACT 1.

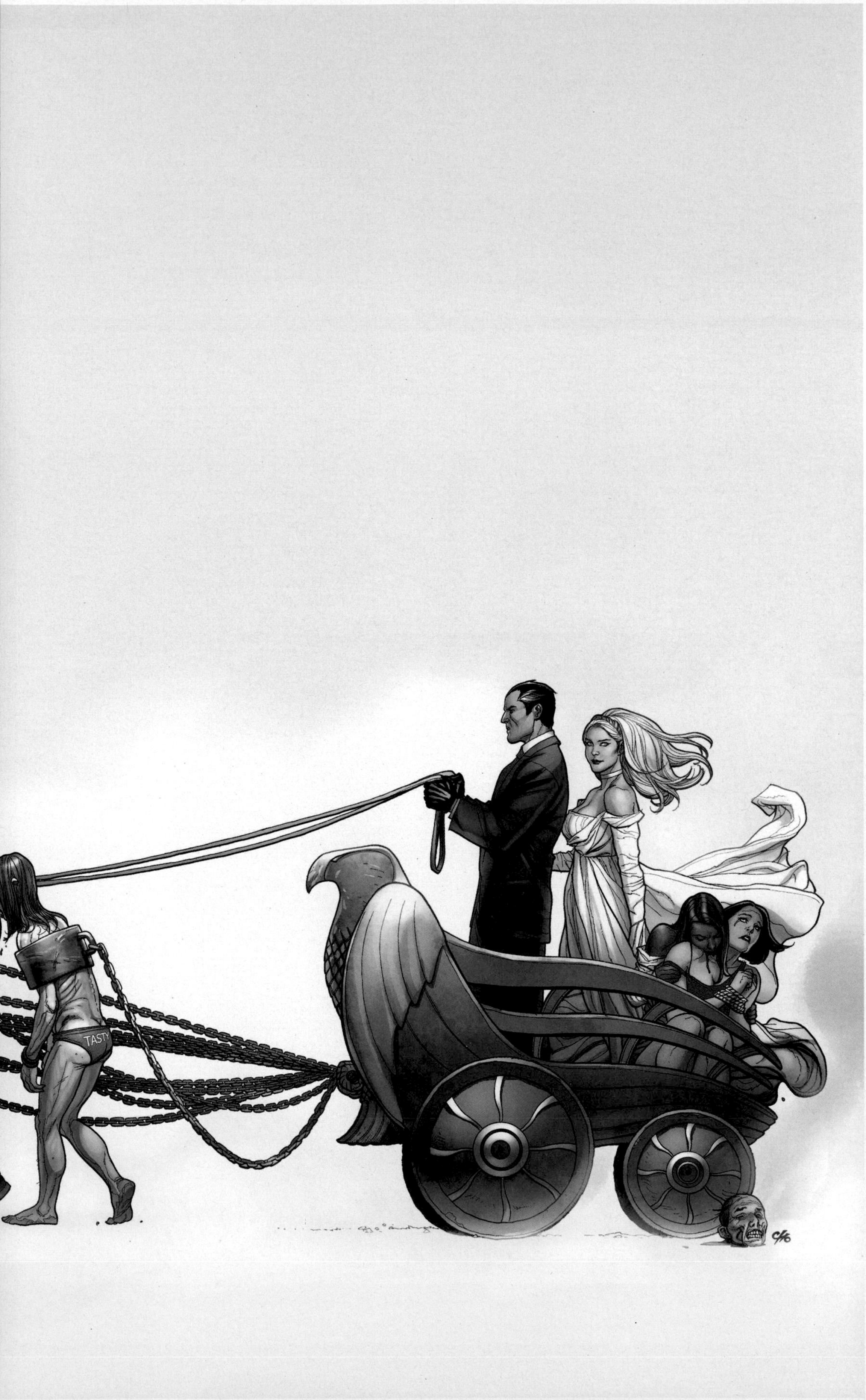
TASTY

#1 VARIANT BY FRANK CHO

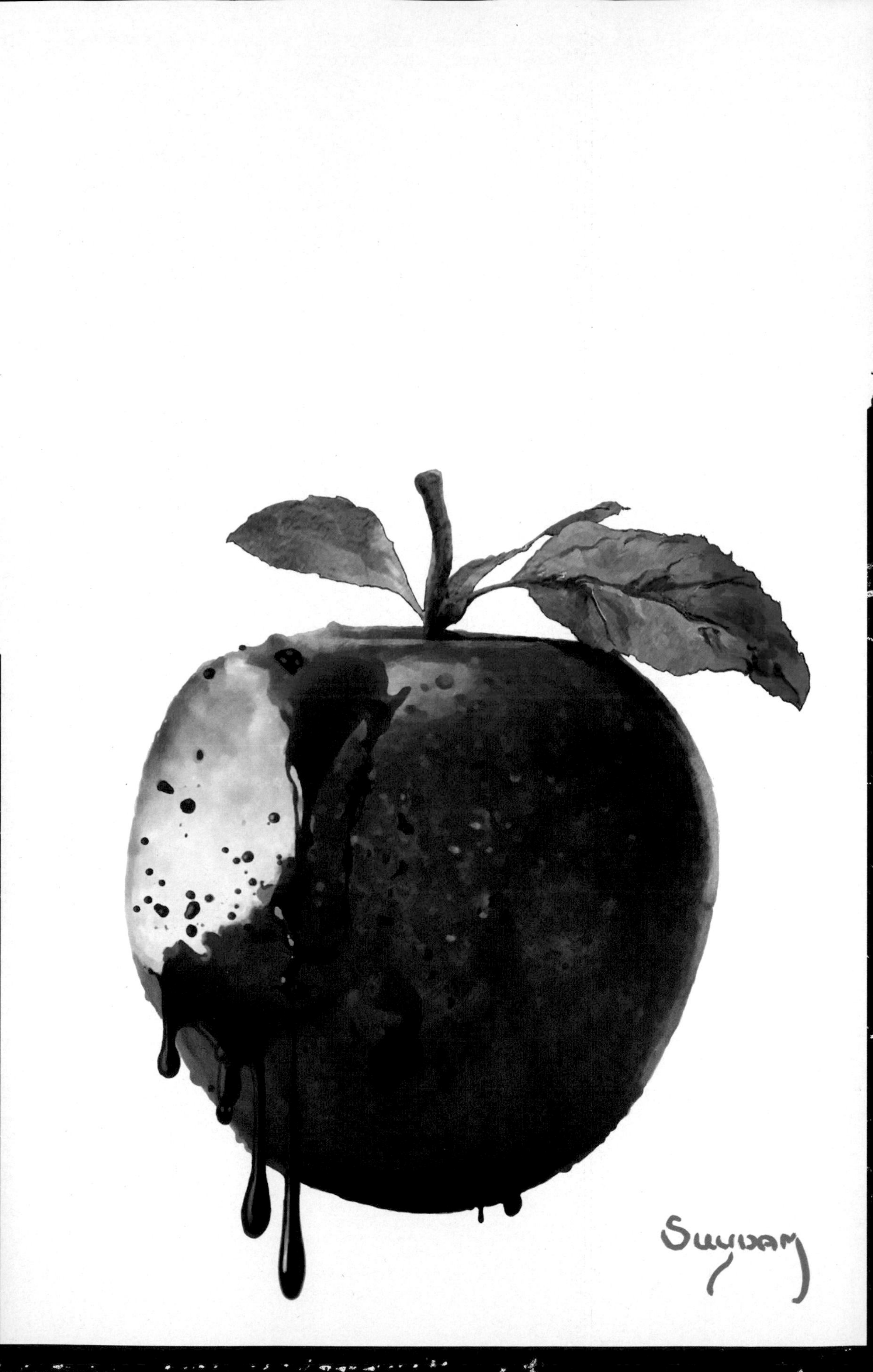
Suydam

#1 VARIANT BY ARTHUR SUYDAM

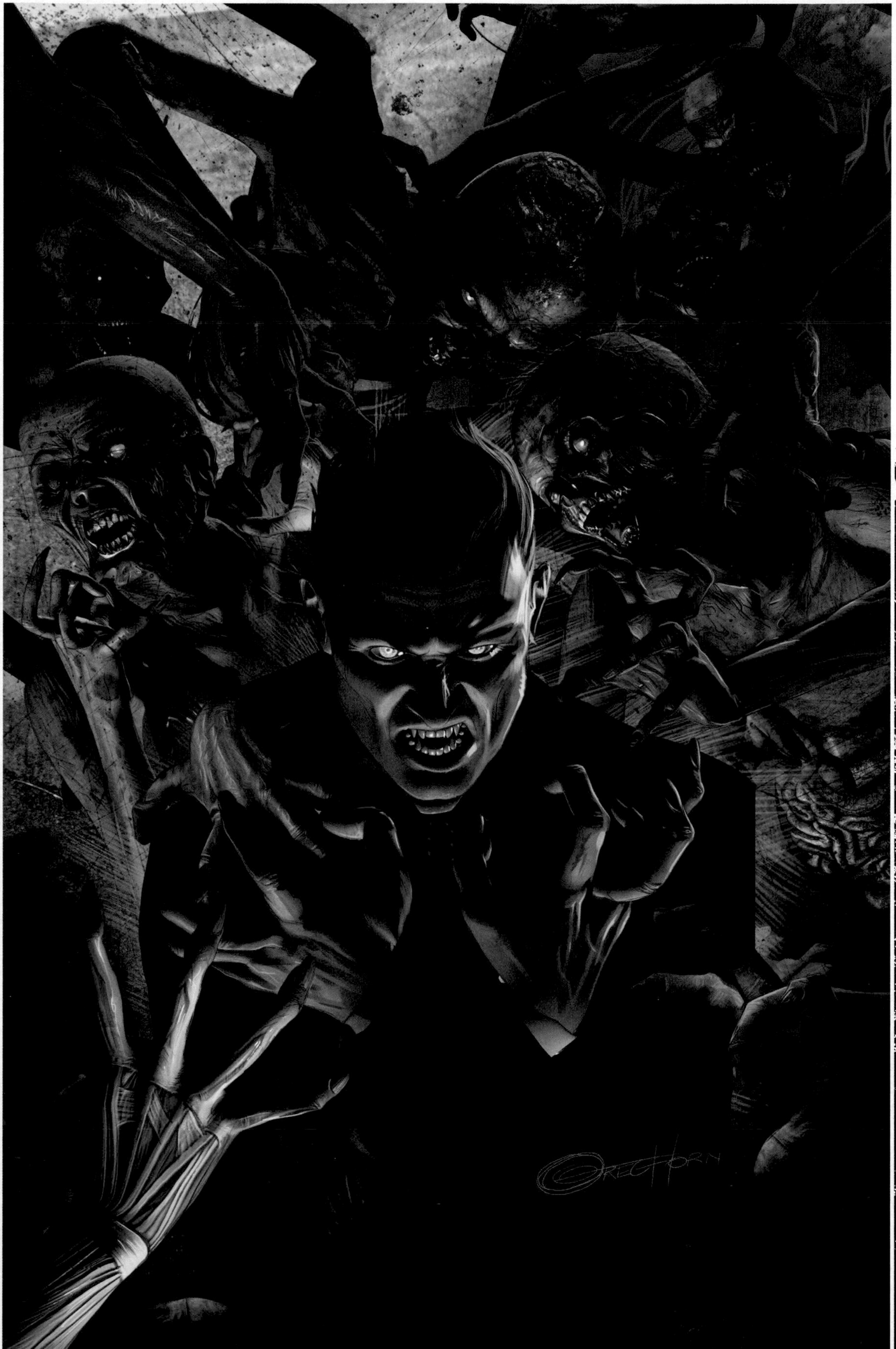

GREG HORN

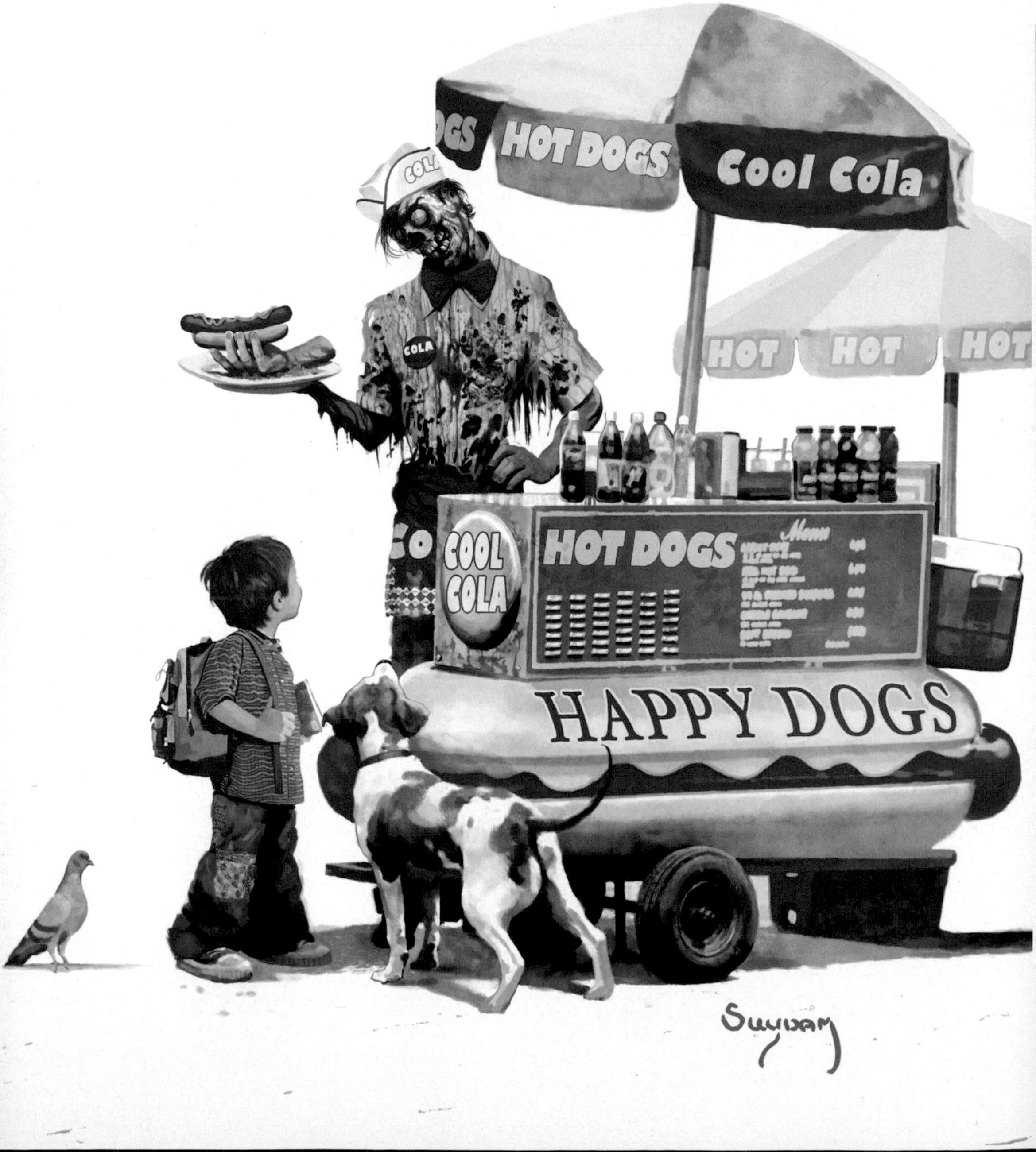
DOGS
HOT DOGS
Cool Cola
COLA
COLA
HOT
HOT
HOT
COOL COLA
HOT DOGS
HAPPY DOGS
Suydam

#2 VARIANT BY ARTHUR SUYDAM

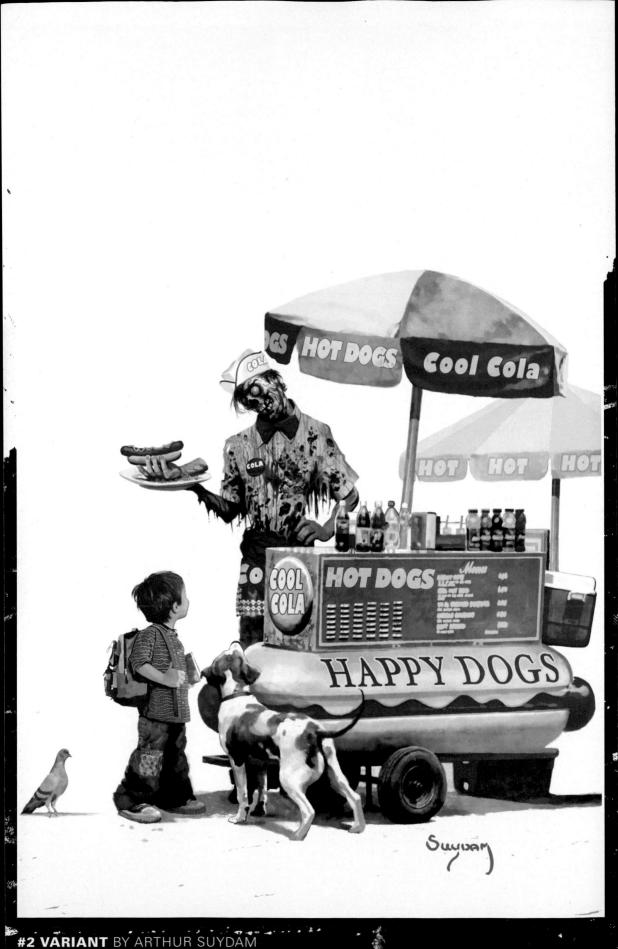

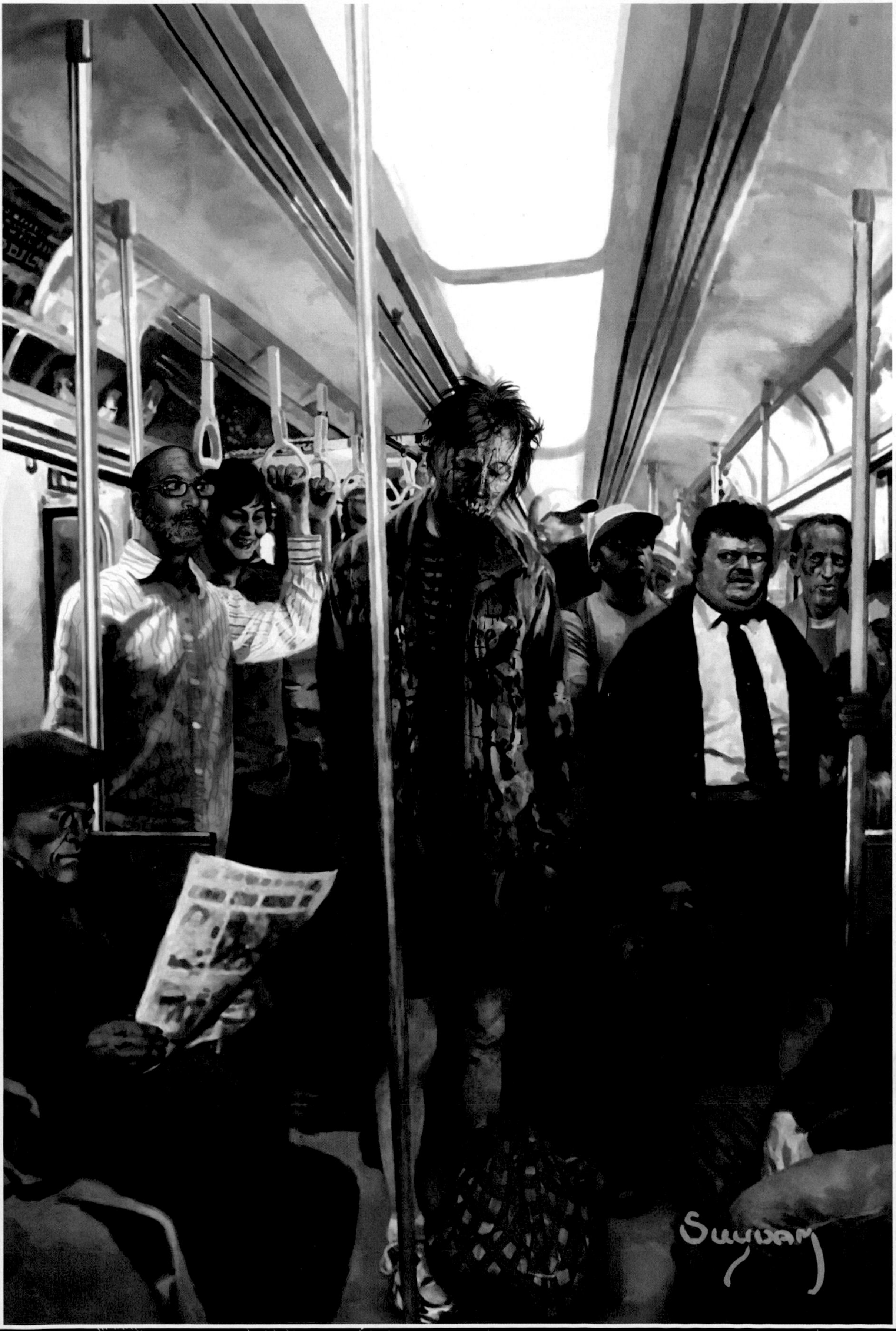
Suydam

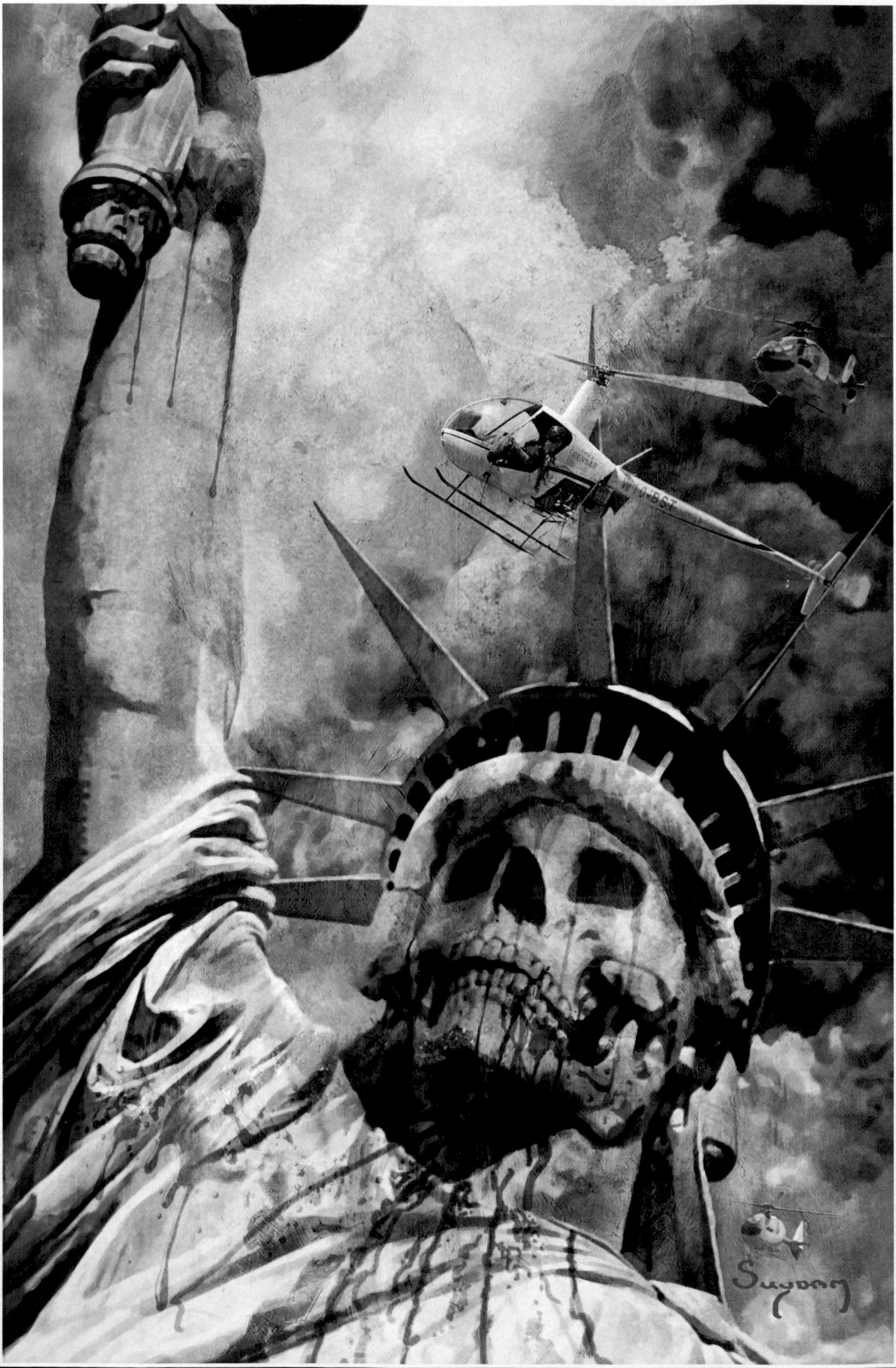

W10-BST
Suydam

#4 VARIANT BY ARTHUR SUYDAM

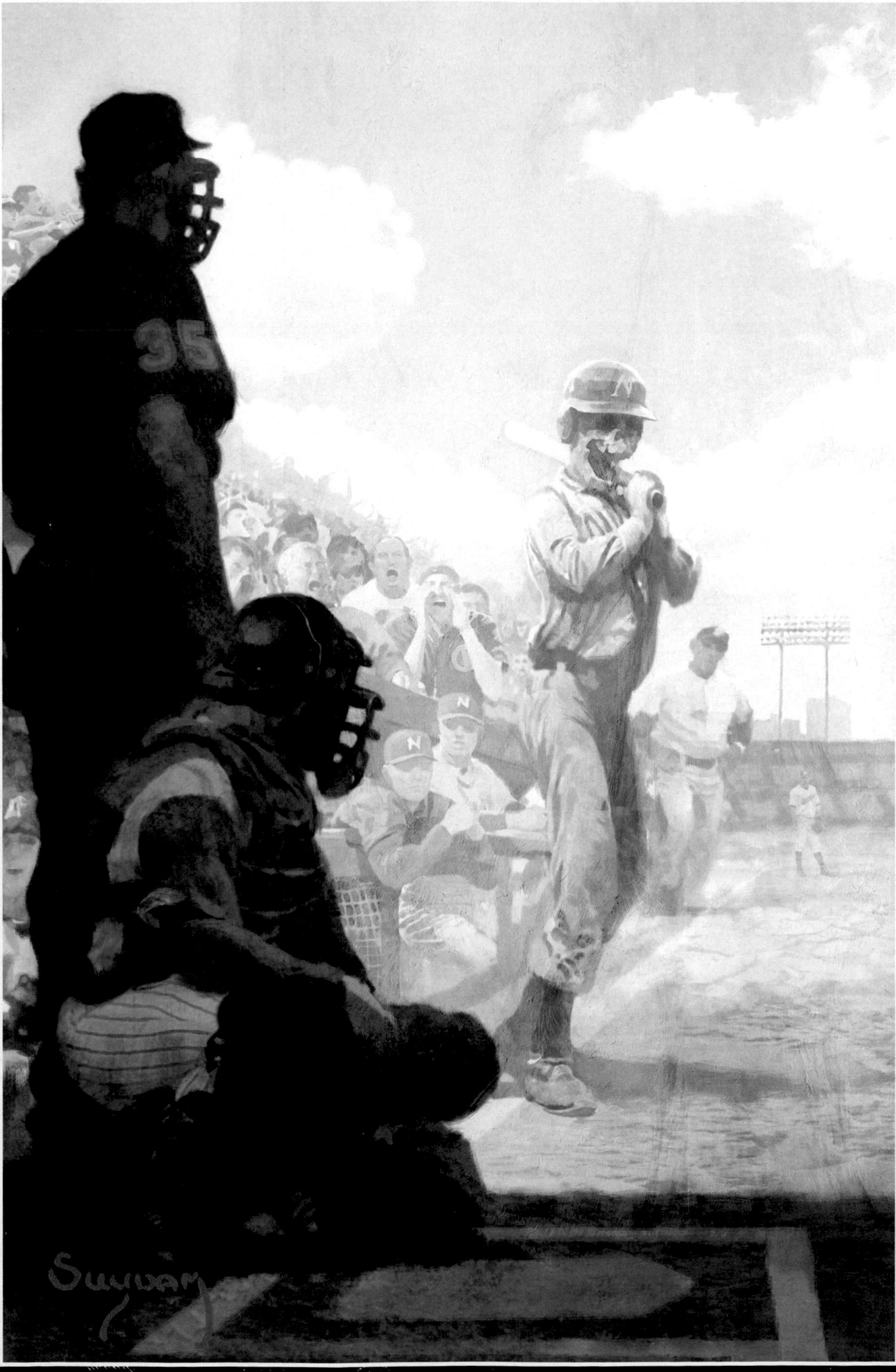

THE STORY CONTINUES IN
GEORGE ROMERO'S EMPIRE OF THE DEAD ACT TWO

MARVEL

MARVEL AUGMENTED REALITY (AR) ENHANCES AND CHANGES THE WAY YOU EXPERIENCE COMICS!

~AUGMENTED REALITY~

TO ACCESS THE FREE MARVEL AR CONTENT IN THIS BOOK*:

1. Locate the logo within the comic.
2. Go to Marvel.com/AR in your web browser.
3. Search by series title to find the corresponding AR.
4. Enjoy Marvel AR!

*AR AR content that appears in this book has been archived and will be available only at Marvel.com/AR — no longer in the Marvel AR App. Content subject to change and availability.

AR
INDEX